Unformulated Experience

From Dissociation to Imagination in Psychoanalysis

D1260756

RELATIONAL PERSPECTIVES BOOK SERIES

STEPHEN A. MITCHELL AND LEWIS ARON
Series Editors

Unformulated Experience

From Dissociation to Imagination in Psychoanalysis

Donnel B. Stern

Psychology Press
Taylor & Francis Group

New York   London

Psychology Press
Taylor & Francis Group
711 Third Avenue
New York, NY 10017, USA

Psychology Press
Taylor & Francis Group
27 Church Road, Hove
East Sussex, BN3 2FA

Psychology Press is an imprint of the Taylor & Francis Group, an informa business

International Standard Book Number-13: 978-0-88163-405-1 (Softcover)

Earlier versions of several chapters appeared in *Contemporary Psychoanalysis*. Chapters 2, 3, and 4 are revised and expanded versions of "Unformulated Experience" (1983) 19:71-79. A version of chapter 10 was published as "The Analyst's Unformulated Experience of the Patient" (1989) 25:1-33. Chapter 11 is a version of "A Philosophy for the Embedded Analyst: (1991) 27:51-80. An earlier version of Chapter 12 appeared as "Courting Surprise" (1990) 16:452-478.
"Good Form" from *The Things they Carried*, © 1990 by Tim O'Brien. Reprinted by permission of Houghton Mifflin Co., Seymour Lawrence. All Rights Reserved.

Library of Congress Cataloging-in-Publication Data

Stern, Donnel B.
    Unformulated experience: from dissociation to imagination in psychoanalysis / Donnel B. Stern.
        p.   cm. — (Relational perspectives book series; v. 8).
    Includes bibliographical references and index.
    ISBN 0-88163-405-0
    1. Psychoanalysis. 2. Consciousness. 3. Subconsciousness. 4. Imagination. I. Title. II. Series.
BF175.3665   2003
150.18'5—dc21   97-25923

Visit the Taylor & Francis Web site at
http://www.taylorandfrancis.com

and the Routledge Web site at
http://www.routledge.com

For Kathe

[T]here is in human existence a principle of indeterminacy, and this indeterminacy is not only for us, it does not stem from some imperfection of our knowledge, and we must not imagine that any God could sound our hearts and minds and determine what we owe to nature and what to freedom. Existence is indeterminate in itself, by reason of its fundamental structure, and in so far as it is the very process whereby the hitherto meaningless takes on meaning . . .

—Maurice Merleau-Ponty
The Phenomenology of Perception

It is when working on movements which are still irresolute, unstilled, which may not either be called diversions or laws, works of art or theorems, movements which, when completed, lose their likeness to each other, that the operations of the mind can be of use to us.

—Paul Valéry,
"Introduction to the Method
of Leonardo da Vinci"

Contents

Preface

Psychoanalysts have always understood that we can reflect on experience only when it exists in verbal form. What we have not adequately considered in American psychoanalysis is the nature of language itself. For if language is not merely a set of tags or labels for experience, but actually plays a role in constituting it, we are challenged to change our conception of what it means for experience to be unconscious. Unconscious experience, under those circumstances, is no longer merely hidden, awaiting only language to bring it out of the shadows. Instead, the form it will eventually take in words is not predetermined by its own structure. The shape of our future verbal-reflective experience is not fully accounted for by its past. We can certainly hypothesize, and with a good deal of confidence, that unconscious experience *exists*; but it does not exist in forms in which we can grasp it in words. It remains to be interpreted. Unconscious experience and meaning is what I call unformulated experience, and unformulated experience has clinical implications. It implies changes in our conception of defense (chapter 3), changes in the way we understand our creation of conscious experience (chapters 4 and 5), particular ways of grasping the process and outcome of clinical interpretation (chapter 9), and a perspective on the analysis of transference and countertransference, or "breaking the grip of the field" (chapter 10).

Unformulated experience is the idea with which this book began 15 years ago. At the time, however, the idea was different in important respects, because I had yet to encounter hermeneutics. After writing and thinking about unformulated experience for a few years, I came into contact with the work of Hans-Georg Gadamer, a modern student of Heidegger's, whose phenomenological or ontological hermeneutics seized my imagination and seemed to me to have much to say to psychoanalysis. I recognized in Gadamer a mentor and soulmate. His way of describing what it is to understand seemed very right to me and still does. His view is historicist and perspectivist, so that he accepts that we can understand only what the language of our time and place allows; but he has an ontology that is not limited to perspectivism. Gadamer envisions a reality beyond the reach of words, but it is not one we will ever be able to sense directly. He therefore allows room for both the relativist and the realist, and does so while simultaneously preserving the imaginative aspects of understanding and offering not even a toe-hold to nihilism.

Perhaps most important to me, with my long immersion in interpersonal and relational psychoanalysis, is Gadamer's insistence that understanding is always and inevitably dialogic, that it happens only in conversation, whether that conversation takes place between two people or between a person and a text, a theatrical production, a painting, and so on. This part of Gadamer's work immediately resonated with my conviction that the interpersonal field is the smallest meaningful unit of human living, which I had absorbed from the work of Harry Stack Sullivan and other psychoanalysts, some of whom were heavily influenced by Sullivan (e.g., Edgar Levenson) and others who probably never read a word Sullivan wrote (e.g., Racker and Winnicott). I was delighted, but not surprised, to learn from philosopher Richard Bernstein (1983) that Gadamer was the single best listener and conversational partner Bernstein ever met.

As I became interested in Gadamer, my previous interest in unformulated experience began to fall away (or so I thought at the time), and I began to feel that I had moved on. Those were the exciting years during which metapsychology was overthrown, Merton Gill began to interpersonalize his thinking, and Roy Schafer and Donald Spence presented the first explicitly hermeneutic formulations in psychoanalysis. I began to think about what hermeneutics could teach us about the clinical conundrums faced by the analyst embedded in the continuous invisible enactments of the analytic situation (chapter 11), and how the analyst in this position could "court surprise," inviting new and unbidden perceptions of the analytic relationship (chapter 12).

When I decided to pull together my thinking into book form, however, I was forced to think through matters that had not previously occurred to me, and I saw that my interest in hermeneutics, which I thought had been a movement into a new area of thinking, was really only an extension of the old. Those who claim we each have one thought that we elaborate endlessly seem to be right.

The link between hermeneutics and unformulated experience was dissociation. First I noticed that unformulated experience bore the same relation to dissociation that fully formed unconscious content bears to repression. That is, unformulated experience is material that has never been *brought into* consciousness, not material that has been ejected from it. This notion, it then struck me, implied that dissociation was a matter of avoiding the *interpretation* of experience, not (as in traditional notions) of avoiding the awareness of preinterpreted material. (Chapter 6 discusses "not-spelling-out," or the unconscious refusal to interpret structured unconscious meanings; chapter 7 is devoted to "narrative rigidity," or the dissociation of all those implicit meanings that are inattended as the result of any narrative choice.) That brought the hermeneutic perspective directly to bear on unformulated experience, because hermeneutics is about understanding as interpretation, or, more precisely, the adoption of an interpretive perspective. It began to seem to me that the way we formulate the unformulated was very much what Gadamer meant by the process of understanding—except, of course, that Gadamer, being a philosopher, did not consider dynamics. The dynamic element fell into place with the recognition that the interpersonal field is the context within which all events of dissociation and imaginative understanding take place, and is the medium that largely determines what material is interpretable at any given moment. I then began to see that this point implies the multiple self and a rethinking of the degree of responsibility we bear for our experience (chapter 8). All that remained was to find a way of thinking about the enigmatic act by which reflective experience is formulated, which I have done by describing formulation as not only the instrumental task of noting the contingency of meanings and events, but the much less easily specified process of creative speech. Inside treatment and outside it, the formulation of experience is a matter of imagination (chapter 5). In thinking this issue through, the evocative language of Merleau-Ponty was important; "creative speech" actually comes directly from him.

That, in briefest *précis*, is what I want the book to say. I set out to accomplish a portrayal of what clinical psychoanalysis might be in an interpretive, constructivist, hermeneutically conceived world. The ideas in the book emerged slowly, sometimes frustratingly slowly, over a long period of time. I certainly wish to spare the reader that part of my experience of writing it; but I do hope that some of the mystery of formulation that I also experienced, some remnant of the sense of meaning as an emergent thing, attends the reading of these chapters.

Acknowledgments

I could not have written this book without the love, support, generosity, critical acumen, and colleagueship of my wife, Kathe Hift, who has always somehow managed to help me find the time to write and has herself found the time to read and comment on what I have written. I am especially grateful to my editor, Stephen Mitchell, whose thoughtful suggestions, emendations, and additions made the book much better than it would have been without him. Philip Cushman, Robert Gaines, and Emmanuel Kaftal all read the final manuscript more than once, and each saw crucial problems and thought of ways to improve the manuscript that would never have occurred to me. I am grateful for their friendship. Muriel Dimen, Adrienne Harris, Lawrence Jacobson, and Emmanuel Kaftal read substantial parts of an earlier draft and helped me to adopt a different and fruitful direction. Our regular discussions have broadened my awareness of the literature, stretched my appreciation of the intellectual scope of psychoanalysis, and deepened my grasp of psychoanalysis as a moral and political enterprise. Conversations with Louis Fourcher and Irwin Hoffman have always enriched my thinking and kept me mindful of the clinical and theoretical problems that attend linguistic relativism. I am especially grateful for Louis Fourcher's generous and appreciative criticism, without which I would not have devoted sufficient attention to the ways in which even unformulated experience has structured aspects. I thank Allan Cooper for many things, perhaps most for his encouragement. I also thank Barry Protter for his help in guiding me into the literature of hermeneutics at a time, years ago, when I had an interest but did not know where or how to begin. From years before that, I thank my first and most important teacher in graduate school, Joseph Reyher, whose passion for the work of Freud and Sullivan sparked my own. And finally, at The Analytic Press, I thank Nancy Liguori for her reliability, good cheer, and command of detail.

PART I

Experience Formulated and Unformulated

1

The Given and the Made

A Constructivist View

The great challenge for psychoanalysis has always been the problem of the given and the made. Somehow we must negotiate the dual claims that experience is discovered, that it is structural and preexists our knowing of it, and that it is entirely understandable in phenomenological terms, by means of grasping the process of understanding itself. At issue in psychoanalysis are nothing less than our conceptions of mind and experiencing: consciousness, the unconscious, the defenses, the nature of representation and interpretation, and the kind of significance we attribute to language. The concept of unformulated experience, which takes center stage in chapter 2 and holds it throughout the book, is the central character in my approach to these problems, and the coming chapters are my attempts to grapple with them. In this introductory chapter, I offer the broadly hermeneutic context, the narrative tradition, so to speak, from within which the main character speaks.

WINNICOTT'S DIALECTIC

Winnicott (1971) taught that the given and the made constitute a paradox. We take given experience and make it into something that is our own; but it is just as true that we make or construct experience only by avoiding violations of the givens that define what the experience can be. Any experience is sometimes given, sometimes made, depending on how and when we look at it. Sometimes, perhaps when we are wisest, it is both.

3

But in day-to-day life, many experiences are more one than the other: for the painter, the painting is more made than given; for a rider, the horse is more given than made. It is true that the love of the rider for the horse and for the feeling of the ride are "made" things, but they are quite inextricable from the very "given" horse, because one loves and rides *this* horse, no other. The painting derives from experiences of the artist's that may have been reworked, recontextualized, and more fully imagined, but that nevertheless have a given reality as well; that is why, for the painter if not for the viewer, the art always exists in the context of the given events of the painter's life.

But even so, the painting remains more made than given, and the horse is more given than made. The import of Winnicott's paradox is not that the contributions of our constructions and given reality are always equal, but that both are always present and inextricable from one another. It does not violate the terms of the paradox to observe that the given and the made are also a dialectic.

To accept that experience *is* made in the present is to accept that other experience *was* made in the past. The givens in experience are not timeless essences; they themselves had to be constructed, once upon a time. And if an organized experience becomes part of a later moment, the organization it brings into that later moment will no longer be entirely appropriate. It will need to be recontextualized—and recontextualization is really just another word for yet another episode of organization, or reinterpretation. Every moment is made anew, although the experiences of moments past have a very great deal to do with what the experience of each present moment will be.

And so another way to talk about the given and the made is to refer to what we *can* make *now* out of what we *have* made *then*, or in the words of François Jacob (1982), the possibilities of actuality: "Whether in a social group or in an individual, human life always involves a continuous dialogue between the possible and the actual. A subtle mixture of belief, knowledge, and imagination builds before us an ever changing picture of the possible. It is on this image that we mold our desires and fears" (p. viii).

PSYCHOANALYTIC CONSTRUCTIVISM

In the recent literature of American psychoanalysis, it has been constructivist or hermeneutic writers who have most frequently considered the problem of the given and the made. Hermeneutic contributors, whose work originates in a philosophical program, have included Jürgen Habermas (1971), Paul Ricoeur (1970, 1977, 1981), Roy Schafer (1976, 1978, 1983, 1992), Barry Protter (1985, 1988, 1996), and Donald Spence (1982, 1987, 1988a, 1990, 1993), and, from a more fully social-constructionist position, Philip Cushman (1991, 1994, 1995).

Hermeneutics and constructivism are very closely related. The term "constructivism" has been used in recent psychoanalysis to designate a perspective with a hermeneutic agenda, but one that originates less in philosophy than in the clinical recognition that experience is at least partially indeterminate and is created in interaction. Contributions to constructivism have been made by Aron (1996), Fourcher (1992, 1996), Mitchell (1988, 1993), and me (Stern, 1983, 1985, 1987, 1989, 1990, 1991, 1992a, 1994, 1996a, b), but the most influential contribution has been the groundbreaking series of papers published over the last 15 years by Irwin Hoffman (1983, 1987, 1991, 1992a, b, 1994, 1996), whose "social constructivism" (more recently, "dialectical constructivism") has left an indelible impression on a generation of clinicians. Along with Edgar Levenson (1972, 1983, 1991)—whose work is not, however, constructivist in orientation (Hoffman, 1990; Levenson, 1990)—Hoffman has been more responsible than anyone else for the widespread acceptance of the analyst's inevitable unconscious participation and embeddedness in the ongoing therapeutic interaction.

However else they may be different, constructivist and hermeneutic accounts have in common the basic tenet that an individual's experience has no natural or intrinsic organization. It does not come prefigured. Until it is organized, which is accomplished by interpreting it, or taking a perspective on it, experience is "fundamentally ambiguous" (Mitchell, 1993, p. 57). This principle makes it quite natural and comfortable for the constructivist unconscious to be conceptualized as unformulated experience.

Psychoanalytic constructivists understand experience as the joint creation of interacting influences from within and without—from the ephemera of social life and the more enduring structures of one's inner world. Internal and external influence also continuously shape each other, partly by changing form and actually becoming forms of one another. One's structured inner world affects the kind of shaping influence one unwittingly selects from the social world; and reciprocally, as relationships in the social world impact on the inner world, they eventually become more inner than outer, by means of the various processes that fall under the rubric of internalization.

The creation of experience in constructivist terms is continuous: each moment's experience arises from the experience of the moment before.

Constructivists also share a view of time. We are used to thinking of the present as the creation of the past. The succession of moments in a life is not arbitrary, after all. There is emotional and intellectual continuity in the way we create each moment from the previous one, so that the past must be contained and reflected in every new construction of the present; and just as the previous moment shapes the present one, the distant past, through a long succession of moments, shapes both, so that our early years have the greatest influence on us. The distant past survives in the shape of the present, as in traditional psychoanalytic thought.

But just as constructivism teaches us to see the inner and the outer as a dialectic in continuous flux, it sensitizes us to the dialectic of time: the past is as much the creation of the present as the present is of the past. History, after all, can only be told looking backwards. In Frank Kermode's (1985) words, "meaning changes, including past meaning; and . . . the past is inextricable from the present of the interpreter. *There and then* cannot be detached from *here and now*, and objectively inspected. The past becomes, at least in part, a construction of the present" (p. 7).

When we talk about the given and the made in psychoanalysis, then, we are referring not to the contrast between humanly constructed meaning and what came before it, but to what we find preconstructed and what we make from it. The events of the moment combine with the preconstructed past, and the world of others falls together with our preconstructed inner life.

The making of a reflective experience from preconstructed materials requires *engaging* those materials, or taking a perspective on them. We can say the same thing from the other direction: to take a perspective on the preconstructed—that is, to think about it or experience it from a particular vantage point—is what it means to interpret it. Novel experience, or discovery, is creative interpretation; cliché is trivial, uninspired, or conventional interpretation. But even the most commonplace and familiar experience is interpretive or perspectivistic activity.

Now, consider that to take a perspective is to back away far enough to gain critical distance. It is not possible, after all, to "know" something we are so fully involved in that we are only living it. Such a state, if it were all we had, would be something like what Freud meant by "primary narcissism" or the illusory fusion with objects that Lacan calls "the

Imaginary." In a world we could not back away from, there would be no such thing as subjectivity. There would be no experiencing at all, just an undifferentiated wholeness of which each of us would be an equally undifferentiated part.

POSTMODERNISM: THE VERBAL IN THE NONVERBAL

We know only one means by which we can create critical distance: symbolic representation. It is only our capacity for symbolization that makes possible interpretation and the adoption of perspective. It is only symbolization that makes possible knowable experience.

To grasp or interpret (or construct or know) experience requires that symbols be related to one another. A symbol unrelated to other symbols, a symbol with a solitary existence, would not *be* a symbol. It would be a *thing*—and a thing without meaning, at that. Meaning depends on the relations and differences *between* symbols, not on fixed identifications of symbols with entities. It is the relations of symbols, or signs, with one another that define them and lend them interpretive power. This was the primary insight of linguist Ferdinand de Saussure (1966; for an introduction, see Culler, 1976), whose groundbreaking work, soon after the turn of the century, is the source of both structuralism and poststructuralism. (Anthropologist Gregory Bateson [1972] made the same point in a different and quite independent way.) When I point to an object and say, "That is a tree," for example, my designation is meaningless unless we also know that this "tree-thing" is not grass, corn, bushes, shrubs, hammers, houses, clouds, and so on. "Green" does not derive its meaning by identification with a particular wavelength of light, but by its difference from turquoise, chartreuse, blue, yellow, and red.

A system of interrelated symbols is a language, and that thought quickly leads us from the conclusion that all experience is interpretation to the thought that all interpretation is linguistic. If experience is interpretation, language is the condition for experiencing.

This view of language, along with psychoanalytic constructivism itself, are outgrowths of the many streams of contemporary thought (philosophy of science, poststructuralism, pragmatism, and contemporary hermeneutics) that join together in the one great postmodern conclusion: all experience is linguistic.[1] The corollary is social construction: Language itself represents the joined voices and perspectives of those who have come before us, and into whose world we are born ("thrown," as Heidegger puts it). In our turn, we will contribute, usually in ways we cannot imagine and seldom come to know, to the ways our descendants know life. Our ancestors' social innovations are "sedimented" (Foucault) in our languages, and therefore in our individual lives, in ways we so take for granted that we tend to accord them the status of objective, essential, unchanging reality. They have become "normalized" (Foucault, 1980), or "legitimized" and "objectivated" (Berger and Luckmann, 1967). Reality is a social construction, though it feels so familiar and inevitable that we can scarcely believe it is anything other than natural.

These are the ideas that inaugurated postmodernism and cast suspicion on the modernist project of discovering the one objective truth through the application of science and reason. If reality is not a simple, objective given that preexists us, and that will go on beyond us in just the same way, there are no essences to search for. Knowledge is a cultural product, a reflection of the values of the culture in which it is made. Knowledge commonly enforces such values, in fact. As examples that are now so thoroughly evident and familiar that they have themselves become part of convention, consider the enforcement effects of our own field's past "knowledge" of the psychopathology of homosexuality and of the "natural" femininity reflected in certain roles and activities. Recent efforts to demonstrate the "objective" inferiority of African-American intelligence are especially to the point, because many of the people who found this "finding" repugnant nevertheless were reduced to attacking it by trying to show that it was not "good science." The very fact that the argument was couched in scientific terms led these people into the reflexive acceptance that it could be challenged only on its own grounds. Now, *that* is knowledge functioning as enforcement: the power of science to shape the "fact" under consideration was accepted unquestioningly by even those who did not believe the "fact" that was shaped. By its very existence, knowledge affirms the sources of expertise that certify and underwrite it in the first place.

One of the lessons of all this is that if there is no one thing to know, there can be no one way of knowing. Methods of knowing, too, are social constructions, and therefore imbued with unexamined assumptions and biases, so that no method or technique can be trusted as the road to truth, as we once trusted science to be. Science remains crucial; but it is crucial as *a* method, one that should be studied for its inevitable political and moral implications, and not as *the* method of producing knowledge.

The traditional metaphor of language as the mirror of nature, a means for representing what is real, has lost all viability. It used to seem that language obeyed human command with the same absence of resistance or will demonstrated by a screwdriver or a knife and fork. No more. In a very real sense, language uses us; *we* have become the utensils. Language is no longer our tool, but the very crucible of our experience. The world has turned upside down, or at least our picture of it has.

HERMENEUTICS AND POSTSTRUCTURALISM

The word "postmodernism" covers a great deal of ground, and only part of that ground lies under the foundation of this book. Poststructuralism, the loosely defined set of ideas most commonly associated with Derrida, Lacan, Foucault, and their colleagues and students, is probably what most people think of as postmodernism. But for the most part, poststructuralism has not been the ground of my thinking, because for most poststructuralists there is no particular truth to be learned, only prior (and basically arbitrary) ways of understanding to be deconstructed, freeing meanings that had been obscured. Understanding, in the usual sense in which it is conceived in psychoanalysis—the direct understanding of experience—is not the aim. Instead, the goal is the uprooting and exposure of the inconsistencies and hidden purposes inherent in the concepts we employ in conventional understanding. Even Lacan, for whom "Truth" is actually of paramount importance, and "recognizing, respecting, and speaking it are . . . unequalled acts of virtue" (Bowie, 1991, p. 112), considers that what is true "cannot inhere in individual states of mind or states of affairs, and can only be syncopated and spasmodic" (p. 114). Truth for Lacan is found in error, misapprehension, nonsense, word-play, and the weird juxtapositions of dreams. Truth "can as easily be fabricated from lies and evasions as from a plain man's report on things as they are" (p. 114). This "truth of the speaking subject" is not what most American analysts mean when they refer to interpretation and understanding, nor is it what either I or the hermeneutic philosophers who have inspired me mean by those terms.

On the other hand, it has been the poststructuralists more than any others, and especially Foucault (1980; see chapter 8), who have brought to our thinking a new sensitivity to the ubiquity of power relations. Power has an unconscious structuring role in every interaction, including every interaction between analyst and patient, because each of us is defined by his or her place in systems of difference: gender, ethnicity, age, and so on. Apart from critical theorists, such as Jürgen Habermas (e.g., 1971), hermeneuticists have not often acknowledged that their analyses are necessarily embedded in power relations. This lack will have to be addressed if hermeneutics is to continue being useful to psychoanalysis.

In the coming years, the rest of psychoanalysis will begin to catch up with its feminists and theorists of gender (e.g., J. Mitchell, 1974; Dinnerstein, 1976; Kristeva, 1980; Fast, 1984; Irigaray, 1985; Benjamin, 1988; Chodorow, 1989; Butler, 1990; Flax, 1990), who have been arguing for years that power relations, especially those revolving around difference, are central to the constitution of subjectivity and interaction. We will see a groundswell of acknowledgment in psychoanalysis of the necessity for searching reflection about the sources and unconscious workings of power—not only the power operative in the cultural settings within which patient and analyst come to be the people they are when they meet one another, but the subtle, moment-to-moment expressions of power in the analytic relationship itself.

I therefore have good reason to cite poststructuralist thinking. But the heart and foundation of the book lies in hermeneutics, which in today's philosophy means the study of interpretation, or the attempt to formulate what it means to understand. For Hans-Georg Gadamer, the hermeneuticist who has most influenced me, there actually *is* a content to be grasped and a sense to be made, and this understanding is always and inevitably a dialogic event—in psychoanalytic terms, a relational or interpersonal one. For Lacan, on the other hand, relationships do not occupy this kind of primary position in life. They have no special status. While analysis of the transference remains key for Lacan, not only the interpretation of the transference, but the transference itself, is a linguistic phenomenon. Relationships are merely one more part of human experience structured by language. These differences make hermeneutics a more easily employed and useful underpinning for clinical work than poststructuralism. Most psychoanalytic practitioners and patients believe their lives are matters of meanings that have a genuine existence. Patients may be willing to agree that those meanings are obscure, and they may even be willing to acknowledge the possibility that they are partially indeterminate. But that some source of meaning is actually *there*, and worth grasping, is something few patients would even think of disputing—nor would they take kindly to the information that their analysts did (cf. Sass, 1992). Hermeneutics allows us to maintain that we are dealing with some variety of the truth while simultaneously acknowledging the socially constructed nature of our understanding of it.

Despite the sharp differences between the two positions, there is an important area of overlap, which is why poststructuralism and hermeneutics can both be cited as postmodern, at least in the very broadest sense of the term. It is this area of overlap I refer to as the postmodern critique of language. Both poststructuralism and hermeneutics participate in the view that understanding is inevitably linguistic, and that language is historicized, perspectival, and socially constructed. The difference lies in what the adherents of these two positions believe language represents. For poststructuralists, language is not a means of representation, but is an arbitrary circuit of symbols that serve compelling impersonal and suprapersonal aims (e.g., power for Foucault, language for Derrida and Lacan). Hermeneuticists take a less radical and more familiar view: although language (and therefore all of experience) is highly vulnerable to political and moral influences, it maintains a representational function. Language offers a perspective on a reality, a means of engaging a personal and social world that actually exists. For the hermeneuticist, to take a linguistic perspective is to take one of the myriad valid (and sometimes contradictory) views that might be taken, so that no single person, and no historical epoch, can ever formulate anything like a full picture of reality. But each perspective is a partial truth, and some perspectives are better than others—more complete, more coherent, more useful. At any particular moment, any single person's perspective manages to represent at least a sliver of reality. This is most particularly the view of Gadamer (1975, 1976), Heidegger's most prominent student. Gadamer's perspectivism, including the place of reality in his work, is addressed in chapter 9, and his thinking is discussed more generally in chapter 11.

POSTMODERNISM AND CLINICAL PSYCHOANALYSIS: A CONTRADICTION?

The postmodern critique of language can be unsettling and distressing. It deprives us of bedrock. When the topic comes up, one of the most common questions posed to me by skeptical and distressed psychoanalytic colleagues is whether the claim that all experience is linguistic means that nonverbal experience, too, must be conceived as linguistic. I readily reply that not only does postmodernism, but also structuralism mean just that. To this the response is often puzzlement, or the feeling that these ideas betray or alienate us from what we know is true, or the retort that such a contradiction makes so little sense that it is, by itself, reason to reject postmodernism as unreasonably esoteric and out of touch with the real world. How can experience that is incontrovertibly nonverbal nevertheless be linguistic? What are clinicians supposed to do with the day-to-day reality of dreams, unconscious fantasy, transference and countertransference, and all the other undeniably nonverbal, and frequently unconscious, phenomena central to analytic practice? Wouldn't accepting that these things are linguistic phenomena be tantamount to denying the reality of the patient, who is quite sure they are not linguistic at all? How can a clinician take such a stance? And besides, and most important, what would such a counterintuitive view look like in the real world? In order to answer these questions, we need to delve into semiotics.

WHAT DOES "LINGUISTIC" ACTUALLY MEAN?

Consider forms of sculpture that are relatively new additions to the art canon, such as contemporary earthworks or Christo's "wrapping" of buildings and geographic features. Or consider the art of Cindy Sherman, who uses makeup and clothing to reconstruct her image, imitating people of many different eras, occupations, and stations in life, and then photographs herself in this regalia. Her gender-bending portraits are always convincing, often funny, and sometimes purposefully bizarre.

Can the experience of looking upon any of these objects possibly be described as linguistic? We can agree that such an experience is nonverbal; besides, these pieces are not art to which we even necessarily *want* to ascribe a precisely worded meaning. To insist on one way of experiencing such work, and especially to insist on one way only, might actually demonstrate a basic *mis*understanding.

But one can hold that view and still maintain the claim that the experience of art, even this art, is a linguistic phenomenon. The reason will become clearer with a quick look at art's history. Quite simply, in any other era within recent memory, earthworks, Sherman's portraits, and Christo's wrapped buildings would have been deemed psychotic—the productions of dedicated people, no doubt, but crazy things without particular interest, value, or evocative power. Yet today they reach people of unquestioned sanity. They are among the most popular and widely known images of contemporary art.

Why do we give serious attention to these productions today? Because the boundaries of the category "art" have shifted, at least for a substantial part of Western culture, so that earthworks, wrapped buildings, and cannily constructed "false" portraits now fall within them. As objects come within these boundaries—or within what hermeneuticists would describe as the "horizon" of art, or the "clearing" within which it exists—we find ourselves having different sets of attitudes toward them. Without any reflection on our part, new categories of thoughts, observations, and feelings toward them begin to feel to us relevant, appropriate, and natural. The experience of these conceptual art pieces—all art, in fact—is therefore determined by a process that is, in the last analysis, linguistic.[2]

The point is not limited to the experience of visual art, or even to art at all. Think of the atonal sound patterns that have increasingly been considered part of serious music since the turn of the century, or the inclusion of nonmelodic, high-amp noise in contemporary rock and roll. These sounds have become linguistically meaningful; they occupy places in symbolic codes, just as words do in speech. Or consider Simon Schama's (1995) recent demonstration that our culture of origin determines which kinds of "natural" landscapes we idealize and respond to with the greatest depth of feeling. Because "ideal" landscapes differ considerably across cultures, and because these differences are not correlated in any simple way with the flora native to the various cultures' geographic distributions, "natural" beauty is not really natural at all. It is closely linked to language and the stories people use language to tell. It is a manifestation of what a particular culture believes and attends to, the values and verbal traditions in which those who live in that world are embedded. Idyllic landscapes are places in which to live idyllic lives, and idyllic lives are not inventions of nature, but of language and culture.

Consider the plight of the 18th century Polynesians, who are said to have been unable to make a coherent visual percept out of Captain Cook's ship as it sailed into their harbors, because they had no cultural preconception for the image. The story goes that they could not tell whether what they saw was a large object at a distance or a small object much closer to them. Was it a dragon? A fortress? The absence of a preconception made it impossible to understand. Here we have an example of a nonverbal happening that could not attain the status of an experience precisely because it did *not* make linguistic sense.

The postmodern view of language is closely related to the much earlier Whorf-Sapir hypothesis regarding the constitutive properties of language.[3] Benjamin Whorf (1942) cites the story of a certain Captain Coon to demonstrate that language is a direct influence, not only on habits of thought, but on perception itself.

> In parts of New England, Persian cats of a certain type are called Coon cats, and this name has bred the notion that they are a hybrid between the cat and the "coon" (raccoon). This is often firmly believed by persons ignorant of biology, since the stress of the linguistic pattern (animal-name 1 modifying animal-name 2) causes them to "see" (or, as the psychologists say, "project") objective raccoon quality as located on the body of the cat—they point to its bushy tail, long hair, and so on. I knew of an actual case, a woman who owned a fine "Coon cat," and would protest to her friend: "Why, just LOOK at him—his tail, his funny eyes—can't you see it?" [pp. 261–262].

Whorf goes on to tell the story of how the woman's friend told her she was ignoring biology, since the two species cannot breed, to which the woman, who apparently had great confidence in her view, responded by consulting a renowned zoologist! The zoologist (tactfully) declined to decide the issue, and the woman remained convinced that her cat was the outcome of an encounter between a "philandering raccoon" and a "wayward cat." Whorf concludes what is, after all, a shaggy dog story by finally letting us in on the fact that "Coon cats" received their name from "one Captain Coon, who brought the first of these Persian cats to the State of Maine in his ship." Here is Whorf's more serious commentary.

> In more subtle matters we all, unknowingly, project the linguistic relationships of a particular language upon the universe, and SEE them there, as the good lady SAW a linguistic relation (Coon raccoon) made visible in her cat. We say "see that wave"—the same pattern as "see that house." But without the projection of language no one ever saw a single wave. We see a surface in everchanging undulating motions. Some lan-

guages cannot say "a wave". . . . Hopi say walalata, "plural waving occurs," and can call attention to one place in the waving just as we can. But, since actually a wave cannot exist by itself, the form that corresponds to our singular, wala, is not the equivalent of English "a wave," but means "a slosh occurs," as when a vessel of liquid is suddenly jarred [p. 262].

The process of recognizing a relevant agglomeration of stimuli as an instance of a particular category and as a certain kind of experience is fundamentally linguistic. That is, to repeat the heart of the postmodern critique, the possibilities for any experience even *existing* as "an experience," including (as we have seen) experiences we refer to as nonverbal, such as waves (sloshing or not), are based in language. At the root of our experience, there is only the always already made. And yet this ubiquitous effect language has on us is no more visible to us on a day-to-day basis than are our own eyes. We cannot step outside language any more than we can experience stimuli outside the range of our senses.

CLINICAL PSYCHOANALYSIS: THE NONVERBAL IN THE VERBAL

Now that we have found the linguistic in that part of our experience that had always seemed exclusively nonverbal, we will never be able to restore the nonverbal to quite the same unique status it used to have in our theories and our psychic lives. But even without full reinstatement, we will see that the nonverbal can be acknowledged without contradiction and used without qualm. In clinical psychoanalysis, that is, we will turn the tables and find the nonverbal in the verbal.

If we pay close attention, there is often a sensation of something coming before language. Whatever this is, it cannot be worded, though sometimes, after the fact, we feel that it was there. We often have the sense that the words we use "fit" the shape of what we wanted to say, or do not fit. There is always a vague meaning-shape, a protomeaning—perhaps part of what Gadamer (1975, 1976) intends when he refers to "forestructures of understanding" and "preconceptions"—that precedes what we say and by which we gauge our success in expressing ourselves.

Nathalie Sarraute, an iconoclastic French writer often described as one of the practitioners of "The New Novel," builds her work around the fragile connection between what is already there and what we wish to express. What we have not yet expressed, she says, is never conventional. It cannot be. It is defined by the possibility of its novelty. And yet the expressions chosen to represent it seldom do more than lay it out in a familiar form. About that which exists before language, Sarraute said, in a symposium on "The New Novel" in 1971, "Scarcely does this formless thing, all timid and trembling, try to show its face than all powerful language, always ready to intervene so as to re-establish order—its own order—jumps on it and crushes it" (quoted by Shattuck, 1984b, p. 1). Later she goes on, "There is always a kind of drying out produced by language. . . . For me . . . there is something prior to language: a sensation, a perception, something in search of its language, which cannot exist without language."

Over and over again, in conducting an analysis, and in life in general, we have the compelling feeling that meaning is emergent and incomplete, the sense that experience melts and verges into words—and escapes them. Sarraute (1939) captures this sense well:

> What I tried to do was to show certain inner "movements" by which I had long been attracted; in fact, I might even say that, ever since I was a child, these movements, which are hidden under the commonplace, harmless appearances of every instant of our lives, had struck and held my attention. In this domain, my first impressions go back very far.
>
> These movements, of which we are hardly cognizant, slip through us on the frontiers of consciousness in the form of undefinable, extremely rapid sensations. They hide behind our gestures, beneath the words we speak, the feelings we manifest, are aware of experiencing, and able to define. They seemed, and still seem to me to constitute the secret source of our existence, in what might be called its nascent state [p. 6].

What are these "undefinable, extremely rapid sensations," these "feelings of tendency" (James, 1890), "felt meanings" (Gendlin, 1962, 1964), "tacit knowing" (Polanyi, 1958, 1959), if not nonverbal unconscious phenomena—or at least, the only direct manifestations of such phenomena that we can perceive in our verbal, reflective mode? And yet, doesn't this point directly contradict the postmodern view of language? If language defines what an experience can be in the first place, how can anything possibly come before words?

It *is* contradictory for us to claim that our nonverbal experience is nonlinguistic, if we mean by that to deny that cultures shape, define, and set the bounds of what can be experienced. Such an attitude would scant the verbal in the nonverbal. But we can also reverse the terms and look at the situation the other way around. From the perspective of reflective consciousness—that is, from the perspective of the consciousness in which we are able to "know" explicitly anything at all, which requires words—much of everyday life, maybe even most of it, *is* truly nonverbal, and often beyond our power to express.

From this latter, everyday perspective, we find the nonverbal in the verbal. And there is a way to understand it that does not contradict the larger conception postmodernism offers us. The solution is that we agree that what we *experience* as nonverbal is nevertheless defined by language in the larger sense, but that we experience it as nonverbal anyway. Just like verbally represented experience, nonverbal experience is coded; it is just not coded in the language of words. Edgar Levenson (1979) writes that

> speech is only a small part of an extensive semiotic communication that takes place between the two participants in the analytic process. I am not suggesting that one merely pay attention to how the patient sits or looks. I am suggesting something far more elaborate—that there are other extensively coded communications, as informational as speech, that take place in the intersubjective realm [p. 72].

And, of course, it is not only communication that can take place in this linguistically defined, nonverbal realm. The nonverbal is just as appropriate for the representation of dreams, fantasy, memory, and so on.

To make sense of this notion of multiple semiotic codes in experience, consider Saussure's (1966) long-ago distinction between *langue* and *parole*. Language, or *langue*, is the immense and ever-changing system of differences between linguistic elements, a system of a size far beyond any one person's explicit capacity to know. It is the existence of *langue* that makes meaning possible in the first place. Speech, or *parole*, is an instance of our use of *langue*. We are users of *langue* even though we do not have an explicit conception of its elements or how it works; it is the symbolic system within which we have an existence. There is no reason why all the elements of *langue* should be visible to us, even theoretically, and there is no reason at all why the various languages of *langue* have to be worded. It was the insight of the structuralists, especially Barthes and Lévi-Strauss (see Hawkes, 1977), that languages can be nonverbal, like algebra, hieroglyphics, or street signs that use pictures—or even like the pictorial elements of a dream, or the actions and attitudes that make up relatedness, and thus transference and countertransference. The structuralists expanded structural linguistics into semiotics.

Go back for a moment to the problem of our experience of changing forms of art and music. These definitions are certainly *connected* to words; today, we can experience atonal sounds and earthworks as something we refer to as "art." But how, exactly, is our experience of the art *defined* in words? That is a different and more difficult question. We would be much better at deciding whether a particular object belonged in the category than we would be at using words to say what our experience is. What does this suggest?

We already have the notion that language is not limited to what we do with words. The examples of our experience of art and music add to that notion the suggestion that one of the unworded ways we encode experience is as *praxis*, or *practice*. We treat art as if it *is* what it *does*. The regularities of art practice, and our knowledge of these regularities, are part of what we mean when we refer to language in the larger sense, or semiotics, and are what make our experience of new forms of art comprehensible to us. And notice that practices are not necessarily commensurable with words; it may not be easy, or even possible, for even a seasoned viewer or listener to explain the experience in words. Language and practice, that is, are often "structurally distinct" (Fourcher, 1992, p. 327), so that meanings formulated in one of these modes are not necessarily even possible to formulate in the other. Think of how hard it can be to describe the events of the analytic relationship. This difficulty, of course, is routinely meaningful in dynamic and intersubjective terms; but the fact that patient and analyst not only encode the interaction in their own, private ways, but have no direct access in words to their own nonverbal encodings, may add to their difficulty in describing such events. It may be quite difficult to "know what's going on," in other words, even when there is no particular motive to avoid the knowing. Reflect on the difficulty of describing in words the details of how you ride a bicycle, play tennis, take a shower, or (ironically) read. The difficulty is due to the fact that these activities are not represented in words at all, but in the semiotic of practice. The same is true for the difficulty of describing how one deals with one's mother, or one's son, or anyone else; these incredibly complex and often affectively charged sets of events are encoded as practices.

This way of thinking also throws new light on Sarraute's references to "something in search of its language, which cannot exist without language" and "the secret source of our existence, in what might be called its nascent state." Statements like these are made with a kind of phenomenological authority that allows us neither to dismiss them nor to judge that they are merely wrong. But now we can see that their rightness does not require us to believe in experience that exists outside, beyond, or before language. We can just as well understand Sarraute's yearnings for full linguistic expression to be the result of the incommensurability of the various ways we have to encode experience. Sarraute simply cannot find a way to make words express fully the nonverbal meanings she knows are there, but that she can only vaguely sense. As far as words are concerned, this nonverbally encoded experience is ineffable—even though, in the larger semiotic context, it is linguistic. And she is right: when words are forced into usage and made to perform tasks beyond their capacity, when they are forced to translate the untranslatable, the effect is no doubt to "jump on" and "crush" what came before them. But the problem in that case is not that words are evil, or that they are not performing their task; the problem is that their limits are not being respected.

In Louis Fourcher's (1992) description, subjectivity is "heterogeneous." There is more than one way for experience to be represented, and the modes may not be translatable into one another's terms. Fourcher offers the useful suggestion that we call one of these modes "knowledge" and the other "action" (the latter term is equivalent to "practice"). Knowledge is encoded in words and can be reflected on; action is encoded nonverbally, but within the broader bounds of semiotics. Both modes directly affect the way we experience and conduct ourselves, though we are explicitly aware only of the influences of the reflective mode (knowledge). To the extent that we are able to describe in words our relatedness to other people, for example, our experience of that relatedness is "knowledge"; to the extent that we are unaware of what we are doing, or cannot "find the words to say it," our relatedness is encoded in the mode of "action."

Modes of semiotic representation are merely different, each not necessarily more nor less developed than another. Both knowledge and action are valid means of representation; but knowledge, of course, is the only one we can know directly and explicitly, because reflection requires verbal language. Or rather, the act of reflection *creates* verbal representation.

A SOURCE FOR THE UNCONVENTIONAL: THE PERSONAL REWORKING OF PUBLIC "ACTION" IMAGES

But there is still something missing. The incommensurability of "knowledge" and "action" does indeed ensure that prereflective experience can exist apart from reflective consciousness. "Action," while it is part of subjectivity, is "other" to "knowledge" in at least a formal sense. Thus, unconscious experience is not merely implicit to awareness. But there is nevertheless something tame and inhibited about the way "action" accounts for the more evanescent or just plain obdurate aspects of nonverbal experience like Sarraute's. What about the raw and nonrational in unconscious life? These qualities are not conferred directly by experience in the outside world. How do they come about?

In criticizing Sartre for his disdain for the unconscious, Merleau-Ponty (1970) says that

> Such a view loses sight of what was Freud's most interesting insight—not the idea of a second "I think" which could know what we do not know about ourselves—but the idea of a symbolism which is primordial, originary, the idea of a "non-conventional thought" (Politzer) enclosed in a "world for us," which is the source of dreams and more generally of the elaboration of our life [p. 49].

Instinct and drive are the most natural psychoanalytic candidates for "primordial" and "originary," but it is precisely instinct and drive that a theory based in social construction—as all "relational" theories (Greenberg and Mitchell, 1983; Mitchell, 1988) are—must do without. Another natural source for unconventional experience is Bollas's (1989) "personal idiom," which is the individual's inborn potential for what Winnicott called the "true self." But a perspectivistic, socially constructed psychoanalysis must do without personal idiom and the true self, too, because in the terms of constructivism, there can be no reality that is meaningful apart from our interpretation of it, no "endogenous motivational core" (Jacobson, 1997).

In the absence of guarantors like instinct, drive, and idiom, then, where does the powerful, bizarre, nonrational language of dreams come from? According to a theory rooted in social construction, which would seem inevitably to conceive meaning as the outcome of some form of convention, how does any truly unconventional form of experience arise?

We can understand such experience as the consequence of our personal and usually nonverbal reworking of imagery that was originally public and consensually validated. The reworking of experience is the rule in psychic life, not the exception, because reworking is the activity by which we carry out our ceaseless attempt to understand. We are always trying to know ourselves and the people around us, and to do so, we interpret and reinterpret, and then we reinterpret again. In the hermeneutic worldview, all experience is interpretation. As a way into nonverbal reworking, think first of verbal reflection. Do we ever finish saying anything? Are we ever satisfied with interpreting our experience once? Do we not continuously rework our reflective thoughts, so much so that it is sometimes hard to recapture "what we used to think?" When writers revise their work, they usually keep separate copies of their old versions for precisely this reason, especially in the computer age when the old copy no longer exists once one "saves" the new one. And when a new understanding replaces an old one in psychoanalysis, as happens all the time, do we remember the old one a week or a month or a year later?

Why should life be any simpler in the mode of action or practice? If a small child encodes in "action" an adult looming over him and shouting (an example Fourcher, 1992, uses), should we expect that the "action" image will be available in pristine condition years later? Perhaps, and perhaps not. But that is not really the point, because even if it is, it will be accompanied by all manner of reworked versions of itself (or of that *kind* of event, assuming it had the salience for the child that one can easily imagine it had), all encoded in the language of action. Such elaborations will concern people and situations other than the originals—people with whom, and situations in which, the child feared the occurrence of similar-seeming events. The child's internal objects (which are "action" images), and the relationships he has made on their partial basis, will have been shaped by just this kind of reworking—which is why, in the transference, images of parental figures, although they are closely related to what the child actually experienced, are not necessarily simple "copies" of the sum total of those experiences. They are, instead, attempts to interpret and predict—and on these bases, to influence.

The images that result from this elaboration are based on fears of (and wishes for) what the event *meant.* What *could* have happened next (after the looming and shouting)? Could the loud voice have turned soft and forgiving? Could dinner just have gone on as before? Or could the loud voice have turned to violence? Could pain or physical injury have been inflicted? In cases in which the incident is not an isolated one, the child is liable to fantasize about themes in the direction of hatred and even death. Toward what images might a child turn in order to render, interpret, and understand such fears in the language of action? To the fearsome images of fairy tales or *Alien?* To broadcasts of the Power Rangers and their enemies? To a public television program in which lions suffocate a gazelle and then rend and tear its body? Then there are all those even more common cases in which the associative connections between the experience that came first and those others to which it is later linked are less obvious, more private and hidden, hidden even from the child himself, and therefore far less easily grasped in words, by him or by anyone else.

Once they are reworked, elaborated, and reencoded as "action," the relatively public meanings of verbal and nonverbal imagery may become virtually irrelevant in one's inner life. A consensually validated meaning, such as whatever meaning children share regarding the nature of the Power Rangers (that they are heroes, for example), may have little to do with the nonverbal symbolic function that such imagery may take on in the mode of "action," in which, for instance, the Power Rangers might transmute into figures inspiring fear. It is at this point that conventional, consensually validated imagery slips into the more private and less easily grasped vocabulary of phobia, fantasy, and dream. Such imagery just might someday be coaxed to reemerge into public view, but only under very special interpersonal circumstances, such as a psychoanalysis that feels safe enough (see chapter 9). And even if it does emerge again, the meaning that finds its way back into words will not be the one that disappeared into the inner world in the first place. It has been used for a new purpose, and will never again be only what it was, even if it can be interpreted in verbal language successfully enough to be understood.

Thus we never finish *envisioning* anything that matters to us, any more than we ever finish *saying* it. It may be true, as Jacobson (1997) warns, that in its eagerness to embrace the socially constructed, relational, two-person model, psychoanalysis is in danger of sacrificing Freud's great insight about the power of the unconscious to generate the unconventional; but if there is reason to be concerned, the threat, it seems to me, is not due to problems inherent in the two-person model, but to problems with how it is used. In combination with one another, the two factors I have just discussed—the incommensurability of action and knowledge, and the continuous reworking that goes on within each of these modes of experience—actually make unconventional experience quite common. We are all inhabited by such experiences; but because even they exist within the confines of the horizon, they are probably less unconventional than we think. What is uncommon is the desire to know about the unconventional. And then, too, there is Sarraute's frustration, which reminds us that it is difficult to know the unconventional, even when one is relatively unambivalent about doing so.

RAPPROCHEMENT: TWO MEANINGS FOR THE WORD "LANGUAGE"

We need not be concerned that the postmodern critique denies the nonverbal phenomena that are the heart of psychoanalysis. That concern, as we have seen, is due to the inappropriate conflation of two meanings of the word "language." In the broadest cultural context, language as semiotics applies to the possibility of any meaning at all. To try to discuss meaning outside the reach of semiotics is meaningless. Reality may very well exist apart from language; it's just that we simply have no way to apprehend it. Languageless reality is what Lacan calls "the Real," and it cannot be directly known.

But this same word, "language," when used in the colloquial sense, the way we use it in everyday conversation, also continues to apply appropriately to the familiar differences between, say, short stories and dreams—between the worded and the unworded, our familiar verbal and nonverbal ways of experiencing. There is no contradiction here, only an overlap of terms representing different levels of experience. What we are used to thinking of as the nonverbal remains nonverbal—but only in relation to worded experience—which is, of course, what we always meant in the first place. And the nonverbal remains part of what is genuinely ambiguous about our experience, but, once again, only in relation to words, which we must use to extract a verbal meaning from the nonverbal by taking a perspective on it.

We cannot overemphasize the significance for clinical psychoanalysis of the hermeneutic-postmodern insight that all experience is interpretive and perspectivist; the idea has quite literally rearranged the broader intellectual world, and is in the process of rearranging psychoanalytic theory and practice. It is certainly the soil within which the view of psychoanalysis presented in this book is rooted. But in day-to-day psychotherapeutic and psychoanalytic work, semiotics is not the definition of language that we use. We use, instead, our more colloquial understandings of what verbal and nonverbal mean. And we do not need to change that practice, because psychoanalysis remains based in verbal reflection. From this point on, throughout the book, the interpretivism of the postmodern critique of language underlies every chapter; but when I use the words "language," or "verbal" and "nonverbal" experience, I will be speaking in the conventional or everyday sense. I will intend by these words what we take them to be in nontechnical conversations. In particular, by "nonverbal" I will mean to refer to experience coded in that other, unworded "language" of action or practice.

THE CONTINUING CENTRALITY
OF SELF-REFLECTION IN PSYCHOANALYSIS

Many kinds of therapeutic change do not require the choice and decision that verbal reflection makes possible. Even in psychoanalytic treatment, the most crucial events are often moments of relatedness that go forever undescribed. But the stated, conscious *aim* of clinical psychoanalysis—what analysts actually set out to do—nevertheless remains the grasp of the nonverbal in words, or the retelling in new words of earlier worded experience. We intend to learn what experience *means* to us and our patients, and in the course of making these meanings explicit, which may involve a significant degree of creation, the experiences themselves may change. Postmodernism does not alter the fact that psychoanalysis is defined by its attempt to expand self-knowledge and widen the range of explicit choice. These aims continue to require that we reflect on our experience, and this kind of self-examination continues to require words. It is this approach to interpretation that leads hermeneutic thinkers to describe taking a perspective on experience as "engaging" it: to engage experience is to struggle with what it means.

As psychoanalysts have special reasons to know, it is much easier to make reference to this kind of self-reflection than it is to accomplish it. The understandings that really matter—those of our interpretations of our own unconscious lives that are most meaningful—are not merely workmanlike and competent, but unbidden, and therefore more truly our own than they would be if we made them to satisfy prosaic, instrumental, or purely willful purposes. Merleau-Ponty (1964b) writes that, "Personal life, expression, understanding, and history advance obliquely and not straight towards ends or concepts. What one too deliberately seeks, he does not find" (p. 83). And elsewhere he says, "there is in all expression a spontaneity which will not tolerate any commands, not even those which I would like to give to myself" (p. 75). Our best choices and decisions about how to speak about ourselves and one another—our most effective self-reflections—are not under our control. They do not necessarily occur when we desire them to; they have their own life. Yet we know we can encourage them. We can do our best to occupy the kind of existence in which spontaneous, generative understanding becomes most likely. That, in fact, is the ideal state in which to free associate—or rather, that is the ideal of free association. As Merleau-Ponty goes on to say, "he who on the contrary has in his meditative life known how to tap its spontaneous source never lacks for ideas and values" (p. 83).

It is only this kind of paradoxically purposeful and spontaneous reflection, which is really our capacity to allow our most deeply felt intentions free play in the realm of words, that leads to conscious choices that are deeply and openly considered. Only the direct engagement with experience that this kind of self-reflection represents gives us the opportunity to lead examined lives, whether we are patients examining our personal lives or psychoanalysts examining our theories and daily professional conduct. We work in psychoanalysis toward an authentic, unforced consideration of what we fear and what we most deeply desire, and of the consequences of these things. We want to know what our lives mean and what meanings are alive for us.

This special kind of spontaneous reflective understanding goes by many names besides *engagement* in this book, and all of them are ways of referring to the articulation of unformulated experience: the unbidden perceptions that we allow to shape creative disorder (chapter 4); imagination and creative speech (chapter 5); spelling-out (chapter 6); the recognition of "fit" and the "shape of absence" (chapter 9); breaking the grip of the field (chapter 10); emerging from embeddedness (chapters 10 and 11); and courting surprise (chapter 12). Imaginative, disembedding understanding and its avoidance, dissociation, are twin themes in the chapters to come. In the end, though, no matter the expression we use, the conclusion we reach is that it is only by bringing one kind of language—that is, prereflective meaning, however much it may already qualify as a linguistically (semiotically) organized scheme of meaning—into the terms of another, very particular kind of language—words—that we can put ourselves in a position to see and think coherently about our lives and the broader values that shape them.

For writers all the way from Freud to Sullivan and beyond, everyday language is a set of labels to be applied to experience. However, if our everyday language does not merely label reflective experience, but is the means by which it is actively shaped, the first-person voice in clinical psychoanalysis is not just the state of mind created by what we allow to cross the threshold from the unconscious. Conscious, reflective meaning is an interpretation, cocreated by verbal language and preexisting meaning, both verbal and nonverbal. And so, *in the perspective of the first person, within the purview of the "I," all unconscious material is unformulated.* The eventual conscious, reflective shape of unconscious material has not been finally determined, no matter how structured this material is, because it remains to be interpreted in words. Experience *is* fundamentally ambiguous, then, just as it is said to be in the constructivist vision—at least our future *reflective* experience is ambiguous, because we have not yet chosen the verbal perspective from which we will shape it.

Roy Schafer, whose large and crucially important body of work over the last two decades (1976, 1978, 1983, 1992) both provoked the downfall of metapsychology and provided the hermeneutic alternative that has reshaped and reinvigorated psychoanalysis, was the first significant psychoanalytic theorist to recognize that language and reflection actually shape experience. Schafer's (1983) summary of his view serves just as well to recapitulate the claims I have just made.

When the analysand is viewed as being engaged in narrative performance, he or she will be understood to be giving only one of a great number of possible accounts that could be given of these life events. Indeed, on this view, one can never have unmediated access to these events, for the events can exist only in narrative accounts that have been or may be developed by the analysand or analyst for different purposes and in different contexts. . . . In psychoanalysis, the versions of significant events change as the work progresses, and with these changes go changes in what is called the experience of these events, for the narrative accounts and the experiences are inseparable. Contrary to the plans and fears of analysands, the analyst never takes immediately available or emphasized subjective experience as the final or definitive version of anything, for the analyst views that experience as always being constructed and reconstructed; it can be encountered only in explicit or implicit narrative accounts [p. 186].

A NOTE OF CAUTION

This makes words sound powerful. And they are: they are the sole means of our engagement with living. To plunge into experience without knowing that one is doing so—that is, to do so without explicit reflection—is less likely to be courageous than merely impetuous. The power of words is one of the primary underpinnings of the chapters to follow. But it is also worth preserving our humility and our capacity to be skeptical of this great reflective capacity of ours. The power of language exists only in its own little context. Language would look less mysterious and far simpler to a deity who could see us as we cannot see ourselves. An all-knowing being, one for whom all possible perspectives existed, would see that whereas each moment of our reflective experience does indeed remain to be created, the possibilities for reflective experience tend to be predetermined, even if the specific forms of the experiences each of us will have next is not. Heidegger and Gadamer describe culture as a "clearing" within which experience carries meaning, surrounded by a tightly circumscribed horizon. The potentially meaningful is a small space carved out of the vastness of the possible, the All. From the god's-eye view of that deity I have just invented, the range within which we can find perspectives to adopt, the bandwidth within which we engage experience, would probably seem absurdly narrow. Outside that range, experience does not exist at all. And even inside it, its ambiguity is not absolute, because the interpretations we can make, and the symbolic tools with which we make them, are limited. If language is a big fish, it is only because it swims in a very small pond. We must maintain our capacity to be suspicious of what emerges through reflection, because whatever else it is, it is also one of the meanings that language was shaped to reveal in the first place.

On one hand, then, our capacity to reflect is revelatory; but on the other, its very existence is the proof of what we lack. Words bring meanings into the light only at the price of leaving others in the darkness. What we know in reflective awareness is defined by what we have not said and cannot say, just as words are defined by what they do not mean. This is a theme all along the postmodern spectrum, all the way from the relativism and fictionalism of Derrida to the perspectival realism of Gadamer.

If being curious is to surprise ourselves with our capacity to reimagine what we already are, it must also be true that we need to keep trying to catch psychoanalysis itself out of the corners of our eyes. Our theories and clinical practice are structured just as surely and thoroughly as we ourselves are by the vast game of living. Part of our responsibility as psychoanalysts and psychotherapists is to struggle to imagine how. What sinister, unwitting purposes, for instance, might even self-reflection serve? (Foucault, 1973). "I have seen the enemy," Pogo said some time ago, "and they is us." There is no solution here, only our attempt to maintain uncertainty, and our continuous skepticism about our success in doing so.

What sometimes saves us, and now and then makes new meaning possible, is that culture is not monolithic. Each of us is an intersection of many cultural and linguistic traditions (see Cushman, 1995). The value of uncertainty is not an abstract principle. Uncertainty is good because its maintenance allows multiple traditions to contribute in unexpected ways to the formulation of the unformulated.

THE GIVEN AND THE MADE, REDUX

We can return now, with a more explicit position, to the problem of the given and the made. The givens or preconstructed meanings that we interpret and reinterpret in words comprise material of several different kinds: structured, nonverbal meanings coded in practice or action; previous verbal formulations that may be used in reformulations; and all those unconsidered, undeveloped, or potential meanings that are implicit to previous verbal formulations—the interpretations that could have been made, but were disregarded. None of these givens spontaneously appear in conscious experience, as they do if they are conceived to represent the return of the repressed, but they all do serve as *constraints* on conscious reflection. The more structured an unconscious meaning is, the greater the role it plays in the partnership between itself and words. That is, the more structured the unconscious meaning, the greater the constraint it exercises on the meanings that can be validly constructed by means of verbal reflection.

Undeveloped implications of earlier verbal formulations, for instance, are themselves implicitly verbal. Whatever structure they have is determined by the verbal interpretations they might have become. To the extent that such material can be said to exist at all, it is something like "verbal possibility." Because it is already defined relative to words, it brings very little constraint to language. Its constraints are really only the constraints of verbal language itself.

On the other hand, structured meanings coded in action or practice may impose a relatively high degree of constraint on language. If we interpret outside these constraints, the words just seem wrong. The analyst who misinterprets an allergic patient's teary eyes as a sign of sadness will be corrected forthwith.

But although we can posit the presence of constraints, and although we may be able to sense when we have violated at least those that are most structured, that is as far as we can ever go toward grasping whatever reality is. Even those hermeneuticists, such as Gadamer, who accept a relation between understanding and some kind of ultimate reality, do not believe we can ever directly perceive truth, only that small piece of it, or "take" on it, that is available in our particular time and place. All that we really have a chance of knowing is when we are wrong. We can never say exactly what constraints are, or when we are most right (cf. Stern, 1985; Gill, 1995).

For psychoanalysis, one very important corollary of this view, and one that has been noted over and over again, is that bodily processes constrain experience. But this is a very complicated matter, because while we may imagine that some aspects of our sexual feelings, the arousal of rage, the autonomic upsurge that accompanies what we call anxiety, and so on, are givens, we can never really know what those given aspects are. Any such statement requires interpretation on our part, and interpretations are the products of the cultures in which we live. Any description of the nature of bodily constraints on experience, then, cannot be simply objective, no matter how irresistibly obvious, sensible, or insightful it may seem. It is instead a political and moral statement. We cannot even know the extent to which the way we shape and define events, such as the examples I just mentioned (sexual feelings, rage, and so on) are themselves cultural constructions. The conception of constraints, although it is useful and perhaps even necessary, can never be illustrated or exemplified in concrete terms.

The principle that language is constitutive means that the constraint exercised by even the most stable and highly structured unconscious meaning can only be partial: no constraint can completely determine conscious formulation. Verbal-reflective meaning is never preordained, and therefore it is always ambiguous prior to its creation in each moment. And the principle that the unconscious continuously reworks and elaborates itself into new forms, which then, in their turn, await interpretation in language, means that we sometimes use even the words of a cliché to engage experience in an authentic way. When the unconscious itself offers something new, its interpretation in conventional terms can be the route to a novel perspective; seeing the new as an instance of the old is sometimes as fresh and useful as seeing the old in a new way.

We now come full circle to psychoanalytic constructivism, for the ambiguity we always face in the next moment is precisely what I mean by the concept of unformulated experience. Thus my answer to the problem of the given and the made is a version of Winnicott's, with which I began the chapter. The given and the made are a dialectic, neither ever excluding the other and both constituting every meaning and moment. Without the opportunity to change previously structured experience, and without that previous structure to feel and think against, new experience would be impossible. We would be trapped in an evanescent subjectivism. But, on the other hand, without our capacity for an imagination that goes beyond experiential regularities, without the animation of spontaneous expression and the continuous reworking that represents our ceaseless effort to understand, we would never be able to redeem our experience from the stasis of dead convention. It is reflection that saves the unconscious from being nothing more than a set of strictures, and makes it a precious resource instead; and it is the unconscious that offers reflection the fecund and ever-changing materials with which to carry out its life-giving mission.

REFLECTION AND THE INTERPERSONAL FIELD

I argue later on that most not-knowing that occurs under circumstances in which knowing is at least possible is best described as dissociation, and that dissociation should be defined as the unconscious decision not to interpret experience, to leave it in its unformulated state for defensive reasons. But how are these interpretive opportunities occluded? How do we construct experience in such a way that opportunities for knowing are invisible to us?

Our conflicts over whether to know are contextualized in every instance; knowing is a function of the interpersonal field. Each moment of the field is defined by all levels of the interplay between the various conscious and unconscious influences we and our interactive partner(s) bring to the meeting. The interpersonal field structures the possibilities of knowing—the potential for what we can say and think and what we cannot. The field is the source of that continuous succession of personal "horizons" or "clearings" within which each of us exists (chapter 8). And yet its role is invisible and unsuspected. We seldom have any awareness that the fields we are always in the process of constructing with other people set the limits on what portion of our own prereflective experience we will be able to engage and formulate in words, and on the particular selection of interpretive formulations of that experience that will be available to us. Actually, we should go even further: we seldom have any awareness of participating in the construction of a field at all, whatever its function.

We do have varying degrees of freedom about whether to know the fields we have already made, however. It is sometimes possible, if we take on risk and bear uncertainty, to reflect on the interpersonal constraints we so easily fall into. With some people, in some situations, especially the psychoanalytic situation, we feel safe enough to know ourselves in ways that set us on the edge of danger (chapter 9). But that is rare, of course; in most of life's situations, we do not.

Analyst and patient together, inevitably and without conscious purpose, but with deep-running intentionality born of both of them, construct an interpersonal context that allows only certain parts of their experience to come within the range of their capacity to know in words, and allows even those that come within range to be submitted to only certain interpretive approaches. Other experiences and interpretations are, quite simply, locked out, banished (until the field changes in the relevant respects) to the far side of one's personal horizon (chapter 11). The only way for the analytic participants to expand the limits of what they can know together is to grasp the unconscious aspects of this interpersonal situation they have made. As patient and analyst become able to notice the underlying regularities that structure their interactions, which is usually the same thing as understanding why these patterns needed to be constructed in the first place, they eventually "break the field's grip" (chapter 10) and arrive at unsuspected possibilities for new experience (chapter 12).

And so here, at the end of this consideration of the given and the made, we see that the most important phenomenon of all is one that is always both. It is made in every moment: it is the endless flux of interaction. But it is also the one given experience upon which we depend most, because it is the context within which all other representations come about, the one constraint that operates in every instance. It is the interpersonal field itself.

2

Unformulated Experience

An Introduction

When we refer to unconscious influence in psychoanalysis, what do we mean? Do we intend to refer to an objective presence in psychic life, a thought or an affect or a memory that somehow exists as a fact, but outside our ken? Or do we intend to refer to an absence, something missing in experience, an unconsidered or undeveloped implication? Is unconscious material fully formed and merely awaiting uncovering or discovery, or is it potential experience that remains to be spelled out? How should we think clinically about questions such as these?

Consider the dream of a man in his 30s going through a divorce and feeling so sad and bereft that he can scarcely imagine a different kind of future. In his dream he is driving very carefully on an icy mountain road. Around him thick snow is falling. It is silent and cloudy, and the landscape is dull and colorless—black, white, and shades of gray, evoking (in his associations) his depression over his divorce. As he rounds a turn in the road, which hugs the shoulder of the mountain, the sun appears very suddenly, shining brilliantly in a cloudless and intensely blue sky, and he is faced with a breathtaking mountainside of glittering snowfields and intensely green trees. It seems to him at that moment, inside the dream, that this vista is the most beautiful thing he has ever seen, and he is filled with a feeling of great happiness and fulfillment.

After listening to other associations to the dream, the man's analyst tells him that he believes the dream is a way of depicting previously unimagined inner resources that the patient will be able to use to make a new life. The patient, deeply moved, feels immediately the truth of this interpretation.

Was the content of the analyst's interpretation already "there" in the patient's unconscious prior to the analyst's intervention?

As a better example: A 21-year-old man, in the first stages of a treatment, reports a dream in which he finds himself on a dark street confronted by several men. There is a sense of menace. He is frightened, but he also has the sense that he has done something that has angered his adversaries, though he does not know what it is. He feels resigned to whatever happens; he feels vaguely in the wrong. The dream ends without an attack actually taking place. In his associations, the patient focuses for some time on what his transgression could have been: perhaps he has tripped over one of the youths; perhaps he has stepped in front of one of them in line; perhaps he has criticized the driving of one of them.

After getting nowhere in particular by looking into where each imagined transgression might lead, the analyst eventually tells the patient that, by comparison to the sense of menace, the transgressions he imagines seem insignificant. The analyst also tells the patient that he knows retaliation can sometimes be out of proportion to the provocation, especially in New York City (which is where the patient and analyst live), but that it is important to remember who the author of the dream is. Why, he asks the patient, does he think he might have portrayed justice so cruelly? The patient responds that he had not noticed the fact that his imagined provocations were paltry, but that he can see it is true as soon as the analyst mentions it. He then tells the analyst that, in fact, he even feels guilty and ashamed if he goes to the store for bread and the store has run out: he should have known in the first place to go to another store. With increasing momentum, and even excitement, the patient begins to put together an interpretation of the dream based on his relationship with his father, who (it now emerges) has always blamed the patient unreasonably for things that could not possibly have been his fault. If the father could not find his shoes, for instance, he might insist that the patient had hidden them, when in fact the patient had not, and never had. The patient was sure his father fully believed his own accusations, because he would scream and sometimes curse at his son, who felt badly, despite his initial certainty that he did not take the shoes on purpose. Perhaps, the patient would think, he had accidentally pushed them under a piece of furniture. Perhaps, even if he hadn't lost them, he should have been able to find them. Or perhaps (if the screaming went on long enough), he would think that he might have forgotten about hiding the shoes.

The father's paranoia and his toxic impact on his son's reality testing become disturbingly apparent. But how should we understand the patient's interpretation of the dream? Did it exist prior to the analyst's intervention? Did it exist prior to the patient's capacity to put it into words?

Here is another example, this time of the patient's perception of the analyst. A young woman reads an article in the newspaper about the thinking of a particular psychoanalyst, then comes to her session and tells her analyst that she wishes for "something more" in his response to her. It is not specific content the patient finds wanting, but a certain kind of understanding that the other analyst (according to the patient's reading of the article) seems to be able to convey. The patient's own analyst does not convey this understanding, the patient says. She muses that prior to reading the article, not only could she not have said what she felt deprived of, she could not even have said that she was missing something. She cannot put into words how she thought about these matters before. In fact, she believes there were no words available to her. She cannot recapture what the "missing" was like then, because she would have to use the words she did not find until later. She recognizes, she says, that this means she can do no more than provide a description in the present.

Was this patient's experience of missing something already present "in" the patient before her reading of the newspaper article? Was that feeling of missing something already "there" prior to her first words for it?

These questions do not have to be answered with a simple yes or no. As a matter of fact, they cannot and should not be answered simply. Unconscious meaning is a slippery idea. On the one hand, we have all those data we have cited for generations: dreams, parapraxes, symptoms, transference—the phenomena that were so compelling to Freud. We are so used to believing that these phenomena are the visible evidence of invisible, nonverbal, and (if we could but see them) clearly defined unconscious structures that we have lost track of the fact that we are making an interpretation when we think this way. The belief that a single, very particular latent content underlies the phenomenon we do see is one of those interpretations that feels like a simple fact. And it feels that way even though, in daily clinical work, we seldom, if ever, have the confidence that we have really captured a preexisting latent content in words.

More often than not, we lack the confidence that we have "nailed down" the unconscious meanings our patients present to us in their conduct and experience. We are uncertain; we consider alternatives. Early in our careers, especially during the years when we are still prone to the belief that someone else, someone more experienced or capable than we are, would know *exactly* what a dream or a symptom means, we lack that comfortable feeling we imagine we would have if we could just see more clearly. Even later on in our professional lives, once we have developed more comfort in not knowing, we tend to understand the ambiguity of our experience as the joint result of our limitations and the complex distortions of the defenses that intervene between the patient's unconscious meaning and its effects. We rarely consider that our difficulty might be, instead, directly related to the nature of that which we are trying to understand, or to the intrinsic ambiguity of our interpretive task. We so take for granted the idea that the content of the unconscious has one particular meaning that we tend not even to imagine alternative theories. Having lost its status as a perspective or a hypothesis, the idea has been taken up into our everyday sense of things and is simply the expectable state of affairs, as if it were a feature of the natural world.

I do not intend to deconstruct the notion of an unconscious merely awaiting verbal labels; that major task is a different kind of effort than the more clinical one I am undertaking. By the same token, though, the idea of a fully formed unconscious influencing conscious experience in ways that are simply objective or factual deserves to be challenged. I here mount a challenge of that sort, but I do so not so much by taking issue with the older view as by exploring the clinical implications of a newer one: What can be gained from a conception of unconscious meaning as unformulated? The inquiry provoked by this question will take us beyond the particular concept of unformulated experience to the hermeneutic, constructivist conception of mind and experiencing in psychoanalysis that I have already begun to present in chapter 1.

WHAT IS UNFORMULATED EXPERIENCE?

When a patient is finally able to think about a previously unaccepted part of life, seldom are fully formulated thoughts simply waiting to be discovered, ready for exposition. Instead, what is usually experienced is a fresh state of not-knowing, a kind of confusion—a confusion with newly appreciable possibilities, and perhaps an intriguing confusion, but a confusion or a puzzle nevertheless. One is curious. Before, one could not even have said there was anything to learn; now one realizes for the first time that one does not know—and, by implication, that one has not known.

Unconscious clarity rarely underlies defense. On the evidence of our observations of them as they emerge in awareness, the perceptions, ideas, and memories we prefer not to have, the observations we prefer not to make, are often murky and poorly defined, different in kind than they will be when the process of articulation has reached the level of words. The moments of confusion may be quite brief, barely noticeable, or they may be lengthy, becoming either deeply intriguing or disturbing. "Unformulated experience" is the label I have chosen to refer to mentation characterized by lack of clarity and differentiation. Unformulated experience is the uninterpreted form of those raw materials of conscious, reflective experience that may eventually be assigned verbal interpretations and thereby brought into articulate form.

The phenomenon is analogous to an experience most people have had at twilight, when the light is dim and unreliable and familiar shapes can be hard to recognize. Once in a while, at a moment like this, or in a dimly lighted room, one sees something, but simply cannot make a coherent visual experience out of it. Whatever one is seeing stubbornly resists coalescing into an identifiable shape, and one hangs in the perceptual lurch. The affective accompaniment ranges from playful interest to a sense of awe, dislocation, and disorientation so severe it can be nauseating. Among children, more rarely adults, fears sometimes shape the ambiguity, so that fright or terror results. For a three-year-old in a dimly lit room, the ambiguous shape of a towel draped over a chair may assume sentience, perhaps malevolence. But most of the time, in a few moments the unformulated percept falls together into some familiar shape, and one is relieved. One may be left, however, with an increased awareness of the ubiquity of interpretation in our psychic lives, a suspicion that even the coherent perception, when it emerges, is an interpretation, just one that happens to fall easily into place.

One seems to develop a coherent percept at the very same moment in which one is first able to give words to what one is seeing. Just as well-formed percepts do not exist "in" or "behind" the indistinct, unrecognizable experiences of twilight shapes, well-formed cognitions do not exist in or behind the unformulated states that precede them. Rather, the well-formed version remains to be shaped. The unformulated is not yet knowable in the separate and definable terms of language. Unformulated material is composed of vague tendencies; if allowed to develop to the point at which they can be shaped and articulated, these become the more lucid kind of reflective experience we associate with mutually comprehended verbal articulations.

But at this point the analogy of the indistinct object fails, because our uncertainty about the identity of such an object can generally be resolved in only one way. With additional illumination, everyone sees the same form. There is very little ambiguity about a cat located directly under a shining streetlamp, for example, even if it can be hard to make visual sense out of the same cat lurking in the shadows; once the lights go on, that towel draped over the chair, so ambiguous a figure in half-light, immediately becomes the same thing to everyone.

But most of what people talk about in psychoanalytic treatment allows a much wider range of interpretation than well-lighted cats and towels. These other kinds of experience, especially social experiences, are not so inevitably bound to a stimulus. They are much less likely to be divided into perceptual units in just the same way by everyone. Once we move on from perception to consider other levels of meaning, the number of different interpretations that can be made of the same stimulus multiplies by leaps and bounds.

The more a particular kind of experience is the result of an implicit interpretive process, the more variation we can expect to find among different people's versions of it. For example, we should expect to find a very high degree of complexity and variability in the comprehension of gesture or the attribution of intention. There are opportunities at almost every turn, literally from one moment to the next, for interpretive variation.

Most of the material of a psychoanalysis can be experienced in more than one way by the two participants involved. This is so even when the two agree on the basic nature of the people and events under discussion. The way each of us shapes moment-to-moment experience is the outcome of our characteristic patterns of formulation interacting with the exigencies of the moment. Because "exigencies of the moment" almost always refers to happenings with other people, real or imaginary—"illusory," in Sullivan's description—the resolution of the ambiguity of unformulated experience is an interpersonal event. That is, what we think at any particular moment is not only a function of our inner worlds—our histories, our characters, the structured unconscious activities that contribute to the organization and continuity of experience. That view is familiar enough: one person characteristically experiences differently than another. What I want to lay special stress on, though, is the formative influence on all of our experience of the ongoing interpersonal transaction, not only on the feelings and thoughts that we react with, but the very nature of what is possible for us to formulate. The analyst, like the patient, can know only what the interpersonal field he cocreates with the patient allows him to know.

The meaning in a particular unformulated experience, if it is ever spelled out, may take any one of the more precise forms toward which it moves. It is content without definite shape. In the words of the philosopher Jacques Maritain (1953), it is "a beginning of insight, still unformulated, a kind of many-eyed cloud . . . a humble and trembling inchoation, yet invaluable, tending toward an intelligible content to be grasped" (p. 99). The poet and essayist Paul Valéry (in Ghiselin, 1952) puts it this way: "The fact is that every act of the mind itself is always somehow accompanied by a certain more or less perceptible atmosphere of indeterminacy" (p. 99). In William James's (1890) metaphor, each of us "sculpts" conscious experience from a block (or a stream, as James would have it) of the unformulated that might have been carved in other ways.

The revelation of meaning is more often creation than the discovery of a preexisting truth. Yet to be useful, the newly created meaning must be recognizable. It must fit the stimulus, and it must fit better than the meaning that came before. "Insight into an unconscious wish," writes Herbert Fingarette (1963), "is like noticing a well-formed 'ship' in the cloud instead of a poorly formed 'rabbit.' On the other hand, insight is not like discovering an animal which has been hiding in the bushes" (p. 20).

THOUGHT AND AFFECT

Experience is all of a piece. One does not think and feel at different times, but rather is constantly engaged in the more inclusive task, usually quite invisible, of constructing experience. Affect is not only a reaction to seeing the "ship" instead of the "rabbit"; it is just as much a part of the process of shaping the new percept. The separation of thought and affect has been a feature of Western philosophical and psychological theorizing since Plato. Indeed, though there is now reason to believe that thought and feeling are inextricable on even the level of neurophysiology (Damasio, 1994), it remains heuris-

tically useful at times for experimentalists and theorists to define
these processes as independent sets of events that interact with one
another. But in psychoanalysis, such a separation is misleading,
because in clinical work the sole concern is how people actually experience. In the end, what matters most is what the participants can
sense or know directly, because it is immediate experience that transforms mere inference into conviction.

Nevertheless, psychoanalysts are obviously members of their cultures, and because the European world has so often unthinkingly considered thought and affect separately, psychoanalysts often have done
the same. As a result, the words "cognition" and "thought" are sometimes used in clinical discussions as if they refer to intellectualization,
which of course is inauthentic by definition; and "feeling," "affect," or
"emotion," when referred to separately, tend to be idealized, as if the
phenomena the words describe are the only genuine or authentic
aspects of experience. Yet neither authenticity nor affect, of course, is
an "ingredient" of experience, as if it could be added like oregano.

If thought and feeling are an indivisible unity, cognition, which it
is convenient to define as an amalgam of the two, should be construed
as a continuous process of worldmaking, a psychic endeavor on the
borderland between psychology and epistemology (cf. Barnett, 1980).
Even when one can observe a separation of thought and feeling, the
separation is a seeming, an appearance, not a natural division.
Consider isolation of affect and intellectualization, which are defined
precisely by the intention to split the unity of experience; or think of
psychosomatic symptoms, conversions, hysterical affect, and inexplic-
able panic attacks, which may be dissociated from words precisely
because that characteristic makes them useful in defense.

And so the process of formulating experience is as much the clarification of emotion as it is the articulation of semantic meaning, and
unformulated experience refers not only to the germs of words, but
of passions as well. When the process of formulation has progressed,
feelings can be worded and language is woven with emotion.

REIFICATION

We assume breaks or separations between cognitive phenomema for
which we have different words—or rather, our culture's inescapable
everyday language of cognition makes the assumption. These
assumptions guide the way language seems to formulate thoughts,

feelings, perceptions, memories, and so on—in discrete units. We have no consensually validated means of expressing the way a memory melts into a thought about the present, or the way one thought or feeling verges into another. To the careful observer, it sometimes seems that there is a pinprick of a moment during this melting or verging during which it is impossible to say where one instance ends and the next begins. And as soon as we have one thought, the next begins to arise from within that one in just the same way. Clinical psychoanalysis, to me, is firmly rooted in phenomenology.

To be accurate, then, at least on the level of the fine-grained introspective account I favor, I would have to accomplish the impossible task of describing experience while avoiding the idea that we experience in chunks or pieces, just as I would have to avoid the division of thought and feeling, because these characterizations require a process of abstraction. I would have to represent consciousness as a smooth and seamless stream, as William James (1890) did. Consider his description of a thought.

> Let anyone try to cut a thought across in the middle and get a look at its section, and he will see how difficult the introspective observation of the transitive tracts is. The rush of the thought is so headlong that it almost always brings us up at the conclusion before we can arrest it. Or if our purpose is nimble enough and we do arrest it, it ceases forthwith to be itself. As a snowflake crystal caught in the warm hand is no longer a crystal but a drop, so, instead of catching the feeling of relation moving to its term, we find we have caught some substantive thing, usually the last word we were pronouncing, statically taken, and with its function, tendency, and particular meaning in the sentence quite evaporated. The attempt at introspective analysis in these cases is in fact like seizing a spinning top to catch its motion, or trying to turn up the gas quickly enough to see how the darkness looks [p. 244].

Generally, we lose sight of the fact that our ongoing habit of breaking experience into discontinuous pieces is a process of abstraction. ("Speech," writes Merleau-Ponty, 1964a, p. 17, "tears out or tears apart meanings in the undivided whole of the nameable.") We take for granted the existence of discrete experiential units as if they were features of the natural world—as if the phenomena the common words describe (e.g., thought, feeling, perception) demand this kind of description and no other.

In our language, it would be extremely difficult to discuss experiencing if we could not depend upon this assumption that "a" thought and "a" memory (a "feeling," for that matter, to recapitulate the argument I just made about cognition) are "real." The very title of this book is itself a reification of this kind. And as I begin to make an argument for a hermeneutic way of understanding what "unconscious" means, at times I will need to resort to even more stubbornly opaque reifications, notions like structured unconscious meaning, unconscious experience, and mental representation.

Yet what we are all talking about, in referring to content or structure or experience, is not a thing at all, but certain processes, ones that have continuity over time. Some have more continuity (organization), some less; but each is a channel, or a current, if you will, along which meaning can flow. Such processes result in our long-term readiness to construct experience in particular, stable ways and, often enough, our insistence on such constructions. In psychoanalysis, we refer to these processes, variously, as character, schemata, transference and countertransference, internal object representations, imagos, unconscious fantasies, and so on. Therefore, when we use words like structure, content, and representation in reference to experiencing, what we really intend to refer to is the plethora of processes in any one person's psychic life that keep reproducing experience in meaningfully similar shapes. We are referring to the interpreter's organizing activity.

Roy Schafer's (1976, 1978) solution to the problem of reification in psychoanalysis is to convert all descriptions of psychological events into a language that recognizes their status as activity ("action language"). I am drawn to Schafer's aims here, and I admire his rigor. But in the end, for me, the awkwardness of action language overcomes its rigor and rightness. Writing and speaking that way forces linguistic expression in directions it does not go by itself, and so, in the attempt to say things correctly, one loses some of the things one wanted to say. That price might be one a philosopher should pay; but for me, ease and flexibility of expression is worth the price I must pay to use it.

PROGRESSIVE CLARIFICATION:
EXPERIENCE AS EMERGENT

Everyday introspection leads us to believe that reflective experience—the kind of experience we can stand back from and observe—

just arrives. It has no precursors. One moment an experience is not there; the next moment it is. It would appear from this impression that experience "jumps" or "leaps" into existence. From nothing comes something, and all at once. The transition from absence to presence, or from one presence to another, is like the change in what appears on a movie screen from one cut to the next. As the camera angle changes, the new perspective is suddenly there, without lag or delay, without the necessity of focusing or developing the image. We are presented with something that is immediately crisp and clear.

When we introspect very carefully, however, attending to our own processes of experiencing on the finest level of differentiation we can muster, our observations tell a different story. Each moment's experience grows from the experience of the moment before; the process of growth is a process of progressive clarification. Progressive clarification, or the process of emergence, is closely related to the idea of "microgenesis," defined and introduced by Heinz Werner (1956) as the sequence of necessary steps that must occur in the unfolding of a psychological phenomenon. When applied to the development of thought from one moment to the next, microgenesis conveys precisely what I intend in referring to the process of formulating the unformulated. As Arieti (1962) states, "Wherever development occurs it proceeds from a state of relative globality and lack of differentiation to a state of increasing differentiation, articulation and hierarchic integration" (p. 279).

But microgenesis describes the minute developmental life of each thought, in and of itself. I want to focus instead on the development of each moment's conscious experience out of the experience of the one before—or, to be more thorough, the development of the present moment's conscious, explicit, linguistically articulable experience out of the conscious and unconscious mental activity, verbal and nonverbal, that took place in the preceding moment. The progression of mental activity, including that part of it that arrives in awareness, is organic and continuous. Sometimes, after the fact, the way one moment developed from the previous one comes to our attention; more often, it does not.

Despite the regularity of this progression, though, the outcome of the next moment is seldom predictable. A welter of futures is alive in each clinical instant; we cannot know which ones will be called into being in the next moment by the unique and unutterably complex combination of factors that we call the ongoing analytic interaction. The fascination of psychoanalysis is precisely the opportunity to study this progression as it occurs. The next moment just happens, and that "just happens" goes on continuously. Sometimes we can then retrace its history, or at least, what we take its history to have been.

Clinical psychoanalysis, then, like its object of study, is an emergent activity. Each moment, for each participant, is implied in some way by the moment each of them experienced just before. Each moment that actually comes alive was one of the unformulated possibilities.

By unformulated experience, I intend to refer to two phenomena. One is molar and long-term: in this sense, unformulated experience is the sum total of all the knowable, communicable implications that have never been spelled out, perceptions that have been habitually passed over, and so forth. The molar conception can be related to the ongoing organizing activities—character, for example—that supply life with continuity. The other phenomenon is molecular and short-term: unformulated experience as the moment-to-moment state of vagueness and possibility from which the next moment's articulated experience emerges. In practice, these two uses of the term often overlap, because a thought that is habitually unformulated is also part of each moment's potential experience, part of the raw materials that may be tapped for the construction of the next moment's experience.

FREUD'S THOUGHT

The idea that cognitions can exist in a less than precise form was not available to Freud (1900, 1915), who based his theory of repression and unconcious conflict on the premise, generally rejected today, that perception is a sensory given and immediately known to the subject (e.g., Eccles, 1970; Schimek, 1975). It was generally accepted in Freud's era that understanding the process of perception was a matter of pinning down psychophysics, the science of the relations between sensory stimulation and perceptual experience. These relations were fixed, it was assumed (that is, they were the same at one time as at another); so, on the basis of accurate measurement, the laws governing them should have been discernible. The assumption was that to the extent perceptual experience was not directly caused by sensory stimulation, it was a function of unvarying mental processes that intervened between sensation and perception (cf. Boring, 1950).

Everyone faced with the same stimulus array, then, ought to have the same perception. Any lack of clarity in a psychic element, or any variation from the perceptual norm, must be the consequence of later events than perception itself. The particular "later events" Freud proposed as the engines of these distorting effects, of course, were the twin pressures of drive and defense. Freud's emphasis was less on the moment-to-moment construction of new experiences than on the self-deceptive recombination of old ones. And these old experiences were lodged in the unconscious.

The contents of the Freudian unconscious and the materials of the primary process, both of which certainly seem to qualify as inchoate, are not actually unformulated. It is true that in Freud's work, the associations between elements and the form of the elements themselves are fluid, but cognitions in the Freudian scheme, even when they are disguised, are never anything less than fully realized. They are well-defined carriers of meaning that could be represented in language if one's ego, or one's defenses, would "allow" it.[1] But there is no evolution in form as meaning reaches consciousness. In the Freudian scheme, as a matter of fact, the "real" meaning—the wish or desire that is the source of the conscious idea—can exist only in the unconscious. The conscious representation of experience is actually the paler form. For Freud, in entering consciousness an unconscious meaning must shed its original (primary process) attributes and emerge tamed. There is a loss of information.[2] In contrast, in order to enter consciousness, an unformulated thought, if it is the unconsidered implication of a previous formulation, or an alternative formulation, may actually become "more itself." In these cases, as the thought arrives in awareness, it sometimes actually attains a greater degree of the kind of structure it already had. A vague narrative, for instance, becomes a precise one. In those other cases in which unformulated experience already has a high degree of nonverbal structure (such as, for instance, an unconscious fantasy), what occurs during verbal articulation is a change in form—but the forms are merely different. One is not superior to the other; there is no loss of information.

A hermeneutic or interpretivist understanding of experiencing, then, is that the act of interpretation gives reflective experience its articulate, verbal form. In such an account, the very process of formulation—the process of coming to know in words—assumes a significance and complexity it does not have in Freud's theory. The process of coming to know is more than the shedding of disguise or the eschewal of distortion. This point may actually give the processes of inquiry and interpretation even greater significance than they had to Freud, because these activities now become part of the construction of new meaning, not just the revelation of the old. Movement and change in a particular treatment is therefore more the reflection of an increasing willingness and capacity to perceive and interpret novelty than it is the outcome of bringing to light previously existing truth. Therapeutic action is more often a matter of greater curiosity and freedom of thought than of increased access to preformulated memories.

Today, partially because of data and theories that have accrued since Freud wrote, it is clear that experience, even at its most basic perceptual levels, is not simply given. Most of those who have considered this question over the last several decades, psychoanalysts and cognitive scientists alike, have conceived perception to be an active process, not just the passive registration of unambiguous stimuli. George Klein (1976), for instance, one of the first psychoanalysts to make this conceptual leap, reviewed the considerable literature on active perception that had already accumulated in the 1960s, and concluded that "a unit of reality is any *perceived and confirmable coherence*" (p. 57). An array of events becomes coherent, he continued, through a process shaped partially by one's intentions. He eschewed the problem of "exact" or "accurate" perception, because he believed that there are an infinite number of ways reality can be viewed. This multiplicity meant to him that not only accurate perception, but even *exhaustive* perception—the mere grasp of the full range of possibilities—was quite impossible. The adequacy of a perception could be judged, he thought, only by the degree to which it served the purpose that gave rise to it. To a significant degree, Klein believed, even in those early days of hermeneutics in psychoanalysis, that what we perceive is significantly determined by what we intend to perceive.

It seems that we continuously construct our pictures of the world according to unconscious cognitive rules, or algorithms. None of us can say, for instance, how we perform such automatized activities as driving a car or riding a bicycle. We just do these things, despite their level of complexity. Another simple example is the accessing of information. We do not know, for example, how we come up with the right sequence of numerals when we are asked for a familiar phone number. And consider more complex processes. We really have no idea how it is that we manage to speak coherently, making our meanings known to others, without paying the slightest attention to how we choose the multitude of words we use to do so. The process is, for the most part, effortless. We do not know how we recognize faces, make judgments, or perceive other people's emotional states or behavioral dispositions. On a very high level of complexity, consider the fact that chess masters frequently cannot specify their strategies (deGroot, 1965; cited by Lewicki, 1986).

Even at its most basic levels, experience is not wholly given; we also make it, or construct it, though seldom do we have a conscious hand in the process. It seems that we can be unaware of cognitive material not only because we refuse to acknowledge that we know it, but also because it has not yet been spelled out. It has not yet attained a form in which consciousness can—or will—grasp it.

STRUCTURE IN UNCONSCIOUS MEANING

But of course, as I have already taken pains to say, in presenting the non-verbal structure of unconscious meaning as a constraint on reflective interpretation, the fact that we have a good deal of latitude in the for-mulation of experience hardly implies that we have complete freedom. There is a range within which our interpretations of the world around us are acceptable and plausible, but there are also boundaries around any kind of experience beyond which we cannot assert an interpreta-tion without appearing grossly inaccurate or downright crazy.

In the treatment situation, beyond these limits, if the analyst claims a relationship between an articulated meaning and the vague or unformulated mental activity that preceded it, this is experienced by the patient as false, or even ridiculous. If you tell a patient that the explanation for his silence is anger when it is not, the patient can generally tell you that you're wrong, even if he cannot yet substitute wording that more precisely and convincingly describes his state. The structure in unformulated experience is like a figure emerging from a dense fog. There is contour there, but it is fuzzy. It could be a per-son. It could be a rack of clothes being pushed toward you by some-one behind it. It could even be a dancing bear. But it couldn't possibly be an elephant or an automobile.

FORMULATION AS THE ATTRIBUTION OF MEANING

Return once again to the image of the towel over the chair in the darkened room: What exactly *is* the coherent percept that one even-tually makes out of it?

The coherent percept is a meaning. It is not as if the sensory information changes when the percept falls together. Rather, one is finally able to see what the image means. As a second, similar example, let me offer the image that greeted me recently on a sidewalk in New York. As I approached a truck parked across the sidewalk, I seemed to be seeing the view ahead through a huge sheet of glass that was being carried on the side of the truck, presumably to repair a window in one of the brownstones on the block. Such trucks and their cargo are not terribly uncommon sights. Yet there was something wrong. The view through the sheet of glass was . . . well, it was just not *right*. I got that same odd, vaguely queasy feeling I have already described, because what I was seeing was supposed to make sense, but it did not. A scant moment later, I realized that the glass was not the huge window I had taken it to be, but an equally large mirror, and that what was being reflected in it was a cockeyed perspective of the street behind me. It was not until I was able to assign the contextually accurate meaning to the mirror, and thus to the view it framed, that I could settle my ontologically jangled nerves.

There is no easily identifiable metaphor for unformulated experience in this example, as there was in the towel over the chair, because the percept that eluded me was preceded, not by a vague, undifferentiated one, but by a quite explicitly inaccurate one. What I want to illustrate by offering this instance is merely how experience depends on the meanings we assign to it. The illustration shows that even when experience just "arrives" in our awareness (that is, when we do not sit and "figure it out"), as it most often does, we have played a much larger role in its formulation than we have any idea. In this example, without any kind of explicit awareness of doing so, I approached the truck with a ready-made interpretation about the view across the sidewalk: it was the kind of view one sees through a window. It was not until I could see both my interpretation, or preconception, and the alternative to it, that I could formulate a different perception. Interestingly, despite a rather large change in the meaning of what I saw, nothing changed in the *appearance* the scene offered me. Analogously, in psychoanalysis we frequently and repeatedly discover new meanings for events that, in and of themselves, never change.

If we are asked exactly *what* is unformulated in unformulated experience, then, we can say that it is meaning. When we accomplish a new formulation, we have created a new meaning. Sometimes a new meaning entails new perceptions, memories, fantasies, and so on; sometimes it does not.

Some time ago, Eugene Gendlin (1962, 1964) described a similar phenomenon, which he described as "felt meaning." The phenomenological quality of felt meaning is very close to what I am describing as unformulated experience, and so I close this introductory chapter by quoting at length one of Gendlin's (1964) particularly evocative descriptions.

> [A] felt meaning can contain very many meanings and can be further and further elaborated. Thus, the felt meaning is not the same in kind as the precise symbolized explicit meaning. The reason the difference in kind is so important is because if we ignore it we assume that explicit meanings are (or were) already in the implicit felt meaning. We are led to make the felt, implicit meaning a kind of dark place in which countless explicit meanings are hidden. We then wrongly assume that these meanings are "implicit" and felt only in the sense that they are "hidden." I must emphasize that the "implicit" or "felt" datum of experiencing is a sensing of body life. As such it may have countless organized aspects, but this does not mean that they are conceptually formed, explicit, and hidden. Rather, we *complete* and form them when we explicate [pp. 113–114].

3

Familiar Chaos

Unformulated Experience as Defense

We know from everyday experience that we have at least some influence over what parts of our experience fail to develop into articulate form. Defensively motivated unformulated experience is a kind of "familiar chaos," to borrow a phrase from Paul Valéry, a state of mind cultivated and perpetuated in the service of the conservative intention to observe, think, and feel only in the well-worn channels—in the service, actually, of the wish not to think. The "chaos" refers to the natural form of undeveloped thought. Experience maintained in this state can carry with it a comforting sense of familiarity. It may be banal and unquestioned, but it feels like one's own. Interpretation is avoided; familiarity is its camouflage. Defensively motivated unformulated experience is a lack of clarity and differentiation permitted or encouraged in conscious experience that, in more fully articulated form, would raise the danger of noxious (or at least undesirable) interpersonal consequences. If one remains ignorant of the conclusions one might draw, or the observations one might make, or the feelings one might have, one sometimes can pursue aims one prefers not to acknowledge while bypassing certain conflictual, anxiety-provoking interactions. In Joseph Barnett's (1980) apt phrase, one maintains "areas of innocence." The masochist, for example, does not refuse to acknowledge a fact he already knows; rather, by interpreting and living his life in a way that allows the fulfillment of a cherished self-characterization—that he is giving, selfless, and perhaps victimized—he manages not to spell out the observations he could make if he were willing to tell a different story and consider alternative interpretations of his own place in it.

Take the example (extreme, but quite true) of the woman who proudly told her analyst that her husband could maintain an erection only with her. The analyst, taken aback because of the absence of any previous reports of the husband's infidelity, as well as by the patient's apparent equanimity, asked the patient how she had come by this bit of information. The patient, in the same calm and straightforward fashion, reported that her husband had told her. She then stopped, looking at the analyst expectantly, seeming to wait for him to continue. But the analyst, no longer merely taken aback, but amazed, was unwilling to supply the missing link and remained silent. "Well?" said the patient finally, apparently a little exasperated with the analyst's lack of further response. And then, after another pause, she suddenly cried out, "Oh, my God!"

Is this woman coming upon a repressed thought or memory, or has she, until this moment, in the service of perpetuating an idealization of her marriage and her husband, avoided spelling out the traumatic implications of what she knows?

Defensively motivated unformulated experience—what I am calling "familiar chaos"—differs in its very nature from repressed experience or experience distorted by the other traditionally conceptualized defensive processes. Unformulated material is experience that has never been articulated clearly enough to allow application of the traditional defensive operations. One can forget or distort only those experiences that are formed with a certain degree of clarity in the first place. The unformulated has not yet reached the level of explicit verbal differentiation at which terms like memory and distortion are meaningful.

Most psychoanalysts seem to operate on the basis of the implicit hypothesis that people resist the clarification of certain aspects of their experience, preferring vague, impressionistic formulations for which there genuinely are no words. We work as if unformulated experience remains to be formed, as if there is not necessarily an underlying and preexisting clarity in experience. Of course, the uncovering of veridical repressed memories has not been the central event in even the most conservative schemes of clinical psychoanalysis for many years. But even when Freud suggested that construction of the past was necessary, he still claimed that useful constructions presented purely historical truth, and that the unconscious was a storehouse of veridical memories. One might have to put up with the making of constructions as a practicality of the treatment, but theoretically speaking, "All of the essentials are preserved" (Freud, 1937, p. 260).

ASSOCIATIONS AND CONSTRUCTIONS

In associationist theories, such as Freud's, new experience is received, clear and fully formulated, and added to the store of memories as if it were an additional crate being stacked in a warehouse. Experience is a series of discrete mental entities, and concepts arise from various combinations, or associations, of these entities (Freud, 1900, 1925). Memory is therefore very much like that warehouse. Nothing need be changed by the addition of something new, and, like objects or entities, experiences are either present and fully formed or altogether absent. There is no place for the shadowy or unformed.

Many classical psychoanalysts, on the other hand, would accept without a second thought the idea that experience can exist in an unformulated mode. As long ago as 1939, Hartmann described a similar concept. In his view, though, unformulated experience was not the natural state of prereflective thought, as it is from a constructivist vantage point, but an indirect result of the repression of earlier experiences that the ego would have needed to make a mature formulation. This view is frequently present in the work of contemporary theorists of drive and defense (e.g., Kernberg, 1980). Many other Freudian writers have conceptualized the defensive process in ways not unsympathetic to defensive lack of formulation. Merton Gill (e.g., 1963), for one, thought this way from fairly early in his career. Also counted among this group are other former students of David Rapaport: George Klein (1976), Roy Schafer (e.g., 1976, 1983, 1992), and Donald Spence (1982, 1987). The basic proposition that the fully formed experience exists unchanged in the unconscious memory trace (Freud, 1900, 1915; Lewy and Rapaport, 1944), however, has been examined and criticized infrequently from within the classical tradition (for an explicit exception, see Paul, 1967). As recently as 1976, as eminent a theoretician as Hans Loewald wrote, in an important paper on memory, that the notion of timelessness in the unconscious requires the assumption that "nothing recorded in the mind is ever truly destroyed—extinguished rather than merely altered." The psychoanalyst "through the alterations . . . can still perceive or guess the original text that continues to be active and have its own impact" (1976, p. 151). Thus, according to Loewald, who otherwise makes the point in this paper that memory is an active, constructive process, everything registered in the mind, although its appearance may change over time, is permanently readable in the unconscious in its original form.

It turns out that Donald Spence (1982, 1987), whose work (at least his first book) lay at the heart of the early constructivist thrust in psychoanalysis, is also committed to the enduring unconscious memory trace. Although the primary point of his first and most influential book (1982) is that language constructs experience and that the task of psychoanalysis, therefore, is to construct a story of the patient's life that carries narrative truth, Spence retains the view that any difference between the linguistically constructed version of experience and the "original" or "underlying" visual images to which the language refers is correctly described as distortion. There is a single, underlying, nonverbal truth to which our verbal statements refer, and only to the extent that verbal descriptions match the images do they bear truth (cf. Sass and Woolfolk, 1988).

Not only for Freud, then, but for many significant contemporary theorists as well, each experience is recorded and permanently stored in the unconscious, which is therefore conceived to be something like a film or tape library. Conscious memories and other experiences are the result of the distorting effects of drive and defense on the permanent unconscious record. This point leads to the familiar psychoanalytic concept of self-deception. Deceiving ourselves means convincing ourselves that we do not know something that we actually do already know. The Freudian defensive processes are always processes of masking, or disguise, or outright expulsion from consciousness. Again, the defenses take this form because all mental contents—conscious, preconscious, and unconscious—are conceptualized as fully formulated. The concept of unformulated experience makes no sense in an associationist theory. For Freud, and for many of those who have followed him—even, as we have seen, for such progressive cognitivists as Loewald and Spence—experiences may be forgotten, transformed, masked or disguised, distorted, blended with other experiences until undetectable, defused by breaking all links to other experiences, or simply denied. But in all cases the experience still exists "in" the psyche. Despite appearances to the contrary, the fully formulated experience is hidden somehow in the form of what we can see, like the prince in the frog. From different critical vantage points, Fingarette (1963) calls this the "hidden reality" view, and Neisser (1967) calls it the "reappearance hypothesis."

Professional practices often change before they are reflected in the theories written about them. Our "theories-in-use," that is, come to differ from our "espoused theories" (cf. Argyris and Schön, 1976). Whatever we say about what we do, though, we often base our actions on theories for which we have no words. We take many wise and correct actions for reasons we cannot specify. Sometimes our reasons qualify as personal motivations; other times, the reason is cultural lag, that gap of months or years that lies between the time a change has begun to occur and the time the culture finds or allows itself the means to represent the change in explicit verbal terms. For many psychotherapists, and probably because of both personal motives and cultural lag, lack of formulation as defense is a theory-in-use. From a constructivist point of view, however, the concept of unformulated experience makes sense as espoused theory as well. Oddly enough, though, the idea that unformulated experience can serve defensive purposes did not come from a constructivist at all, but from a writer whose interest in constructivism, despite the central role his work has had in my own thinking, would have ranged somewhere between slim and none: Harry Stack Sullivan.

SULLIVAN AND UNFORMULATED EXPERIENCE

Sullivan, who made many references to the defensive use of unformulated experience, was the earliest contributor in this area, and his work remains the most complete clinically derived description.

Because the approach was a new one at the time, and not clearly differentiated from the classical theory of the defenses, it is not always obvious when Sullivan means repression (expulsion or exclusion from consciousness of a fully formulated psychic element) and when he means lack of formulation. Nevertheless, the idea of defensively motivated lack of formulation is natural to Sullivan's theory, particularly to his notions of anxiety and the self system.

The self system or self dynamism (Sullivan, 1940, 1953) includes all those experiences and ways of relating to others that have been found to be safe and secure. Or from the other direction, the self system rejects all experiences and modes of relating that might be associated with anxiety. The task of the self system can be described even more simply as the refusal to perceive or formulate novelty, because novel experience may be dangerous. Safety lies in familiarity.

The predominant characteristic of the self system, then, is that it perpetuates itself. In an interpersonal dilemma, once one finds a solution, or an apparent solution, that minimizes anxiety—a mode of perception, thought, feeling, behavior—one may from then on, in circumstances that appear roughly similar, slap on that solution roughshod. New experiences come to be mistrusted simply because they are new. One does not know what they will bring, and so one extracts from them only that which is already within the purview of the self system. When this happens, the new disappears without ever having been noticed—or without being formulated. Like the woman who didn't think through the implications of her husband's impotence with other women, we avoid anxiety by searching out the familiar in experience and throwing away the rest.

Sullivan's (1940) clearest statement about lack of formulation is as follows:

> One has information about one's experience only to the extent that one has tended to communicate it to another or thought about it in the manner of communicative speech. Much of that which is ordinarily said to be *repressed* is merely unformulated [p. 185].

That is, one *keeps* certain material unformulated in order not to "know" it. What is more, Sullivan seems to be suggesting that this is not material that has *ever* been formulated. Unlike repression, in which at least the original defensive act is an expulsion from awareness, material affected by the process Sullivan describes here was never banished from consciousness, because it was never "there" in the first place.

This is a very different notion of defense, and Sullivan is only able to come to it because of his (surprisingly modern) position that lack of formulation as defense is merely a special use of processes that serve far more general cognitive functions. This position is never stated in just these words, but it is implicit in Sullivan's (1940, 1953) concept of the three modes of experience.

The *prototaxic mode* appears chiefly in infancy and consists of a continuous present, a succession of momentary states without a "before" or "after." The *parataxic mode*, one of the two primary ways experience is organized after infancy, is also nonrational. Experience is broken into parts for the first time, but different kinds of experience are not related to each other in a logical way. "They 'just happen' together or they do not, depending upon circumstances. . . . What is experienced is assumed to be the 'natural' way of such occurrences, without reflection and comparison" (Mullahy, 1948, pp. 287–288). This is the personal, subjective language of dreams and fantasies, but it is also the mode of a great deal of other experience. We cannot pay explicit attention to every meaning, after all, and so there is a certain efficiency in being able to experience and behave on the basis of meanings upon which we have not yet reflected. Quite often, once they are consensually validated, one sees that parataxic meanings have been useful and accurate guides. The trouble, of course, is that precisely because parataxic experience is not consensually validated, it also carries the potential for representing meaning in a way that, if it could be introspected, would not seem accurate at all.

The *syntaxic mode* is the realm of consensually validated meaning, meaning embodied in symbols that have the same significance to all the members of a given social group. Language, as in Freud's secondary process, is the vehicle of the syntaxic mode, though words (again like Freud) can also be used a parataxic way. For Sullivan (1940, 1954, 1956, 1964), words often appear to be conventionally meaningful while actually serving as vehicles for private ("autistic," in Sullivan's vocabulary) meanings, unknown even to the person who is seemingly trying to communicate. Such private meanings, in the absence of explicit inquiry and mutual willingness to reconsider them, bear only an arbitrary relationship to the usual meaning associated with the word. Therefore, meanings that are essentially undecipherable by either party in a conversation may be encoded in language that appears to have conventional, easily apprehended meaning. And of course, what goes for speaking or writing goes for listening as well. Just because one party uses language consensually doesn't mean the other party understands it that way. The parties in a conversation may assume they are understanding one another when in fact they are talking past each other. Human affairs, according to Sullivan, are rife with misunderstanding. Parataxis is rampant.

Not only that, though. The worst of it is that, more often than not, neither party has any idea that misunderstanding is taking place. Sullivan somewhere describes most interactions as feeling "seamless" to their participants. By this delightfully appropriate word he means that gaping holes in history, logical contradictions, even violations of consensual reality and aspects of relatedness that might appear inappropriate or downright strange in other contexts, are all woven together, in most ongoing interactions, in such a way as to seem utterly natural to both parties, and are therefore often virtually invisible. Human relationship is defined as a matter of communication, and communication is almost always inefficient, sometimes inaccurate, often inadequate.

Sullivan actually did not fully develop the implications of this idea for psychotherapy and psychoanalysis, because he did not see the immense significance of countertransference. He had a more or less traditional understanding of the analyst's experience, feeling that the analyst should be capable, on a consistent basis, of remaining the "expert" in the relationship. Like the classical analysts of his day, Sullivan believed that, if psychotherapists were well trained and had learned enough about their blind spots, they could know directly their own ongoing experience with the patient and should be able to avoid emotional involvement. Their experience should be under their control and (at least usually) transparent to their own introspection. Therefore, for Sullivan it was realistic to believe that experts in interpersonal relations could know pretty much everything that was important about their own participation in the treatment, and could, on this basis, plan their impact on their patients. To my mind, however, and in the view of many other contemporary analysts, the analyst's greatest difficulty lies just in perceiving what is most important to investigate. One cannot possibly know as much about one's own participation as Sullivan believed one could.

What Sullivan means in the passage, quoted above, about repression and lack of formulation is that, if one keeps a meaning at the parataxic level, one prevents oneself from reflecting upon it. Reflection is a function of what Mead (1934) called the "generalized other"; it requires the symbolization of meaning in a publically appreciable form. It requires that one either communicate a meaning to another person in a comprehensible linguistic form, or that one be able to do so. If we cannot say a meaning to someone else in terms the other person can understand, we cannot think about that meaning ourselves. To the extent that we define knowing as our capacity to think intentionally about something, we literally do not know whatever meanings we cannot say. Parataxic meaning, then, is unknown even to oneself, and insight is not therefore simply a matter of learning what we already know. Parataxic meaning does not exist in some sector of the mind that has been barricaded off; rather, it has never been formulated. Because we mistrust the unfamiliar, fearing it will threaten our security, we are particularly prone not to symbolize novel experience in consensually valid terms. Such experience remains organized at the parataxic level, the fully formulated meaning never coming into being.

Apart from Sullivan's work, the earliest and clearest exposition of this idea is probably Ernest Schachtel's (1959) notion of "secondary autocentricity," according to which, in order to avoid the anxiety of separation—of individuating and thereby growing away from what is familiar—one tends to conventionalize experience, seeing in it only what one needs on the basis of the past. In the process, one often misses whatever is novel in the present. On the other hand, just as Sullivan suggests about parataxis, life would be impossible without the automaticity that secondary autocentricity makes possible. We would constantly be deeply involved in examining details we can much more efficiently handle in an unthinking way. We would trip over our own feet.

For Sullivan, then, defense is an adaptation of processes also used for other, less affect-laden purposes; defense is essentially "not thinking about it." Avoidance of formulation is accomplished by means of selective inattention, a process upon which he (1950, 1953, 1956) lays heavy emphasis. Focal attention, which helps separate the wheat from the chaff in everyday experiencing, can also be used to keep something out of awareness. If one's focal attention is never trained on this "something," one is never aware of it; and if one is never aware of it, it remains parataxic—or unformulated. Sullivan (1956) writes, "When things go by rapid transit through awareness into memory without the development of implications, those undeveloped implications are not there for the purpose of recall" (p. 58).

One simply does not notice what one does not wish to know. And if one does notice, the implications of what is noticed cannot be drawn. Selectively inattended experience, along with all the implications this experience might have had, were it articulated, are never elaborated, never transformed into an experience in the syntaxic mode. In turn, this fact means one can never reflect on the material. Anxiety is prevented, of course, but the strategy is equally effective in the prevention of learning.

Selective inattention is an aspect of most security operations and what Sullivan (1953) calls "substitutive states," and is used in situations of threat. In the course of development, the most severe insecurity may require entire motivational systems to be dissociated. As life proceeds, it is selective inattention that performs the function of preserving the separation of this dissociated experience from awareness by preventing attention being paid to anything that would tend to bring that dissociated material closer to consciousness. Such experience is simply "gone." It is screened out. It never existed.

Freud (1900), too, proposed that attention was the final gateway into consciousness. But for Freud, this gateway was merely the entry into consciousness of material from the preconscious. Sullivan is proposing something more radical—in Freud's terms, something like keeping the material unconscious. Selective inattention, in fact, is the means by which dissociation is maintained. Dissociation for Sullivan is largely a matter of keeping certain of one's interpersonal engagements from being spelled out. That is, one is involved, but any recognition of the fact is dissociated; the action, in Schafer's (1983) language, is "disclaimed." Only experience that is "reacted to" (either positively or negatively) by the parents and significant others in the child's life becomes part of the self-dynamism. Such experience is "marked," which is to say, capable of being registered, known, and reflected on. To other, "unmarked" impulses, desires, needs, the "self refuses awareness, so to speak" (Sullivan, 1940, pp. 21–22). In other words, this ignored experience, which significant others in the child's life do not notice or respond to because of their own anxiety and the accompanying dissociations and selective inattention, never enters awareness in the first place.

But notice that this process is not an active banishment of experience from consciousness. Rather, the experience is never conscious at all, because it does not receive the interpersonal imprimatur it would need to be cognized. Such experience is screened out prior to its articulation; it remains undeveloped, prototaxic (rarely) or parataxic (usually) in form, and is excluded from the self-system, along with whatever implications it might have had. It can never be elaborated.

Sullivan's thinking suggests (but does not actually articulate) that dissociated material makes people anxious for two reasons: There is the original historical reason for the dissociation, of course, and then there is the tendency we all have to avoid the unfamiliar. The dissociated, though it might have become familiar under different circumstances—that is, if one had grown up with a different interpersonal history—becomes over time an important part of that which is unfamiliar. Thus one is eventually afraid of dissociated material, not only because of its specific place in one's history, but also because of its novelty.

Dissociated material makes people anxious because they have never thought about it. One has built one's whole sense of self around these gaps in experience, which means that sudden awareness of one of them could be devastating, disequilibrating, throwing off a whole system of self-definition and anxiety avoidance. Thus, in consequence of the self system's powerful tendency to perpetuate itself, dissociation, too, must be permanently maintained. In the beginning of life, dissociation may be simply an "empty space" in the developing structure of experience, but as time passes and the self system grows, the dissociation is no longer just "a place where something isn't," but is an element of the sense of self, a piece of the structure of the ongoing story one tells about one's life. The dissociation becomes as vital to the integrity of the self and its story as, say, the white space is to the visual integrity of a painting. In novelist Bruce Duffy's (1987) pithy expression, "The hole, too, is part of the doughnut" (p. x). It thus becomes a matter of some delicacy to raise a patient's curiosity about this kind of material without simultaneously raising anxiety to unbearable intensity.

Sullivan's views are compatible with the observation that when resistance abates, disavowed thoughts do not suddenly pop up, fully formed, ready to take their place in the continuing unfolding of the treatment. Parataxic experience remains to be formed. But Sullivan also seems to assume, with most of the other writers of his day, a point-to-point correspondence between parataxic meaning and the language that could be used to spell it out; parataxic experience, that is, can be formulated validly in only one way. It is a form of unconscious experience, like the contents of Freud's unconscious, that merely remains to be paired with verbal labels to enter awareness. The process of bringing it into language is not constructive or generative, and the resulting meaning is not emergent. Language allows mutuality and reason, but it is not constitutive; it merely labels meanings that already exist in a linguistically immature form.

CURIOSITY, UNCERTAINTY, AND ACCEPTANCE OF THE FAMILIAR

A respect for uncertainty and the difficulty we face in maintaining it appears throughout Freud's work. Uncertainty has always been one of the guiding values of psychoanalysis, in theory and the ideal of practice, at least, if not always in its day-to-day exercise. It has been pointed out, in fact, that the amount of uncertainty psychoanalysts must create and tolerate is directly proportional to the proliferation of psychoanalytic theories: the more ideas we have, the more uncertainty we must create if we are to avoid treating theories as if they were matters of faith. The more we learn, the more difficult and important it becomes to create the recognition that we don't know, and the more difficult it is to resist the reassurance belief offers (Witenberg, 1978).

The same point can be approached from a clinical perspective. There is always, of course, more than one meaningful interpretation of an event, but nevertheless, with disconcerting frequency, we all (patients and analysts alike) find ourselves talking and acting as if only the particular one we have selected could possibly be true. These constructions, defended so doggedly, may be the only visible evidence of lack of formulation being used defensively. Uncertainty can be stifled just as effectively by forcing an interpretation, usually a safe, conventional one, as by refusing to make one at all. Assumptions carried from one situation to the next, applied over and over again, are methods of structuring the world in such a way that one can avoid having to think about it. These assumptions and expectations are ways of keeping the process of attention reined in, fixed in a routine of illuminating only that which one already knows it will illuminate. If uncertainty cannot be made to disappear altogether in this way, it certainly can be dampened.

Everything often seems perfectly clear in this kind of world, though it may feel nearly unbearable. It is hard even to conjure the questions one might ask oneself. *In extremis,* this is the world of psychosis, of the psychotically depressed person, for instance, who is absolutely sure of his or her failure and complete lack of worth. It is the world of the paranoid schizophrenic, peopled with beings who menace one terribly, but who always behave in predictable ways.

Every psychotherapist and psychoanalyst has worked with people who, when they begin to ask themselves questions about the way they live, perhaps for the first time making a concerted effort to define and challenge the interpretations of their own experience they have always taken for granted, are surprised to find that they have never done it before. Looking back on it, they say, to paraphrase Patrick Mullahy's (1948) description of Sullivan's parataxic mode, "That's just the way things were. It didn't require explanation." The restriction of thought is a kind of self-imposed stupidity in which everything smoothes out, and questions disappear into the familiar. Even the "sharpening" attitude of the vigilant paranoid implies a "smoothing out." There may be such attention to salient details that the person gives the illusion of perceptiveness (it is a clinical truism that paranoid people can be devastatingly insightful within the constricted range of their focus), but the vastness of experience is actually left nearly untouched. Unquestioning acceptance of the familiar ensures that there will be no inadvertent deployment of curiosity.

The familiar swallows anything. It is bottomless. When experience fades into the familiar, it loses substance, it becomes a ghost of itself. It may be gone forever, irretrievable in its original form. Bartlett's (1932) classic memory experiments show that as time passes, people remember a more and more conventionalized form of a story they have been told, even if the original form of the story deviates radically from conventionality. "The known," Hegel wrote somewhere, "just because it is the known, is the unknown." Unquestioning acceptance of the familiar is the attitude by which maintenance of unformulated experience as familiar chaos is accomplished.

If what is dreaded remains unformulated, one does not know what it is, of course, but one may very well sense that whatever it is, it is dreadful. Similar things can be said of situations that cause more prosaic kinds of discomfort, far down the scale of urgency. If one has a preference that one wants very badly to believe is a necessity, for example, or at least a wise judgment, one may avoid formulating certain aspects of the situation that would suggest otherwise. One may be sorely tempted to buy some item at a time when it is financially unwise, for instance, and one may convince oneself that one absolutely *must* make the purchase; the price will never again be so low. Of course, one ignores all the while the fact that one cannot really afford even the sale price.

The refusal to formulate—to think—is a different solution to the problem of defense than repression, which is a matter of keeping unconscious thoughts that already exist. Instead of positing the intentional removal and continuing exclusion of content from awareness, as the repression hypothesis does, lack of formulation as defense means never allowing ourselves to interpret our experience in the first place. The refusal to formulate is quite simple; one just restricts one's freedom of thought, and the "offending" experience is never created.

The process is self-perpetuating—in Sullivan's terms, an aspect of the self system. One has more to fear from freeing thought itself than from any particular constructions thought might make. The capacity to see the familiar in the unfamiliar, one of the great achievements of infancy, becomes in adulthood an equally great impediment to thought's growth.

4

Creative Disorder and Unbidden Perceptions

Unformulated Experience as Possibility

The most intriguing thing about how we tell the stories of our lives, and one of the things that makes storytelling particularly fascinating as an account of living, especially to a psychoanalyst, is that we are virtually never aware of doing it. The process of telling one's own life story—at least as long as it is authentic and not merely "made up" or forced—is not volitional in any simple way, any more than is our construction of dreams, or, for that matter, our construction of the next moment's experience. Yet, also like our dreams, our deepest intentions inform and shape our stories. An authentic narrative of self is so thoroughly imbued with these intentions, which are themselves lived, and thus not necessarily reflectively considered prior to being enacted, that it reflects them without symbolizing either the motivations that underlie them or whatever cognitive processes immediately precede them. Well or poorly told, rigid or flexible, coherent or fragmented, complex or simple, our life stories are simply there. Their events, sequences, and meanings generally seem—purely at face value—the outcome of impersonal natural forces, forces as little our own as the "march of history" itself.

The comparison with history is not only apt but ironic, because history, which my generation grew up understanding as the epitome of that kind of human event that is simply "there" and certainly not told, turns out to be just as much a tale as the stories of individual lives.[1] Revisions of our collective pasts have the same power to startle us that convincing retellings of our own personal histories do. Even Columbus and the cowboys are not heroes forever.

the process of discovering
what you are going to write

Interestingly enough, it is professional writers of fiction, people who are so drawn to telling stories and so good at it that they do it for a living, who have most often given us accounts of stories as unbidden phenomena. The following examples are all the more remarkable when one considers that these writers are referring to the stories they tell purposefully. That is, even when one is *aware* of telling a story, one does not necessarily know what will happen next. "This sense of being in the service of the imagination—not its master," writes Patricia Hampl (1989), speaking for creative people everywhere, "is a trademark of an authentic experience of creativity" (p. 37).

Take Joyce Carol Oates (1982): "If I say that I write with the enormous hope of altering the world—and why write without that hope?—I should first say that I write to discover what it is I will have written" (p. 1). Or Gabriel Garcia Márquez: "I'm very curious, as I'm writing this book, to see how the characters go on behaving. It's a true investigation. I could almost say that one writes the novel to see how it will turn out. And to be able to read it" (quoted by Simons, 1985, p. 18). Brian Sibley (1986) tells us that, though Lewis Carroll did not dream the story of Alice, it did "come into his mind with an unconscious effortlessness akin to dreaming" (p. 140). Carroll wrote that he had sent his heroine "straight down a rabbit hole . . . without the least idea of what was to happen afterwards" (quoted by Sibley, 1986, p. 140). And here is Raymond Carver, in his essay "On Writing," convincing and a little touching in his surprise at discovering that he is not alone in not knowing what he will write next.

> [Flannery] O'Connor says she most often did not know where she was going when she sat down to work on a short story. . . . When I read this some years ago, it came as a shock that she, or anyone for that matter, wrote stories in this fashion. I thought this was my uncomfortable secret, and I was a little uneasy with it. For sure I thought this way of working on a short story somehow revealed my own shortcomings. I remember being tremendously heartened by reading what she had to say on the subject [quoted by Hampl, 1989, p. 37].

In the passage that heartened Carver, which appeared in the essay "Writing Short Stories," O'Connor was discussing her story "Good Country People." When she began the story, she did not know "there was going to be a Ph.D. with a wooden leg in it. I merely found myself one morning writing a description of two women I knew something about and before I realized it, I had equipped one of them with a wooden leg." Then, also with no particular plan in mind, she invented and introduced a Bible salesman. "I didn't know he was going to steal that wooden leg," continues O'Connor, "until ten or twelves lines before he did it, but when I found out that this was what was going to happen, I realized it was inevitable" (quoted by Hampl, 1989, p. 38).

And consider this passage from novelist Tim O'Brien, whose *The Things They Carried* (1990) is, among other things, a meditation on what it is to tell war stories.

> You take your material where you find it, which is in your life, at the intersection of past and present. The memory-traffic feeds into a rotary up in your head, where it goes in circles for a while, then pretty soon imagination flows in and the traffic merges and shoots off down a thousand different streets. As a writer, all you can do is pick a street and go for the ride, putting things down as they come at you [p. 38].

And then there are the many famous examples of nocturnal illuminations seemingly foisted upon their sleeping discoverers, such as Coleridge's (1816) "Kubla Khan," and Hilprecht's sudden comprehension of Sumerian cuneiform writing (Newbold, 1896). Robert Louis Stevenson (1925, p. 44) regularly received completed stories in his dreams from "the Brownies." The process of copper engraving was bequeathed in a dream to William Blake by his dead brother (Raine, 1971, p. 43). Particularly well known is Kekulé's dream of snakes devouring their own tails, from which the dreamer suddenly awoke knowing that the image of the reptiles depicted the elusive molecular structure of benzene, a problem he had been struggling unsuccessfully to solve for a long period of time (MacKenzie, 1965, p. 135).[2]

Let me add examples of the dreams of ordinary people, just to underscore the point that unbidden experience is not the private province of genius. Any dream would do as an example, since all are unbidden. But there is a particular kind of dream that has always especially fascinated me, because dreams of this kind make it incontrovertible that we create our own experience, even at those times when, as in dreams, we have that odd sensation of being inhabited by it.

The dreams I am thinking of are those in which an explicit experience of surprise at one's own creations, and often delight, is prominent. Take the example of a brilliant and highly cultured woman, in treatment, who was romantically involved with a married man who claimed he intended to divorce his wife. For a considerable time, the treatment revolved around the vagaries in this relationship. The patient could not decide what to do. She did not doubt the sincerity of her lover, but she did doubt that he could really bring himself to go through with the divorce. She was a pragmatist, not the starry-eyed type at all; nevertheless, she could not bring herself to take her perception seriously enough to take action on it. Meanwhile, she was in daily agony. Things eventually came to a head the day after the following dream, which solidified for the patient what she believed. She was attending the performance of a play, which she somehow knew was Elizabethan. As she entered the playhouse, the stage came into view. On the stage was an easel, and on the easel rested a placard that spelled out the name of the play in ornate calligraphy: "Too Much Married."

The dream was hilarious, because of the perfection with which the patient had expressed her own message in Elizabethan style. The title of the dream could very well have been the title of a play by Marlowe or Shakespeare. She told me the dream with more wistfulness than amusement, of course, because she knew very well what it said about what she really thought.

The second dream is one of my own. I was in a gathering of people somewhere. Also in attendance was a certain woman who happened to be a new patient of mine at the time. Gesturing wildly, and with a desperate, wide-eyed look, she rather frantically cried, "Let's all have a party!" Standing next to me was a colleague whose clinical acumen I particularly respect. He whispered to me in a confidential tone, "What *she* needs is to have a party in her *soul.*" This was a sound and very apt observation, for when I awoke the next morning and remembered the dream, I realized that this woman's seeming liveliness, which had begun vaguely to grate on me, though without my explicit awareness of what was bothering me, was actually a kind of desperate attempt to obscure from herself the fact that, in her inner life, she felt more dead than alive.

For my present purpose, the particular meanings these dreams seemed to have are less relevant than the more general phenomenon of the unconscious creation of explicit meaning. My colleague's "observation" came as a complete surprise to me in my dream, but it was obviously just as carefully constructed as the name of the Elizabethan play in my patient's dream. The words surprised both of us, just as if they really had been written on a placard or spoken by someone else.

The psychoanalytic discourse itself can be described in this same way. Once seen, a new clarity may seem so inevitable that it is experienced as having "been there all the time," deceiving us into believing that it actually was (the "hidden-reality" view I referred to in the last chapter). The previous lack of awareness is astonishing. The right words, once found, pull the figure out of a background that, until a moment before, seemed homogenous. Alternatively, if the meaning remains implicit or felt, as in the case of many dreams, the moment may pass with only the awareness of the presence of a vague something. Yet enough is left that we recognize the thought if we have it again; and if someone else says it, or the thought appears in print, we have a reaction of puzzlement and surprise that we ourselves have thought of this very thing, something like, "I *knew* that."

It must be obvious by now that from the perspective I am beginning to lay out, marginal, shadowy, vague experiences—subjectivity and cognitive disorder, even including what Sullivan refers to as "the autistic"—have to be more than what Sullivan made of them. They are more than the absence of communicability and mutuality. Unformulated experience is not only parataxis; it is also the source of novelty. It is creative disorder as well as familiar chaos.[3] Prior to the moment we can articulate an invention, a new idea, a line in a poem—or for that matter, a new thought about ourselves or a dream—it is less accurately described as "immature," as we must characterize it if we use the terms of parataxis, than as "potential," existing in a state of possibility. Interpretations we are emotionally and intellectually equipped to make are the raw materials of the next moment's new experience.

According to Sullivan's theory of selective inattention, if we can train our attention on unformulated experience, we should be able to formulate it. Of course, training attention on certain parts of experience, such as experience relevant to dissociated motivational systems, is often impossible, at least without what Sullivan would call "grave consequences." But however difficult it may be to attend to the unformulated, attention by itself, contrary to Sullivan, just does not seem to be enough to bring the unformulated into reflective awareness. After all, if the unformulated is not assimilable by consciousness, what is there to attend to? We know how uncommon it is for the ineffable to spring suddenly into the realm of the communicable as soon as resistance relaxes. Unlike Freud's repressed, which is always trying to return, it is not as if the unformulated is forever leaning against the door of consciousness, just waiting for a chance to overcome resistance and tumble into the room.

The unformulated must organize itself first. It must somehow begin to coalesce. Eventually, as this process of coming-together proceeds, hints of the existence of new meaning are apprehensible in consciousness. For the prepared mind, one that is interested in the vague new meanings that might, with effort, be clarified, these hints of new meaning are like the unfurling tendrils that appear in a garden in the spring, their existence signifying that a seed has germinated underground. When the process of formulation reaches this point, the function of attention can be focused and used to help and coax a fully formed product to emerge in awareness. It is only after the initial period of invisible germination, however, that volition can contribute. Prior to that time, though the process of creation is always within the purview of personal agency (who else but oneself, after all, could be responsible for one's autonomously percolating thoughts?), it is fruitless to force it. In Leslie Farber's (1966) terms, the initial part of formulating new experience goes on entirely inside the "first realm of the will," which is the kind of will that can sometimes be grasped, but never directed. It is the deepest kind of intentionality, the intentionality that moves each of us in the directions that are most authentic for us. It is a paradox: what we most want is what we must simply allow to move us. Once the hints of our own thoughts emerge into awareness, however, will of the second realm—consciously directed will, what we are used to calling "will power"—can be deployed.

As examples, Farber reminds us that we can will ourselves to lie down in bed, but we cannot use volition to go to sleep; we can force ourselves to sit and look at a book, and even to read the words, but we cannot force ourselves to learn; a man can will the activity of sex, but not an erection. In just this way, one can will the further development of a thought that has already reached a certain degree of articulation, but conventional effort is of no use in initiating the process of making new experience.

Paul Valéry (1952), writing about the composition of poetry in an essay that Farber would have held in high esteem, approaches from one direction after another the point that we cannot force creation. After we have prepared ourselves as fully as possible, he says, the only thing we can accomplish by the application of will (will of the second realm) is the limitation of whatever naturally occurring creative powers we have. There are implications here not only for literary creation, but for psychoanalysis. There is a point beyond which analyst and patient cannot progress by directed inquiry. The inquiry may lead them to new experience that can be used in the creation of new, good questions, or it may lead them in a direction that somehow results in the profound understanding of an old question, but the construction of those questions and understandings, at least the best of them, cannot be made to happen. The application of force results in aridity, convention, and intellectualization. Many of the most important experiences in psychoanalysis must simply be allowed to take place. Here is Valéry.

> [W]e can act only upon the freedom of the mind's processes. We can lessen the degree of that freedom, but as for the rest, I mean as for the changes and substitutions still possible under our constraint, we must simply wait until what we desire appears, because that is all we can do. *We have no means of getting exactly what we wish from ourselves* [p. 102].

The unbiddenness of experience is one of Valéry's themes. He writes elsewhere (1950):

> The surprising thing is that one sometimes gets an impression of poise and consistency in human constructions made with an agglomeration of apparently irreconcilable materials, as if he who had arranged them had known that they had secret affinities. But astonishment passes all bounds when one realizes that the author himself, in the vast majority of cases, is unable to give any account of the lines he has followed, that he is the wielder of a power the nature of which he does not understand [p. 102].

And yet again, from a third source (Valéry, 1920):

> I do not know what I am going to do; yet my mind believes it knows itself; and I build on the knowledge, I count on it, it is what I call *Myself*. But I shall surprise myself; if I doubted it I should be nothing. I know that I shall be astonished by a certain thought that is going to come to me before long—and yet I ask myself for this surprise, I build on it as I count on my certainty. I hope for something unexpected which I designate. I need both my known and my unknown [p. 142].

Valéry is hardly alone. The mathematician Marston Morse (1951) offers a lyrical description of the same sequence of events.

> Out of an infinity of designs a mathematician chooses one pattern for beauty's sake, and pulls it down to earth, no one knows how. Afterward the logic of words and of forms sets the pattern right. Only then can one tell someone else. The first pattern remains in the shadows of the mind [p. 608].

Although these passages are especially pithy and beautiful expressions of the point, artists commonly tell us that the unformulated coalesces this way, without conscious intervention; but, they say, the unformulated must brew first, and it takes its own time to do it. Mozart is one famous example. He apparently could compose in a room full of noise and traffic, and could be interrupted at any point without being disturbed, because by the time he sat down to write, he was merely copying onto the page a piece of music that already existed in its entirety in his mind. About his ideas he wrote, "Whence and how they come I know not; nor can I force them." The poet Marina Tsvetaeva wrote that a poet's hand does not belong to her, but "to that which wants to exist through [her]." In a letter to Boris Pasternak she said, "We dream and write not when *we* please but when it pleases: a letter to be written, a dream to be seen." The poet, writes Keats, "does not know what he has to say until he has said it." Lamartine puts it that, "It is not I who think, but my ideas who think for me." Mallarmé rhapsodizes, "Words rise up unaided and in ecstasy." Gertrude Stein, ever straightforward and down to earth, says simply, "It will come if it is there and you let it come." The painter Helen Frankenthaler, referring to a small book of her prints, organized around a poem, commented that it "just fell into place like a little rose" and that she had "very little to do with it." Orpingalik, an Eskimo poet, showing that the autonomous crystallization of unformulated experience is not a culture-bound phenomenon, writes that "We get a new song when the words we want to use shoot up of themselves."[4]

These accounts describe the sudden appearance of more-or-less fully formed creative products; they omit the hints of ongoing unconscious formulation that so frequently come before. Along with Valéry, William James (1890) describes these glimmers more often and more fully than anyone else I have come across. He calls them "feelings of tendency" or "signs of direction in thought." "The truth is," he writes,

> that large tracts of human speech are nothing but signs of direction in thought, of which direction we nevertheless have an acutely discriminative sense, though no sensorial image

plays any part in it whatsoever. . . . One may admit that a good third of our psychic life consists in these rapid premonitory perspective views of schemes of thought not yet articulate [pp. 251–252].

Now what I contend for, and accumulate examples to show, is that "tendencies" are not only descriptions from without, but that they are among the objects of the stream (of consciousness), which is thus aware of them from within, and must be described as in very large measure constituted of feelings of tendency, often so vague that we are unable to name them. It is, in short, the reinstatement of the vague to its proper place in our mental life which I am so anxious to press on the attention [pp. 252–253].

Great thinkers have vast premonitory glimpses of schemes of relation between terms, which hardly even as verbal images enter the mind, so rapid is the whole process. We all of us have this permanent consciousness of whither our thought is going. It is a feeling like any other, a feeling of what thoughts are next to arise, before they have arisen [pp. 255–256].

It seems, then, that knowing we author even the most startling of our own thoughts does nothing to demystify the common experience of merely recording them. Even if we sense glimmers, we do not know with any clarity or certainty the articulate meanings these glimmers will assume when they attain a firmer shape. We have no choice but to wait for what the following moment will reveal. Quite literally, we do not know what we will think next. Thoughts, images, and feelings come to us; they arrive; one feels like a conduit.

We are used to the notion that ideas simply arrive in the mind of the genius. The madman, too. But the idea that everyone thinks this way is less familiar. Though it has indeed been creative people who have most often captured and conveyed the experience, the phenomenon of finding oneself faced by one's own thoughts is by no means limited to exalted or otherwise altered states of consciousness. Thoughts need not be sublime, nocturnal, or psychotic to be unbidden. As a matter of fact, surprise is not the exception, but the rule. The "unconscious thought" revealed in artistic inspiration and creative dreams is not as unusual or mysterious as it seems. These events are best understood as particularly graphic and dramatic instances of a process that occurs with regularity, and in waking hours as often as in sleep. All thought, in this sense, is unconscious thought. It happens, in Heidegger's phrase, "behind one's back." We are onlookers at our own ways of grasping the world. Even if we are not writing fiction or poetry, or furiously pursuing a scientific problem, all of us, without even knowing we are at work, are continuously in the midst of constructing stories.

Once in a while, if we are alert to James's feelings of tendency and signs of direction in thought, we can see, out of the corners of our eyes, something like clouds of vaguely defined meaning. In addition to my own personal and clinical experience of worrying at something vague until it coalesces into a thought, it is other people's descriptions of this sort of hazy protomeaning that makes me prefer the idea of unformulated experience to the simpler notion that new experience just arises *de novo*. Referring to amorphous cognition as "endoception," a kind of nonrepresentational mental activity from which creative products emerge, Silvano Arieti (1976) writes that, "this endoceptual cognition is an indeterminate entity in search of a form, a groping for some definite structure. When a suitable form is found, this activity is transformed into creative work" (p. 62). "The endocept of the future creative work," he continues later, "contains no more than possibilities of what can be actualized in different ways, according to what the author may choose to do" (p. 64).

Most of those who have made similar observations have been artists and writers of one kind or another. Isadora Duncan, for example, referred to "a state of complete suspense" as one of the stages in her invention of a dance. Brewster Ghiselin suggested that, "In order to invent, one must yield to the indeterminate within him." Stephen Spender, when he came close to a new poem, said it was "something still vague, a dim cloud of an idea which I feel must be condensed into a shower of words." Alfred North Whitehead described "the state of imaginative muddled confusion which precedes successful inductive generalization." Rainer Maria Rilke writes that the thing to do is "to let each impression and each germ of feeling come to completion quite in itself . . . beyond the reach of one's own understanding."[5] And once again, it is perhaps Paul Valéry (1952) who is most eloquent of all in his evocation of the way articulated creations arise from vague precursors.

> The instability, incoherence, inconsequence of which I spoke, which trouble and limit the mind in any sustained effort of construction or composition, are just as surely also treasures of possibility, whose riches it senses in its vicinity at

the very moment when it is consulting itself. These are the mind's reserves, from which anything may come, its reasons for hoping that the solution, the signal, the image, or the missing word may be nearer at hand than it seems. The mind can always feel in the darkness around it the truth or the decision it is looking for, which it knows to be at the mercy of the slightest thing, of that very meaningless disorder which seemed to divert it and banish it indefinitely [p. 101].

Let me add two more sentences from that same remarkable little essay.

All may be summed up in this formula: that in the making of a work, an act comes in contact with the indefinable [p. 104].

[D]isorder is the condition of the mind's fertility: it contains the mind's promise, since its fertility depends on the unexpected rather than the expected, on what we do not know, and because we do not know it, than what we know [p. 106].

Despite the fact that Sullivan's conception of the parataxic mode of experience is at the heart of the idea of unformulated experience, the idea of parataxis, and Sullivan's single-minded aim of bringing all parataxic experience into language, must be reconsidered and broadened. Our aim, in life and in psychoanalysis, is the formulation of the unformulated, but that is not all it is. We aim also at a state of being in which we accept unformulated experience as creative disorder. We have no choice but to accept that our most authentic and informative experiences are simply not under our control.

TWO USES OF UNFORMULATED EXPERIENCE

In practice, broadening Sullivan's aims beyond consensually validated linguistic symbolization means that when the function of a particular piece of familiar chaos is successfully understood, what replaces it, and what makes new formulations possible, is not a sudden inrushing of words, but the acceptance of previously rejected uncertainty. In psychoanalysis we tend to believe that understanding is the natural event, as if meaning would be obvious if defense were resolved. Misunderstanding from this vantage point is a corruption, an interruption, of what comes naturally. When a defense is resolved, therefore, it is easy to imagine that understanding, having been artificially dammed, explodes into the new space and finds its own level without any particular effort on our part.

Not everyone thinks of the process of understanding in this way. Most hermeneuticists take the point of view that *mis*understanding is effortless; it is *understanding* that requires work and accomplishment. Understanding is an act, and it is easier, less effortful, *not* to carry it out than to carry it through. When resistance is resolved (substitute whatever wording you prefer to signify achieving a readiness to understand), one does not simply *know;* rather, one arrives in that moment at a position from which it is possible to consider that some new way of understanding may fit better than the understanding one had been (unconsciously) insisting upon. In the use of unformulated experience as creative disorder, uncertainty is accepted, and feelings of tendency are encouraged, valued, and nurtured. One tries to capture in symbolic form as many feelings of tendency as one can.

In familiar chaos, by contrast, there is little interest in what may emerge, and in fact, as Sullivan suggested, one is interested primarily in keeping the unformulated experience just as it is. Feelings of tendency are avoided. What is defended against is not a thought, not exactly, because no thought has been formed. What is defended against is rather the process of thinking itself. When one prevents attention from focusing on feelings of tendency, the possibility and uncertainty of creative disorder are frozen into the autistic certainty of parataxis.

Some of the experiences that emerge when resistance is resolved are no more predetermined than the daubs and streams of color in a Pollock painting. One may have only intimations of the mental activity that will take place when obstruction vanishes. The future of unformulated experience, as a matter of fact, does not exist prior to its articulation. That is, while we can hardly deny the familiar unconscious influences on how we construct the future, influences is all they are, even when these influences are structural in nature; they are not determining factors.

It is true that the future pulls us along behind it, and in that sense the future makes itself. Valéry (1952) again: "A poem is a discourse that requires and sustains continuous connection between the voice that is and the voice that is coming and must come" (p. 98). But it is equally true (and entirely consistent) that we construct the future as we go, out of the immensely complex combination of our present views of our pasts and futures, the views we believe others take of our pasts, and the views we and others (we believe) have of our own presents and futures. It is possible to predict no more than certain broad trends in a life, and even on that level of abstraction, behavioral prognosticators, like meteorologists, have reason to maintain a good deal of skepticism about their powers, although they sometimes advertise otherwise.

Lack of formulation, then, is lack of verbal symbolization. Not to have a thought means not to give linguistic shape to unformulated experience. In the case of defense, it amounts to a refusal to make this leap into meaning, whereas in the case of the invisible interpretive predispositions that represent the shaping effect of culture, we are actually unable to make meanings of a different nature. Language is constitutive of experience, but it also seduces us into accepting a mythology of the world around us that is based, solipsistically, on the properties of language itself. In these ways, language and culture (which are in this instance synonymous) set the limits beyond which even creative disorder cannot spread.

CURIOSITY AND CREATIVE DISORDER

In constructivist views, since each person is the unwitting author (or at least coauthor) of her own experience, the only thing to be learned about oneself that can really be counted upon to be the truth is that one is afraid or unwilling to be curious. Along with uncertainty, curiosity has always been a guiding value of clinical psychoanalysis. The ideal patient and the ideal analyst are curious about everything, and to be curious requires the toleration of uncertainty. Curiosity preserves the uncertainty in unformulated experience; it is the attitude by which unformulated experience is maintained as creative disorder. In these terms, psychoanalysis is the progressive awakening of curiosity, a movement from familiar chaos to creative disorder.

I have said that curiosity means allowing oneself to make constructions. "Allowing" may seem like strange wording—or it may sound like some kind of conscious granting of permission to oneself to "go ahead and work on" thinking. To "work on" thinking is precisely the meaning not intended. Curiosity is an active attitude of openness (Schachtel, 1959), not a focused search, at least not to begin with. It means that rather than employ a focused beam of attention, a searchlight to look *for* things in experience, which in one way or another usually seems to result in conventionalizing, one allows the possibilities implicit in experience to impress themselves on one's consciousness. One takes one's hand off the tiller and lets what Schachtel (1959) calls "global attention and perception" drift as it will. When an interesting construction begins to form itself out of this preattentive material, one may stop and perform a more focused search on and around this construction to fill in the detail and give it the convincing quality Freud (1937) knew it had to have to be useful.

Of course, it is no accident that this description of "allowing" is essentially a description of free association; but it is the ideal of free association. Seldom do either psychoanalysts or patients find themselves in possession of such powers of openness and observation. We make do with much less. In fact, it seems that much of our work is an inquiry into what happened to the rest of it. Nevertheless, there is value in a description of the ideal, because we can aim at it—or at least toward it.

In this view, then, psychoanalysis is not a search for the hidden truth about the patient's life, but is the emergence, through curiosity and the acceptance of uncertainty, of constructions that may never have been thought before. Furthermore, these constructions are not merely sensible stabs at history and description; they are part and parcel of the new world patient and analyst are creating between them. This fact permeates them and is at least as significant as their degree of historical accuracy. Actually, the interpersonal world of patient and analyst has just as much effect on the new constructions created within it as the new constructions have on the interpersonal environment. The idea that new understanding, especially a new understanding of the analytic relationship, influences the field is familiar. The reciprocal of this idea, however, is not; namely that the field already may have modified to allow the new experience to come about in the first place. A new understanding therefore may be as much the occasion for a new inquiry as it is an accomplishment of an older one.

Each new and convincing construction in psychoanalysis has something of the quality of "effective surprise," a term Jerome Bruner (1979) uses to describe the result of a creative act. The term might suggest high drama at first glance, but Bruner intends nothing of the kind. It is partially for that reason that Bruner's description is particularly apt to the discussion of understanding in psychoanalysis, a process that is indeed creative, but that more often than not goes on from one day to another with neither agony nor ecstasy.

> An act that produces *effective surprise*—this I shall take as the hallmark of a creative enterprise. The content of the surprise can be as various as the enterprises in which men are engaged. It may express itself in one's dealing with children, in making love, in carrying on a business, in formulating physical theory, in painting a picture. I could not care less about the person's intention, whether or not he intended to create. The road to banality is paved with creative intentions. Surprise is not easily defined. It is the unexpected that strikes one with wonder or astonishment. What is curious about effective surprise is that it need not be rare or infrequent or bizarre and is often none of these things. Effective surprises . . . seem rather to have the quality of obviousness about them when they occur, producing a shock of recognition following which there is no longer astonishment [p. 18].

Effective surprise marks the symbolization of unformulated experience, the creative use of language, the flowering of explicit meaning. The formulation of experience is a mystery: it belongs to us more truly than anything we own, but we do not control it. It decides for itself when to occur. It provokes in us the feeling of recognition, the *shock* of recognition, because we have seen its outlines before—in parataxic, amorphous, felt form, in our feelings of tendency. And yet we may become aware of this feeling of prior acquaintance only in the moment of its transformation, its disappearance. We feel as if we had been looking through poorly focused binoculars without realizing it. Somehow the adjustment is made, and suddenly and unexpectedly, the view leaps out at us in fine detail. In just this way, by creating between them a world of thought and curiosity, patient and analyst rescue unformulated experience from the oblivion of the familiar.

POWER AND CURIOSITY

Of course, we also know that seldom do either psychoanalysts or patients find themselves capable of such complete openness and observation. The reality of both power relations (Foucault, 1980, 1988a, b, c) and dynamics means that we make do with much less than full curiosity in psychoanalysis. Certain kinds of participation (an authoritatively delivered interpretation, say) are typically "masculine," for example, and defined by their difference from other, "feminine" kinds (consider empathy or acceptance). And although these different kinds of participation may be correlated only loosely with the actual genitalia of the participants in any particular analytic interaction (men are often enough empathic, after all, and women authoritative), gender differences almost always have some kind of implication for dominance, submission, and the exercise of authority. This is clear enough in the case of the authoritatively delivered interpretation; it may be less immediately obvious that to practice empathy is to let the other person dominate—in this case, to establish meaning.

The same goes for the influences of race, ethnicity, and sexual orientation. Each of us is multiply defined by the ways we belong to our cultures, and these various identities influence our participation in ways that are very difficult for us to formulate. What is the effect, we need to keep asking in every instance, in every context, of bringing together different configurations of identities in the psychoanalytic situation? What kinds of interaction, what exchanges of ideas and feelings, are encouraged and foreclosed between two men? Between a man and a woman? Between an African-American female analyst and a white Jewish male patient? Between a white female analyst and a gay Latino patient? Perhaps most complex of all, in what ways might analytic technique itself be the unseen result of power relations that seemingly have nothing to do with it? It is the necessity for this reflexivity in our postmodern world, for example, that leads Irwin Hoffman (1996) to the conclusion that we must submit to analysis the authority we invest in the the role of the analyst, authority that, even when we are willing to accept it, can now only be ironic. The same kind of reflexive examination leads others (e.g., Price, 1997) to criticize even the limited degree to which Hoffman preserves the analyst's authority.

Knowledge is a prime effect of power. Knowledge, that is, is an *expression* of power, and so all knowledge carries political and moral consequences. To accept a body of knowledge is unwittingly to adopt a moral stance; thus, because we must select one knowledge or another just to get along in the world, we had better ask ourselves continually about the moral consequences of these selections.

When psychoanalysts think of "knowledge," they think first of theory. But knowledge in the sense in which I mean it here just as easily encompasses our conduct with our patients. Our interventions have moral and political effects, whether we think we intend such effects or not, and whether or not, in any particular instance, we consider those effects important enough to draw analytic attention. The conduct of an analyst in the consulting room is shaped by various knowledges, not only the explicit professional ones, but also all the other implicit ones we embrace as a consequence of the various aspects of our identities. Power relations are shaping influences on the experiences that seem merely to arrive in our minds. Unbidden perceptions, in this sense, are not only the most authentic experiences we have, they also express the unconscious workings of power.

And so we are in a quandary. If we depend on nothing but our unbidden perceptions, we tacitly accept the power relations in which we are embedded—which is to say, the status quo. But the status quo and its conventionality are precisely the problems for which I have claimed that unbidden perceptions are a solution. What are we to do with this contradiction, coming up so late in the argument?

The only real solution—a solution that is really only the recognition that a real solution is impossible—is for analysts to be actively and consciously suspicious and skeptical of the ways they may be enacting culturally sanctioned group relations in their professional work. To maintain that kind of skepticism requires us to find our way to formulations of some of the automatic workings of power, and alternatives to them. To formulate in that way—which is to say, against the grain—requires that we keep ourselves educated about thoughtful opinion regarding power relations, especially opinion that challenges the status quo.

Therefore, the curiosity or freedom of thought I am proposing as the guiding value for psychoanalysis—the kind of curiosity that expects obstructions at every step of the way and is commodious enough to encompass even the things we do not want to know—is an ideal. It is well worth aiming at, but should not be mistaken for a goal that is really achievable. I must end this chapter with a qualification, one meant to apply with the same degree of appropriateness to the discussion of "imagination" undertaken in the next chapter: effective surprise in psychoanalysis must be tempered with consciously directed, highly informed reflection about psychoanalytic participation in power operations. The analysis of what comes naturally must be supplemented by the analysis of what does not.

POWER AND COCONSTRUCTION

The reality and ubiquity of power means that we must not allow ourselves too much confidence in the egalitarian intentions that underwrite psychoanalytic constructivism. An idealistic embrace of democracy is tempting, because it transforms analysts, in one fell swoop, from authoritiarian decoders of the unconscious to collaborative healers. But neither characterization is supportable in pure form. Egalitarian intentions are too easily compromised by the unconscious workings of power (not to mention conventional countertransference), and those compromises are too often invisible to those who make them, and too easily rationalized.

Whenever a term becomes a "buzzword"—that is, when it is used so often that it begins to stand as much for a movement as for a specifiable idea—it is liable to be obscuring something significant. "Mutuality," "coconstruction," and "cocreation," although all three terms refer to conceptions dear to me, are in danger of becoming just that kind of word. They can seem to suggest that it is within the power of psychoanalysts to create a constructivist democracy in the consulting room. We must not believe in that democracy too easily. We hardly need to question the contemporary dictum that analyst and patient both participate in the construction of the analytic experience; that point will remain as long as perspectivism endures. But we must be careful not to assume too quickly that the contributions of the analytic participants are either equal or freely chosen. Egalitarianism, like curiosity, is an ideal.

PART II
Reconsidering Self-Deception

Toward a Theory of Dissociation

5

Imagination and Creative Speech

Thoughts on Dissociation and Formulation

Usually we think of consciousness as the natural state of experience. We imagine that if we are unaware of something, we must have taken some action to be unaware. It is as if experience were a beach ball. It just naturally floats along the surface. If we want to keep it underwater, we have to push it down there and sit on it; and that takes work. We assume that active exclusion of content from awareness requires effort, as if it were any other kind of action—running, thinking, and so on.

Freud's theory certainly encourages us to continue thinking this way: repression and the other defenses force into unconsciousness experiences that would otherwise appear in consciousness as naturally as the beach ball pops up from underwater. It is hard and tricky to force that ball down; we often lose our balance. And once we manage to find our balance, it is just as hard to keep the ball down there. Freud makes these two activities—forcing material out of consciousness and keeping it out—the heart of his theory of experiencing. After an initial act of repression, defense is continuously necessary to beat back the drive derivatives that are ceaselessly cast "up" toward consciousness—the return of the repressed.

But what if we reverse the terms and look at the appearance of experience in awareness, not as the state of affairs that occurs "naturally," "by itself," or without intervention, but as the effortful event in itself? What if things are the other way around? What if the natural tendency is for experience to remain *outside* awareness? What if action and effort are required, not to keep experience *out* of consciousness, but to bring it *in*? What if conscious experiencing is not so much like stifling the uproarious beach ball as it is like lifting a rock from the bottom and hauling it to the surface?

From this point of view, consciousness is closely related to language. To haul up a rock from the bottom—to make a piece of experience conscious—is to construct that experience in words, to interpret it, wittingly or unwittingly. We know about ourselves to the extent that we can spell out in words what we are like, what our experience is like—very much as Sullivan (1940, 1953) wrote long ago, and as contemporary psychoanalysts influenced by Sullivan hold today, in particular Edgar Levenson (1972, 1983, 1991).

This is also precisely the perspective on consciousness (minus the beach ball) taken by philosopher Herbert Fingarette (1969). Fingarette reminds us that the language of consciousness in Western civilization is shot through with visual metaphors. "To see" is to understand, for example. When we want to draw someone's attention to our own thoughts, we say, "Look here." We "turn our attention to" a subject as we "turn our eyes toward" something. Vision, as a matter of fact, Fingarette contends (along with a long list of Western philosophers), is actually the model for our notion of consciousness; because of this connection, we think of experience "falling" on consciousness the way light falls on the eye. We have to make an effort *not* to see. And just as in everyday life we assume that seeing is the passive registration of light (though today's psychology of perception would certainly take issue here), even today we tend to assume that consciousness is the passive registration of the contents of the mind. We do not credit consciousness with constitutive or shaping properties, in other words, but see it only as the receptacle for what we will allow to fall into it. In this way we come to take for granted that we must make an effort *not* to be conscious. Instead, says Fingarette, we must conceive consciousness as active, not passive; it is something we "do." We are "doers," and consciousness is the exercise of a skill.

> The specific skill I particularly have in mind as a model for becoming explicitly conscious of something is the skill of saying what we are doing or experiencing. I propose, then, that we do not characterize consciousness as a kind of mental mirror, but as the exercise of the (learned) skill of "spelling-out" some feature of the world as we are engaged in it   [pp. 38–39].

To "spell-out" is often, but not always, to produce detailed verbal representations of something that is becoming conscious. Though Fingarette refers to "allusive" and "cryptic" forms of spelling out that are not transparently verbal, spelling-out always bears a "close relation" to "perfectly straightforward examples of linguistic activity" (p. 40). In any case, spelling-out is always a matter of becoming explicitly conscious of something. Spelling-out is, in the terminology I have been using, interpretation in reflective consciousness.

It is a very short step—in fact, it is more like dropping the last piece into a mosaic that is already intelligible—to the conclusion that, in a frame of reference in which consciousness is active interpretation and not passive registration, the basic defensive process must be the *prevention of interpretation* in reflective awareness, not the *exclusion from awareness* of elements that are already fully formed. If reflective experience is created by interpretation, such experience is avoided by not interpreting, or by not-spelling-out. And not interpreting, or not-spelling-out, are essentially ways to define dissociation. Defensively motivated unformulated experience, then, or what I have referred to as "familiar chaos," is the way the dynamic unconscious looks in a constructivist, dissociation-based model. Familiar chaos is to dissociation what repressed content is to repression.

This is a definition of dissociation as an active defensive process. In many discussions, especially those centered on trauma, dissociation is portrayed as the result of "breakdown"; it is not a defensive measure itself, but is instead the result of the *overwhelming* of one's capacity for active defensive measures. It is the personality's last fallback position; there is nowhere else to go and absolutely nothing else to do, at least nothing consistent with continued sentience. Dissociation in this frame of reference represents an *inability* to reflect on experience, not an unconscious avoidance of doing so. It is about survival and necessity; there is no element of unconscious preference involved. I want to find in the use of dissociation, however, the same kind of active and preferential world making we take for granted in thinking about the traditional defenses, something on the order of what Philip Bromberg (1993, 1996b) describes as a kind of "normative," or perhaps better, *expectable*, dissociation (see also Mitchell, 1991, 1993; Hirsch, 1994; Davies, 1996b; Harris, 1996b; Flax, 1996). That is, whether the unitary self is an accomplishment or an illusion (and it has been repeatedly described as both), it is at the very least an effort. What is difficult or painful to put together we tend to leave apart.

WHAT IS DISSOCIATED?

Dissociation is the avoidance of certain formulations of present experience. It is part of the activity by which we organize experience; it is part of our readiness to construct experience in particular, stable ways. Like the processes we call "mental contents" or "representations," dissociation is a channel or current along which certain meanings can flow and others cannot. To dissociate is simply to restrict the interpretations one makes of experience. Or perhaps better stated, because the interpretation is hard to separate from the experience itself, dissocation is a restriction on the experiences we allow ourselves to have. Even memory is an experience in the present, so that a dissociated memory is one we will allow to be constructed only in certain ways—and especially not in other ways.

NEW MEANINGS

As far as it goes, it is true to describe dissociation as the unconscious refusal to make verbal interpretations; but going that far is not enough. Although technically accurate, that kind of account, at least unembellished, would turn away from what I have been at pains to emphasize: the clinical import and subtlety of the constitutive properties of verbal language. We would again find ourselves in jeopardy of falling back into a psychology of mental essences and linguistic labels for them. There is nothing in a purely mechanical account of language, in other words, that helps us understand in what ways a verbal interpretation can be more than a label, nothing to tell us why spelling-out is more than spelling. A hermeneutic or interpretivist theory of dissociation should help us to understand, in a more phenomenologically compelling way, what it means to have a new reflective experience and what it means to prevent one.

To be capable of new experience is to be capable of not knowing what will come next. It is when one actually has some kind of sensuous contact with William James's (1890) "movements" or "feelings of tendency" in thought that expectation and the conventionality it breeds are weakest. At such times we have an interested sense of what might arise from these vague "movements"; we have an unworded and unwordable sense of what we might think next—unwordable because to word it would transform it into what it merely tends toward. But at the best times, we are more interested in allowing "movements" to become meaning than in forcing them in any particular direction. Reflective consciousness under these conditions "happens," which is to say that we feel comfortable letting language take its own shape, in the way that in fables, smoke streaming from the mouth of a bottle takes the ultimately recognizable, but utterly unpredictable, shape of a djinn. Rigid perceptions of the other and oneself are least likely at such moments.

Of course, we are certainly interested in being more than conduits. We hope that over time we and the patient, within the confines of our own little universe, and then in the larger world, come to use language more flexibly and precisely than before. We hope that we come to a greater acceptance that speech and thought are always incomplete and imperfect, and to an appreciation that saying and thinking one thing always means not saying or thinking another—that language constantly requires us to burn bridges to meanings not selected and articulated. And we hope that, however precisely we are able to express ourselves, we will be able to tolerate knowing that we never finish saying anything.

Language structures reflective consciousness. We have only the categories and processes of language within which to construe reflective meaning, which is the only meaning we can know directly. If a meaning cannot yet be spoken, it does not yet exist in a form in which we can grasp it; and if it is not among that virtually limitless crowd of phenomena that language has the capacity to represent, it can never become reflective meaning at all. It can be a different kind of meaning, and it is certainly meaning*ful*, but it cannot enter reflective consciousness.

There are many moments between patient and analyst—of intimacy, say—which are complete in and of themselves, and which cannot be adequately spelled-out by verbal description. Words would often ruin such moments, and those moments play a very important part in creating the mutative effects of psychoanalysis. But we cannot strive for them. In this way, they share the quality that makes reflective consciousness authentic: they must just happen.

For the most part, what we and our patients are trying to do is to bring into words experience that has existed before that time in a different, inarticulate form. And often, the meanings we work with are less than fully expressed until they reach such a stage—until they can be said. We and our patients are not aiming at the unnameable bliss of mysticism, nor are we trying to create art. What we do bears the same relation to nonverbal experience that the work of the critic bears to a play or a piece of sculpture. Like the critic, we would not be drawn to our work unless we had a greater appreciation and love of the subject matter than most people do. Psychoanalysts love the forms experience can take as critics love art. And it is true that to become and remain good analysts, we must retain that direct and unmediated appreciation. But our relation to our subject of study—to experience—does not remain merely appreciative. We are driven to understand. Creating experience, by itself, does not satisfy what we want from our work; we must say things about what we create. We acknowledge how often the important parts of psychoanalytic treatment occur in the shadow of the interpretive task, spontaneously and apart from verbal representation; we hope, and even pray, that we and the patient will find our way to that kind of authentic experience. But we do not know how to make authenticity happen. So, while we are grateful for the unexpected and inexpressible benefits along the way, we focus our conscious attention on trying to say things.

Even when we limit our task in this way, however, we are immediately aware of invisible obstacles. How very difficult it is to say things that matter! In psychoanalysis, an activity in which the affectively charged nature of what we are trying to say means that we are often ambivalent about formulating experience in words, we use a generic term, *resistance*, to describe our difficulty. But resistance is not limited to the clinical situation. In both everyday life and clinical psychoanalysis we are constantly tempted to say things before they are ready to be said, to force the matter by the use of conventionalized or stereotyped language. Such use of language is, in Mallarmé's metaphor (quoted by Merleau-Ponty, 1964b, p. 44), the worn coin placed silently in the hand. It is precise, agreed-upon, consensually validated; it is what it is, nothing more. There is nothing suggestive about it, nothing that points beyond itself. The conventional use of language, however central it is to the smooth operation of our day-to-day lives, does not give birth to meaning; it counts it, notes it, passes over it. This use of language reveals nothing new, but it does grease the tracks. Life is easiest when we use language in a way that reveals only what we already know. All of us are prone to this temptation.

Merleau-Ponty (1964b) distinguishes "empirical speech," the established usage of conventional expressions, from "creative speech," which "frees the meaning captive in the thing." "To speak," he says about authentic speech, "is not to put a word under each thought. . . . We sometimes have, on the contrary, the feeling that a thought has been *spoken*—not replaced by verbal counters but incorporated in words and made available in them" (p. 44). He goes on to discuss the creative use of language this way: "Language signifies when instead of copying thought it lets itself be taken apart and put together again by thought. Language bears the meaning of thought as a footprint signifies the movement and effort of a body" (p. 44). And earlier (1964a), he tells us that speech

> tears out or tears apart meanings in the undivided whole of the nameable, as our gestures do in that of the perceptible. To make of language a means or a code for thought is to break it. When we do so we prohibit ourselves from understanding the depth to which words sound within us—from understanding that we have a need, a passion, for speaking and must (as soon as we think) speak to ourselves; that words have the power to arouse thoughts and implant henceforth inalienable dimensions of thought; and that they put responses on our lips we did not know we were capable of, teaching us, Sartre says, our own thought [p. 17].

This is hardly a vision of language as passive, docile, or merely categorical. It is instead apocalytic, intuitive, antic, possessed. Language is no servant; it is disobedient and revelatory. Language is a dervish. It belongs to us and it carries us away, all in the same instant. There can be discomfort in the realization that we really don't know what we will experience next. We do not even know what we are going to *mean*, what we will *want* (intend) to say. This uncertainty is the price we pay if we choose to wait for our thoughts to come to us of themselves. If we want to become able to reflect upon some portion of whatever exists apart from words, or if we want to reword what we have worded before, that previous experience must remain unformulated until it can be said in a way that does it justice. It must feel right to say it. We know to treasure what comes before speech, particularly when we can feel its stirring, because then we know we are inhabited by some sort of nascent meaning. A worthwhile interpretation is not one the analyst (or the patient) has arrived at by "figuring it out."

Experience that we know directly just appears. We have the experience of receiving it. We can try to reconstruct its history, and there is certainly something to be gained in this way, as Freud (in the case of his self-analysis), William James, and many others have shown us. But we cannot observe directly whatever implicit or nonverbal forms or structures of experience occur apart from our capacity for reflection. However close we may sometimes feel (or even be) to nascent meaning, we will never be able to see what it is. For it occurs outside the range of the categories at our disposal; and as soon as it comes into view, it is not what it was. Unconscious meaning outside the reach of words is like light or sound that occurs at frequencies and wavelengths outside the range of our senses; we have ample evidence that it exists, but we do not have the equipment to experience it directly.

THE PRAGMATICS OF CREATIVE SPEECH

An essay by the literary critic Denis Donoghue (1981) offers a hint about the nature of creative language. Donoghue writes,

> We often assume that the problem of interpreting words is a matter of knowing what they mean and linking their meanings together in some reasonable order in our minds. But it's not quite like that. The problem is to decide at any moment what our relationship to the words should be, even when we know what they mean [p. 14].

Then, later in the essay, Donoghue brings up a television play called *Spend, Spend, Spend*, the fictionalized true story of Vivian Nicholson, an English woman who won a huge amount of money in the football pools and proceeded to live up to the title of the play. The play deals with whether the money changed Vivian, and it answers its own question with a resounding negative. Why doesn't the money change the lives of the Nicholsons? Donoghue sugggests that Vivian is the product of her emotionally barren life, which has left her in a position in which, "If the structure of her feeling doesn't change when she comes into big money, the reason is that nothing that happens to her amounts to an experience. Vivian is locked in her feeling as in her language" (p. 17).

An example of how Vivian is "locked in her language" is the way the word "bugger" is "shouted again and again, as verb, noun, adjective, and adverb" (p. 17). "Most of the feelings in the play are violent, but the violence never finds an authentic form for itself; it's always vented in the same few ways. Every expression is belated, a cliché; Vivian's only speech is the speech of others" (p. 16).

And then, after a brief foray into literary criticism, Donoghue writes an intriguing couple of sentences. "But many events casually called experiences are merely happenings. The test of an experience is that it alters the structure of our feeling; if it doesn't, it has been merely a circumstance, it hasn't entered our lives in any radical sense" (pp. 17–18).

Here we have a perfect statement of what I want to say dissociation is—and by implication, what formulation is, too. As if to confirm it, Donoghue goes on to discuss an essay by Walter Benjamin about soldiers who came home from World War I with "nothing to report, no stories to tell." "The reason is that their months or years in the trenches never became real in the sense of altering their structures of feeling; or they overwhelmed whatever structures already obtained, rendering the soldiers numb" (p. 18). Good war fiction, Donoghue remarks, is usually written years after the war has ended. It takes that long for the experience to be made one's own,

> because the events become experience only with time, distance, memory, and imagination. At that point they are incorporated for the first time in the person who, surviving them, has been changed by the reception of their force. Not by the force itself, but by its reception [p. 18].

The mere contingency of events, even if we are aware of the contingency, is not necessarily experience. Experience must be made *from* contingency, and that requires the articulation we can only accomplish by the creative use of language.

We are now in a better position to understand what it means to refer to language as creative or authentic. Language is being used creatively when we do not try to send it anywhere in particular, but allow it the freedom to follow the lead of our feeling, when, as Merleau-Ponty says, we allow language to be taken apart and put together again by our thought. "Language is much more like a sort of being than a means" (1964b, p. 43), he says elsewhere; "we do not have to consult some inner lexicon that gives us the pure thoughts covered up by the words or forms we are perceiving; we have only to lend ourselves to its [language's] life, to its movement of differentiation and articulation, and to its eloquent gestures" (p. 42). What a wonderful phrase: "we have only to lend ourselves to its life." That phrase is precisely what I want to say, for it contains within it the recognition of the power of expression we can have in language, but only if we give ourselves over to it and do not force meanings, allowing them to arise within it.

We use language creatively or authentically, in other words, when we treat unformulated experience as "creative disorder." By cultivating uncertainty and following the lead of our feeling, by following the point of emotional urgency on whatever path it charts through the time it takes to make a narrative, we create the best, truest stories, and they heal us by bringing what has hurt us into a meaningful relation with experience we already identify as our own. Our pain thereby becomes part of what we identify as ourselves—as our "self"—and ceases its disembodied, unstoried wanderings, what Loewald (1960) called its "ghost" existence.

It is not necessarily true, then, that a dissociated memory is unremembered. It may very well be possible to recapture the contingency of the relevant events, but the sequence is merely a fact; it has no place in our experience. To spell-out is not merely to bring an event into reflective consciousness, but to create for it what Donald Spence (1987) so aptly refers to as a "narrative home." And the opposite of dissociation is therefore not really the articulation of experience, at least not in the sense in which articulation means the creation of mere clarity, as in Sullivan's ideal of consensual validation. The opposite of dissocation is the particular kind of vivid and feelingful articulation we describe as imagination.

TRUE STORIES

I have said all these things: the best stories create experience; simple contingency is not experience; true stories heal. But what *is* a true story, if we are linking it with experience, and if we are not necessarily linking experience with what "actually" happened? Is an objective appreciation of events to play no role at all in our construction of narrative? And what, then, is dissociation, if not simply the refusal to acknowledge the contingency of "real" events? Do we skate here along the edge of an unchecked subjectivism or relativism in which the truth of stories is merely what we wish it to be, and the content of our dissociations is open to endless debate?

A certain degree of subjectivism is inevitable for anyone who seeks meaning in life and not the mere sequence and conglomeration of events—and when we get down to brass tacks, that includes pretty much everyone, even those who, like Vivian Nicholson, don't know how to do it. Why? Because when it comes to the measurement of reliability and validity, meaning is uncooperative. This is not to say that facts do not have their own truth. Of course they do; and that truth is often essential, as in the current controversy over adult memories of childhood sexual abuse (e.g., Davies and Frawley, 1994; Davies, 1996a; Harris, 1996a). But psychoanalysis has no magical, truth-serum way to establish the facts, and does not pretend to. Psychoanalysis deals with meanings.

So what is a true story? What is it that imagination creates and dissociation prevents?

The only good answers to these questions are allusive. Any concrete set of criteria would destroy what it sets out to describe, just the way an insistence on words can ruin certain moments in treatment. We can say that true stories represent something important, even essential, about what they describe. But that is so pale and generic a statement as to be useless. We can say that true stories are either full of feeling or, if they are not, like Raymond Carver's purposefully flat-toned short stories, that they cause us deep feeling, or anguish over its absence. But once again, as right as this answer is, it, too, is too concrete to be very useful in any particular instance.

The best answers I have run across are from *The Things They Carried* (1990), one of Tim O'Brien's novels of the Vietnam War. Rather than try to paraphrase O'Brien's language, which is irreducible, I quote two passages at length. The book is fictionalized autobiography, although it is never entirely clear what is fiction and what is fact, and O'Brien places this ambiguity, which he believes is inescapable, at the book's heart. O'Brien is never generic: he always refers to "war stories" when the stories are about war. But there are other stories in his book as well. O'Brien's work is about all of us. And despite the ambiguity in his side-by-side presentations of story truth and "what actually happened," it is also true to say that these horrific and deeply moving stories of war are unimaginable without "what actually happened." The facts, it turns out, are essential, in war as they are in the rest of life. The meaning of "story" for O'Brien therefore reminds us that though reality is there, always, we have no choice but to grasp it through the very particular lenses offered by our time, place, traditions, and personhood. Nevertheless, each picture that convinces us, that furthers a dialogue between people who seek the truth, is true and objective. A good story, as Irwin Hoffman (1983) writes in a different context, "gives meaning or shape to something 'out there' that has among its objective properties a kind of amenability to being assimilated in just this way" (p. 409). In the following passage from O'Brien, he and several others, including a young man named Curt Lemon, are on patrol in a quiet forest in Vietnam in 1970, when Lemon steps on a mine.

It's hard to tell you what happened next.

They were just goofing. There was a noise, I suppose, which must've been the detonator, so I glanced behind me and watched Lemon step from the shade into bright sunlight. His face was suddenly brown and shining. A handsome kid, really. Sharp grey eyes, lean and narrow-waisted, and when he died it was almost beautiful, the way the sunlight came around him and lifted him up and sucked him high into a tree full of moss and vines and white blossoms.

In any war story, but especially a true one, it's difficult to separate what happened from what seemed to happen. What seems to happen becomes its own happening and has to be told that way. The angles of vision are skewed. When a booby trap explodes, you close your eyes and duck and float outside yourself. When a guy dies, like Curt Lemon, you look away and then look back for a moment and then look away again. The pictures get jumbled; you tend to miss a lot. And then afterward, when you go to tell about it, there is always that surreal seemingness, which makes the story seem untrue, but which in fact represents the hard and exact truth as it seemed [p. 78].

Should we call this "psychic reality"? That trivializes it, and, just as bad, it is inaccurate. To call it psychic reality implies a contrast between private and public versions of what is true, as if we could see what was "really" true about O'Brien's version if we could just compare it to the "official," depersonalized one. But that separation is precisely what O'Brien denies.

Later in the book, a very brief chapter describes what it is to tell a story. Note that O'Brien makes the same distinction here between experience and happening that Donoghue does, calling it the difference between story-truth and happening-truth. I quote the chapter in full.

It's time to be blunt.

I'm forty-three years old, true, and I'm a writer now, and a long time ago I walked through Quang Ngai Province as a foot soldier.

Almost everything else is invented.

But it's not a game. It's a form. Right here, now, as I invent myself, I'm thinking of all I want to tell you about why this book is written as it is. For instance, I want to tell you this: twenty years ago I watched a man die on a trail near the village of My Khe. I did not kill him. But I was present, you see, and my presence was guilt enough. I remember his face, which was not a pretty face, because his jaw was in his throat, and I remember feeling the burden of responsibility and grief. I blamed myself. And rightly so, because I was present.

But listen. Even that story is made up.

I want you to feel what I felt, I want you to know why story-truth is truer sometimes than happening-truth.

Here is the happening-truth. I was once a soldier. There were many bodies, real bodies with real faces, but I was young then and I was afraid to look. And now, twenty years later, I'm left with faceless responsibility and faceless grief.

Here is the story-truth. He was a slim, dead, almost dainty young man of about twenty. He lay in the center of a red clay trail near the village of My Khe. His jaw was in his throat. His one eye was shut, the other eye was a star-shaped hole. I killed him.

What stories can do, I guess, is make things present.

I can look at things I never looked at. I can attach faces to grief and love and pity and God. I can be brave. I can make myself feel again.

"Daddy, tell me the truth," Kathleen [O'Brien's ten-year-old daughter] can say, "did you ever kill anybody?" And I can say, honestly, "Of course not."

Or I can say, honestly, "Yes" [pp. 203–204].

DISSOCIATION AND IMAGINATION

This seems to leave us a long way from conceiving dissociation to be a matter of the defensive refusal to interpret unformulated experience. And yet—perhaps not so far. Dissociation is the unwillingness to allow one's imagination free play. It is the unwillingness to allow oneself freedom of thought. Yes, it is true, dissociation sometimes does involve nothing more than the defensive refusal to formulate or interpret. Sometimes, that is, dissociation is a simple matter of preventing a certain kind of experience or memory altogether. That is the meaning of dissociation with which we are most familiar. But it is not the most frequent kind of dissociative event. To conceive the most common sorts of dissociation, the kinds we see in psychoanalytic practice every day, we must add that dissociation is the refusal to allow prereflective experience to attain the full-bodied reflective meaning it might have if we left it alone and simply observed the results of our own capacity to create it. Dissociation is an intervention designed, in advance of the fact, to avoid the possibility that a full-bodied meaning will occur. Dissociated meaning is style without substance, the story that accounts for what it addresses but tells us nothing we don't already know, the conversation we can fill in without having to listen. Dissociation is the deletion of imagination.

Sometimes we refuse to imagine fully the unstructured possibilities and alternatives that are implicit to the stories we already tell about our lives, the possibilities that would be apparent if we were to allow ourselves to loosen the ties that bind the ways we live. To allow ourselves this kind of imagination might provoke in us the generic anxiety we feel about any kind of freedom (e.g., Fromm, 1941), but it would not necessarily be specifically noxious. Other times, we refuse to imagine memories and other aspects of our experience that we have encoded as action or practice. Now, these experiences, if we reflected on them with real feeling, would be likely to lead us into something ranging from the quite specific anxiety associated with selectively disavowed experience to outright terror. In either case, however, the alternatives—fully imagined, partially articulated, or dissociated—are the outcomes of the language we use.

What determines when we use creative language? When do we think with our full capacity for imagination? This question seems clinically crucial, because I am saying that our reflective experience is really only full-blooded when we do use language this way. Should we not know whatever we can about how to encourage it?

We should, of course. On the other hand, this is probably another one of those questions that should not be answered too precisely. A precise answer would trivialize the question and, more than likely, would seem clumsy or foolish, something like trying to paraphrase a poem.

Who can say how we come to say exactly what we mean? Our capacity to use language well is probably more accurately understood as our willingness to let language serve our deepest intentions—and those, of course, are always beyond any easy description. Merleau-Ponty (1964b) writes that

Expressive speech does not simply choose a sign for an already defined signification, as one goes to look for a hammer in order to drive a nail or for a claw to pull it out. It gropes around a significative intention which is not guided by any text, and which is precisely in the process of writing the text [p. 46].

What we can do as clinicians is to be sensitive to the evidence of dissociation, which we note as absences, gaps, contradictions, stereotypes, repetitions, and dead spots in the material. In an atmosphere of safety, the patient then collaborates with us on the task of understanding if this is, indeed, a dissociative process, and if so, why it is necessary and what it obscures. During the process, with patience and luck, the patient may gain access to imagination. We cannot make language do our bidding, at least not in any but the most superficial sense; but to some degree, we can clear the field so that we do the least possible to prevent the eruptions of our own "wild logos" or "wildflowering mind" (Merleau-Ponty, quoted by McCleary, 1964), our spontaneous and unpredictably engaged capacity to speak the truth.

A man in his early 30s, quite devoted to his analysis, used to refer to certain brief and precious periods in his treatment as "speaking from the heart." He never knew when speaking from the heart would start, and once it did begin, he never knew how long it would last. But it was both serious and exhilirating, because during these times, he knew that he meant every word he said. Every word, magically, was exactly what he *wanted* to say; his language and his intention were one. He and I never could identify what set off these episodes, which lasted somewhere between two and seven or eight minutes. They did not seem reliably related to the content under discussion, and there was no accompanying variation in the transference-countertransference that either he or I could identify. Speaking from the heart came and went on its own schedule, the way writers describe an "opening" into their material that suddenly allows them to type furiously for a little while, knowing that what they are writing will be good when they read it back, but having no idea why it is suddenly given to them.

Who is it that speaks from the heart? Whose language is creative language? Who is it that imagines? Is it consciousness itself? It must be. But it can't be, at least it can't be consciousness alone, because what we say at such times is beyond our power to predict. Is imagination, then, the sudden appearance of that unconscious organizing activity I have been discussing? Is it the unconscious that takes hold of speech and makes it true? In the most concrete sense, it can't be, because that unconscious activity is nonverbal. And yet—yes, too; it must be, at least in part, because we have no better way to refer to our deepest intentions than to defer to the mysterious authority of the unconscious. Conscious and unconscious: that brief catalogue seems to exhaust our parts. But once again: is it perhaps some other thing that possesses us and speaks at these moments? Are we taken by the Muse? But no: this way isn't adequate, either, because we know it is we ourselves who mean what we say, not someone else, and certainly not an anonymous presence. And yet, we must admit that it is indeed the Muse who speaks, or the spirit of culture itself, because we find that when we speak from the heart we are suddenly using the semiotic tools at our disposal in ways we could never have imagined.

The one who speaks from the heart must be all of these and none of them alone. It must be a voice that knits together all our parts, if only for a little while.

IMAGINATION AND CONSENSUAL VALIDATION

I can now be more specific about a theme sounded in earlier chapters: the inadequacy of Sullivan's account of language. Now I can say that the problem with Sullivan's theory of consensual validation and the syntaxic mode of experience is that it does not recognize imagination and the creative use of language.

Sullivan himself was unquestionably imaginative, and his writing, which is never dull, shows it (though whether it is bane or balm is a matter of taste). But when he moved from the practice of language to its conception, he sheared off everything that is quirky, poetic, and difficult about linguistic expressions, all in the interest of his operationism. Yes, of course, language must be understood by others; and so, yes, of course, consensual validation is desirable. But Sullivan missed something essential about consensual validation: he didn't see that it could easily degenerate into empirical speech, the worn coin placed silently in the hand. He didn't see that language was most important when it was revelatory, and that, at those moments, it was less important for it to be understandable to others than for it to be generative to one's own sense of experience. Imagination brings thoughts alive. It is important, later on perhaps, that one be able to say them to someone else, of course, but that comes with the territory; that is a consequence that follows naturally from the fact that the kernel of the self is Mead's (1934) "generalized other"; other people always understand us when we clearly understand ourselves. What is more important, especially for psychoanalysis, is that one be able to say one's thoughts to oneself, even if they are messy, incomplete, and a bit confused. The capacity to say one's thoughts to oneself (and, in the case of free association, to the other) is what spells the defeat of dissociation. And if one's thoughts are densely poetic, or even just plain opaque, and if that poetry or opacity makes one's interlocutor's work difficult, and even makes the interlocutor wonder about whether the speaker's language is autistic—well, then, so be it. Eventually a meaning for the speaker's utterance will come clear in the mind of the listener, or the listener will think of questions to ask that will help along the process. Communication is always the eventual point, just as Sullivan said. But there is no reason that it should always be easy. To communicate about a matter of substance is liable to be difficult. Maybe it even *should* be difficult, because, after all, the thought hasn't been spoken before. Difficulty should not too easily be attributed to parataxis. In "A Prayer for Old Age," William Butler Yeats wrote,

> God guard me from those thoughts men think
> In the mind alone.
> He that sings a lasting song
> Thinks in a marrow-bone.

And Sullivan's most frequently quoted aphorism (though I do not know where it comes from) is, to his everlasting credit, and despite what I have just said, "God save me from a treatment that goes well!"

DISSOCIATION AND THE INTERPERSONAL FIELD

It is a clinical commonplace today that the patient and the analyst cocreate their experience of the analytic situation, but it is less often pointed out that patient and analyst cocreate the environment in which it becomes possible to think certain thoughts and not others, to have certain feelings, perceptions, experiences. It is the ongoing nature of the relatedness in the analytic situation that determines when experience must remain unformulated and dissociated and when a new perception can be articulated. Reflective meaning, in other words, is an interpersonal event.

This is a view Sullivan pioneered. "Selective inattention," says he (1956), in reference to people's omission of crucial parts of both their histories and current events in their lives, "is so suave that we are not warned that we have not heard the important thing in the story—that it has just been dropped out" (p. 52). He goes on to say that the important thing simply has been overlooked, "so that we just do not notice the gap where it belongs" (pp. 52–53).

Dissociation always goes on without the the awareness of either the patient or the analyst. That is its nature. Analyst and patient build a relationship together that seems natural and seamless, and the longer it goes on, the more natural it seems. Its naturalness is not as simple as it feels, though, because as Sullivan (1940) puts it, "there is nothing else as powerfully motivated as that which is happening" (p. 190). In other words, what seems natural, and therefore unworthy of remark, has come about for reasons that lie at the heart of the reason why the patient came for treatment in the first place. The very naturalness of the relationship obscures some of what is most important to know; often it takes some kind of problem, or even upheaval, to bring the obscured to light. Time and time again, when I have learned something unexpected about a patient, or about the relationship that is taking place between us, it has seemed to me that my capacity to understand was potentiated by a shift in the nature of the interpersonal field. I have not necessarily intended such shifts in any conscious way and cannot take credit for them. Yet they are often responsible for my capacity to transcend a dissociation and articulate a new understanding.

If, as psychoanalysts, we were able to satisfy directly our motives to grasp what we do not know, it could only be because we were successful in a direct exercise of will. And we know how much good *that* does. Anything like "a *will*, in contradistinction to the vector addition of integrating tendencies" (Sullivan, 1940, p. 191) is bound to be illusory. We take for granted our inability to force self-understanding. But we can depend no more reliably on our capacity to grasp what is transpiring between ourselves and the other person in a relationship, because we do not have the power to decide these things for ourselves. "Situations call out motivations" (p. 191), says Sullivan, reversing the usual polarity. Here we have the core of the thinking that Sullivan himself never found a way to articulate, but that he would eventually inspire in others (e.g., Levenson, 1972, 1983, 1991). Sullivan did not understand that the analyst was embedded in the analytic relationship right along with the patient, but what he did say about the matter allowed succeeding generations to extend his ideas to embrace that insight (see Levenson, 1992).

A CLINICAL ILLUSTRATION

At the time of the clinical incident I recount, I had been seeing Bob for several years, three times a week. I would have liked to see him even more often, and he felt the same, but as it was, even though I charged him a reduced fee, his treatment was a great sacrifice of both time and finances for him. He was deeply involved in the analysis, though, and with me, so despite the sacrifice, he never had any question about continuing—until the episode I narrate.

Bob's feeling about me was usually warm and appreciative; he said more than once, with real feeling, that I was the father he had not had. I was a father who appreciated how hard he tried to be good and how much he sacrificed for others, including me; Bob badly wanted me to demonstrate a continuing understanding of how staying in treatment strained his time, money, and emotional resources to the limit. In fact, it did not feel difficult most of the time for me to provide that understanding. I felt paternal toward Bob, and it was gratifying to feel helpful. Bob's appreciation merely added to all that. It seemed likely enough to me that our relationship was an enactment of something important in his past, but I was content to wait to find out the signficance of what it was we were doing. I did not find the assumption that we were involved in an enactment objectionable, and the thought did not make the very real emotional contact between us mean any less to me, because I believe enactment is continuous, even when we cannot see any particular problematic involvement with the patient. We know that most enactments are invisible; to that I will add that they are invisible because they constitute nonlinguistically structured organizing activity that is dissociated, or Schafer's (1983) "disclaimed action." All we can do is continue the work with the hope and intention of perceiving what we and the patient are up to, and of eventually interpreting and understanding it.

I knew that Bob's father most often had been silent, withdrawn, and depressed, a state frequently punctuated by episodes of rage. It turned out, though, that the warmth between the patient and me was not entirely absent from the patient's actual experience of his father, who was the more emotionally available parent. The boy had managed to be with his father at certain times, usually just before the father would fall asleep, when an uncharacteristic calm and content on the father's part allowed the two of them to spend a few close, silent minutes together. The boy would tell his father some of the things that were on his mind, and at these times, unlike others, the father could tolerate listening. It hurt when, invariably, the boy realized as he talked that his father had fallen asleep; but these times were precious nevertheless, and understandably so.

Despite these times with his father, though, the duration of warm feeling between Bob and me was new for Bob, and the continuity was probably always fragile. I realized that it would be easy for me to fail him in some way. It was probably even inevitable. And I did. Every now and then Bob felt I had betrayed him in some fashion, or did not appreciate him, and he responded with disappointment and rage.

One day Bob arrived for a session and, as he lay down, told me blithely (as it seemed to me then) that he would not be paying me on time when I billed him next; he would be several weeks late. I have an agreement with patients that they pay me the session after they receive the bill, and I had sent him that month's bill two weeks before. It was also my impression that Bob had not yet paid the previous month's bill.

But this situation was not simple, because I had several times stretched my payment policy considerably with Bob; I knew he was, if anything, more interested in paying me than I was in being paid. He dreamed of being able to "hold up his end," by which he meant being able to pay a full fee. Over and over again, sometimes angrily, he expressed the concern that I probably resented having reduced his fee, and that if I did, then I should just say so and he would leave. He refused to be a burden.

Of course, no matter how sincere Bob was in wanting to hold up his end (and I did have the impression that he was sincere), the reduced fee was also dear to him, because it meant I was doing something for him. And I was doing it for a reason he liked: I wanted him to be able to come more than the once a week he could have afforded at my regular fee. That is, the fee was evidence that I cared about him. I was to find out that, unbeknownst to me, I wanted his appreciation for my generosity, just as he wanted mine for his sacrifices.

Anyhow, laying aside all the complexity about the fee for the time being, the upshot was this: if Bob was late paying, I knew it was always because he simply did not have the money.

Yet in this instance I found that his announcement irritated me. It seemed to me, as I thought back on it, that he had not asked me if he could defer *last* month's payment, and here he was announcing his intention to defer *this* month's payment. This was not a request at all. I would probably not have thought twice about his tone if he had paid the previous month's bill; but this entitled assumption that I would be delighted to put up with any payment schedule he chose seemed outrageous. I was annoyed.

In a tone that expressed my annoyance, I asked Bob what he thought it was about to just assume my compliance with his wishes. Why had he not asked me if it was all right to defer payment?

Bob was immediately enraged and went on the attack, telling me I should know he would pay me, that he always paid me, that I had no right to question his integrity. This attempt to turn the tables on me, for that is what it seemed, did not have the effect, let us say, of dampening my annoyance. I returned to my original point and tried to tell Bob that I was not concerned in the slightest with his integrity, but with his apparent assumption that he did not need to ask me about deferring payment. He responded by saying that he guessed I had a point; but within a few seconds he had said something subtle that denied that very point. He then repeated his accusation. I responded by repeating my own point, and he once again agreed, then subtly took it back. I felt that he was trying to have his cake and eat it, too— that he wanted to appear to agree, thereby complying with what he thought I wanted, while simultaneously but indirectly suggesting that what he *really* thought was that he should be able to do as he pleased. My attempt to draw his attention to this process, needless to say, only fanned the flames.

Bob was soon in the midst of an eruption of volcanic proportions. He spent much of the remainder of the session shouting at me, and we ended having made almost no headway. Before he left, we both made efforts to reconnect by trying to express concern for one another, but neither of us had an effective grasp of what had happened.

We chewed over this incident unproductively for the next two sessions. Bob remained very angry, and I was unable to find anything more effective to do than to tell him there must be something more to the situation than met the eye, because (I said) all he seemed interested in doing was punishing me. That remark was true, but none of the ways I thought to say it helped. Once in a while Bob agreed with me, because even he could see that there was simply nothing I could say that he did not deride; but within a moment or two he was once again telling me that I, as the analyst, should simply never have become irritated with him. It had been either wrong or a demonstration of incapacity. I told him that, at this point, we should try to understand what we had been enacting. We could try to understand what he was looking for in my response. Was he missing something from me? What accounted for the extent and power of his reaction?

Bob would momentarily be mollified by the tone of what I said, but my invitation fell on deaf ears, and within a few minutes he would start up again in the same way. Things were going nowhere. He remained angry, and I was frustrated and very distressed and guilty. It seemed possible that this treatment that had been so important to Bob, and to me, had been irreparably damaged. I felt I should have handled things differently, though I wasn't quite sure how.

In the meantime, it was time for me to do my billing again. As is my custom, I sent Bob a bill that listed both the current charges and the balance he was carrying from the month before. Over the weekend, before he came for his next appointment, Bob left a message on my answering machine expressing shock at the size of the bill. As far as he was concerned, he had paid the previous month's bill. On the day he paid it, he had not thought to write the check before the session, he said, and in order not to inconvenience me, he had written it in the waiting room after the session, put it in an envelope, and slipped it under the door of my office. He had done this before, usually telling me his plans as he left the office at the end of a session, and I had accepted the practice without comment, so he simply assumed the bill had been paid. Now he was afraid that maybe he hadn't paid it, and he said he was panicked about where he could possibly get the money to satisfy his responsibility.

The next time we met, I told Bob it was terribly unfortunate that this issue should come up at a time like this, but that I had no record of the payment. I told him that because of the financial burden this imposed on him, I hoped the mistake had been mine, but because I had never made this kind of error before, I could not simply assume it was my doing. I told him I was sorry to put him to the trouble (and you can imagine, under the circumstances, that I was), but that I would have to ask him to locate the cancelled check. Even if he had left it in my office, I told him, I needed to make sure that I was the one who endorsed it.

The next session, Bob came in waving the cancelled check, which did indeed have my signature on the back of it. I had apparently not recorded in my account book half-a-dozen checks I had grouped together and deposited in the bank. I was unhappy with myself and I told him so.

The expected attack did not come. Bob's fire had subsided somewhat. Instead of continuing to express his rage, which I actually might have preferred, he reported, simply and calmly, that he would be terminating at the end of the month. He spent a good deal of time shaking his head over my lack of responsibility, and he went back to the earlier episode again, making the same points but less furiously. Of course, I asked him what my most recent error meant to him about me, or about my feelings about him, but he just rather sadly repeated the charges he had already made.

I was not entirely surprised by this turn of events; I had worried about something on just this order, especially after my accounting error. Privately, I thought that the fact I had neglected to record his check was probably not a meaningful reaction to him in particular, because his check had turned out to be one of several in that batch. But I still believed, and told Bob, that we needed to understand what exactly had happened between us, and that it would not be in his interest, if he did terminate, to do so prior to recovering the positive feelings we had had between us for so long. I told him that it seemed to me, no matter how angry he was at me now, and no matter how badly he felt I had behaved, that we had spent several positive years working together, and that if he left, I wanted to make sure he took those experiences with him, too. I reminded him of some of the most important things that had taken place over the years. I was very sad at the prospect of his departure, and I expressed it.

In response, Bob said bitterly, "You made me dig up the check. It was such a pain. I had to spend an hour and a half looking through boxes in the garage. You couldn't just believe me."

I don't know exactly why this remark accomplished something that none of Bob's accusations had. It's not as if the remark awoke some dormant empathy for him, because there was nothing vulnerable in it; quite the opposite. What he said certainly did not express, in any direct way, a fear on his part that I did not trust him any more; he did not even suggest such a thing, at least not in so many words. But somehow, in response to his reference to my not believing him, that is the thought that came into my head. Suddenly I realized that the fact that he had already paid the bill for the month before meant that the entire disturbing interaction had been built on false grounds. I saw that I had reacted to him with irritation to begin with, because I had believed he was being *blasé* about a debt to me that in fact did not exist. Had I realized he did not owe me for the extra month, I now knew, I would not have been irritated when he told me, with that apparent lack of concern, that he would be late paying the next month's bill.

I remember feeling intensely relieved, because I finally thought there might be a way to get a foot in the door. I did not know what the answer to the question I wanted to ask would be, but I knew I had a good question, and it seemed like the first one I had come up with in weeks. Asking a patient to join in an open-ended inquiry (e.g., "What might it be about, do you think, that your reaction to what I did is so intense?") is not helpful when the patient is stymied, because the patient, even if he can manage a degree of collaboration at a bad moment, really has no idea where to start. Yet, up to now I had been reduced to taking just this posture with Bob, because I could not see how to ask a more meaningful question about the problems we were having.

I had been suffering from a lack of imagination, a disturbance in my capacity to think and speak creatively about this problem. I have no doubt that I would have remained frozen on that same unproductive path, too, if Bob had not said what he did, allowing me, for whatever reason, to breach the dissociation. Perhaps my imagination could not reawaken until I felt the kind of concern I could only muster once the demise of the treatment was imminent. Or perhaps Bob's remark, which had consciously struck me as bitter, was mournful as well, and I had responded to that aspect of it without knowing it.

At any rate, at this point I could ask Bob—and I did so tentatively—if it was possible that he thought I didn't trust him. Almost immediately, his eyes filled with tears, and he said, still angrily but with a certain surprise, that yes, it certainly *did* seem that I had lost trust in him over the last few weeks, though that thought had not directly occurred to him before this. The atmosphere in the room softened rapidly, in an almost tactile way. Armed with this new point of view, we quickly went over the events of the previous weeks. It had seemed to him that I had chided him for not paying his bills more quickly. I had tried to explain to him that the irritation I had felt on that first occasion had not been about that issue, but he had never really believed me. Bob had felt betrayed, because he felt that I, knowing how important it was to him that he hold up his end, and be a good son, should never have doubted that he would pay me as soon as he could. And then, when the error took place in my accounting, I had not believed his insistent claim that he had paid his bill, which of course simply compounded the problem and the hurt.

I explained that my request that he bring in the cancelled check had not been a matter of belief in him or lack of it, but of figuring out which of us had made an honest error. This time my explanation made sense to him.

In that same session, I reminded Bob how badly he had always wanted his father to appreciate his efforts, and how badly he had wanted the same thing from me in the past. I told him that during the previous weeks, seeing matters as he had, he must have felt I did not appreciate him at all.

Bob agreed. We had clearly reestablished contact. He said he had apparently not seen the events of the previous weeks very clearly; however, he pointed out, neither had I. Why was that? Had I really understood nothing at all? Why had it taken so long?

I told him I did not have a complete answer to that question (though a more or less complete answer was to arise soon enough, as will be clear), and that I would be interested in whatever thoughts he had about it. (Be warned, reader: stay with the weird analogy I am about to report—it was useful in the context of its invention.) I *could* tell him, I said, that the way I had experienced the situation was as if he had shown me a hardboiled egg in the palm of his hand, representing his implacable rage at me, and had expected me to see that it was not actually a hardboiled egg at all, but an artichoke—that is, that his rage was not rage at all, but hurt feelings. I could tell him nothing more, I said, than that it had looked like a hardboiled egg until it suddenly looked like an artichoke. Bob laughed. In their ludicrousness, these metaphors convinced him that during the past weeks it really was true: I had had no inkling of the conclusion we had just reached.

No doubt you have already seen the last point I want to make. It turns out that it was not only Bob who wanted to be appreciated. Apparently I wanted to be appreciated, too—in my case, for my willingness to give Bob a financial break. That is one good understanding of why I would have been irritated with Bob for taking my flexibility for granted (that is, if my records had been accurate). We each apparently wanted the other to appreciate him, and we were each prone to feeling that the other did not.

From this formulation, which I suggested to Bob and he accepted, it was a short step to the interpretation that Bob was not the only member of his family who felt unappreciated. We were able to see, for the first time, that Bob's sad and distant father must have wanted Bob's appreciation, just as Bob wanted his father's.

Even now, the story is not entirely told. There is a coda; or maybe it is a beginning. Why did I dissociate this particular enactment? Why did I not articulate it sooner, as Bob asked? Better yet, why did I not just avoid it altogether? Did I not bring some motive to the interaction that would help to answer these questions?

I did. Like Bob, I am a son who wanted to be appreciated by his father more than he was. To one degree or another, most of us are sons and daughters with unrequited yearnings for parental love. It did not occur to me, however, that Bob and I had this piece of feeling and history in common until I had already formulated the interaction I have described. In retrospect, it appears that Bob and I had been passing the roles of appreciative father and appreciative son back and forth for years; that is one way to formulate the content of that affectively positive, long-running enactment I had been content to wait to understand. Enactments are routinely gripping; but no enactment grips either the patient or the analyst unless it somehow taps into a compelling part of both their histories. Analysts do not use only their well-analyzed experience to understand patients; as Racker (1968) described so eloquently, we also continue our analyses with our patients. I do not believe the analyst always understands himself first, as a condition of understanding the patient, as Racker believed; but whatever the order of the events, the substance of the point is the same.

A fully interpersonal conception of treatment is a field theory. The psychoanalytic relationship, like any relationship, takes place in a field that is defined and ceaselessly redefined by its participants. It is not only the intrapsychic dynamics patient and analyst bring to their relationship that determine their experience with one another. The field is a unique creation, not a simple additive combination of individual dynamics; it is ultimately the field that determines which experiences the people who are in the process of cocreating that field can have in one another's presence. It is the field that determines what will be dissociated and what will be articulated, when imagination will be possible and when the participants will be locked into stereotypic descriptions of their mutual experience. Each time one participant changes the nature of his or her involvement in the field, the possibilities for the other person's experience change as well. When Bob became enraged with me and could only repeat the same accusations, I could not see further than the stolid and stereotyped observation that his reaction seemed more intense than made sense. It is meaningless, really, to claim that I *should* have been able to see beyond his rage. The field is the only relevant context. In the field Bob and I had constructed, I could not do it.

Meaning, then, is an interpersonal event. The meanings that can be explicitly realized, articulated, or reflected on at any particular moment depend upon which interpersonal field(s) one is participating in at that moment, and upon the shape of that field at that time. Because it suited the purpose of an illustration, which must be simplified, I have written as if imagination is all or none, but most of the time, of course, that is not true. Any relationship is made of multiple fields, with their corresponding multiple selves, so that at any one moment, it is possible to use language creatively about some things and not about others; and the distribution of those areas of light and darkness changes a moment later.

It is also worth noting, in the context of the illustration, that empathy is not a stance one can necessarily choose to take toward the patient's experience, however desirable it may be (Stern, 1988, 1994). Especially when the analyst is under intense emotional pressure, what I have elsewhere called "the grip of the field" (see chapters 10 and 12), all he can do is to stay as open as possible to whatever new meanings float within range, waiting until something makes it possible to tell a more imaginative and convincing story of the events transpiring in the field—sometimes, in fact, waiting just to be able to *see* the events. Often the enabling episode, as in this illustration, is initiated by the patient. No matter which participant it is who eventually manages to exert the influence that destabilizes the previous perception, however, neither patient nor analyst usually knows, before the fact, how to do it. Sometimes destabilizing episodes are large, as the one I have recounted here; more often they are small. And to the extent that a treatment is moving well and imaginatively, such episodes must be nearly continuous, though seldom actually formulated. We are grateful for abilities we apparently have, but cannot understand. We are grateful when we can speak from the heart. We know not to sneeze at serendipity—if that is what it is.

6

Not-Spelling-Out

Dissociation in the Strong Sense

TWO KINDS OF DISSOCIATION: "STRONG" AND "WEAK"

From the perspective of language—from the top down, so to speak—there is only a single question about the formulation of experience, and it is always the same: Is language being used stereotypically or creatively, empirically or authentically? The stereotypic use of language is always dissociative, because it precludes new experience; the creative use of language just as surely and dependably results in the articulation of new experience, because creative language wants to accomplish nothing else. There is, then, only one kind of formulation. Language is always interpretive; the question is only whether the interpretation is hackneyed or from the heart.

From the perspective of prereflective content, however, the question is complicated by a factor of two. First, we must understand the relationship of both stereotyped and creative language to unconscious experience organized in the language of action or practice, a process I take up in this chapter and call "dissociation in the strong sense." Second, we must understand the same relationship between the two uses of language and implicit, unstructured unconscious content, the kind of meaning that remains unformulated only because attention has never been drawn to it. This process I call "dissociation in the weak sense" and address in chapter 7.

DISSOCIATION IN THE STRONG SENSE

Dissociation in the strong sense refers to an active defensive process, an unconscious avoidance of the verbal articulation of certain kinds of experience that already has some kind of nonlinguistic unconscious structure—experience that exists as action or practice, such as transference and countertransference. And I repeat: it is not the nonverbally organized experience itself that is denied reflective consciousness (because that kind of experience, being inconsistent with reflection, can never enter reflective consciousness at all) but all or some of the verbal interpretations that could be made of it.

Sometimes a dissociated meaning is highly organized, and in those cases dissociation in the strong sense takes place in virtually pure form. Such is the case in the instance of a highly organized but disavowed intention, or in those instances of dissociated memories that are actually recovered in specific form at some later point. At other times, the meaning in question is not specifically disavowed at all, and is entirely implicit; it simply has never been attended in such a way that it could be formulated. Here the dissociative act occurs in the weak form.

Many acts of dissociation, however, are composed of some combination of the strong and weak forms. In many dissociative episodes, that is, two things happen at once: the formulation of a meaning that is already highly structured (or a range of such meanings) is intentionally (defensively) prevented; and unintentionally (but just as effectively) the possibility of formulating other meanings simply never comes to light. One kind of story, in other words, *must* not be told; as a result, other kinds of stories *can*not be told, because they escape notice altogether. The material dissociated in both ways remains unformulated.

As examples of phenomena in which both the strong and weak forms of dissociation occur simultaneously, think of transference and countertransference. Quite often we find out, with analysis, and in the long run, that particular interpretations of the analytic relationship had to be avoided earlier in the treatment; equally often, we see in retrospect that other interpretations, which might have been at least as plausible as the one we and the patient used at the time, were quite invisible—not specifically disavowed, but rather obscured by the consciously embraced interpretations already in place. That is, some stories of the relationship *had* to be told, and those stories, simply because they dominated our attentional processes, prevented our formulation of alternatives to themselves (the weak form of dissociation); but one or more of these alternatives *could not* be told, having been actively forbidden (the strong form of dissociation).

Verbal interpretations of experience organized as action or practice cannot be made at will; if they could, we would merely be talking about a process of translation from one language to another. Instead, such interpretations occur unbidden, the result of imagination and creative use of language. To breach a dissociation is to allow oneself greater interpretive freedom; it does not necessarily mean that one constructs any particular interpretation. Active or defensive dissociation therefore can be understood as the restriction or stifling of imagination, accomplished by the stereotyped or empirical use of language. *What* is dissociated in this way can range from the entire experience (so that it either is never allowed to occur in the first place, or so that it seems as if it never happened) to much more subtle emotional resonances that leave the perceptual part of the experience intact, but make it feel unalive. The portions of the experience that are dissociated remain unformulated.

Dissociation in the strong sense poses major difficulties for our understanding of self-deception. Or rather, self-deception, as it is usually understood, poses a challenge to a theory of defensively motivated unformulated experience. How can it be feasible to "choose," albeit unconsciously, to force nonlinguistically organized experience to remain unarticulated in language? Isn't "someone" doing the choosing? And if so, doesn't it follow that some "part" of oneself would have to formulate the experience in language to begin with, just in order to be in a position to choose what *not* to formulate? How can one select what not to interpret in linguistic terms without first converting the relevant experience into language?

SELF-DECEPTION FOR FREUD AND SARTRE

Self-deception has always been a contradictory idea. The paradox at its heart is that to accomplish it, one must decide not to be aware of something about oneself and simultaneously to *be* unaware of it. Does this process not seem to require two people? Does it not at least require that two independent consciousnesses inhabit one body? When I "decide" to become unaware, what do I do with the knowledge of the decision? You might conceivably say that I *repress* the decision to repress. In that case, though, what becomes of the decision to repress the repression? Infinite regress does not qualify as either explanation or understanding; it merely pushes a grasp of the issue continuously into the future.

This paradox was a large part of the reason that Freud (1923) added his structural model, in which the dynamics of mental contents could be understood by reference to their psychic jurisdiction (id, ego, superego), to his topographic model, in which mental contents were characterized only descriptively (conscious or unconscious). The change allowed Freud, by overlapping the two schemes, to conceive the ego and superego as partly unconscious. By taking this step, he argued, he could posit that a portion of the ego, an internal authority that he had earlier (1900, pp. 505–506) called the "censor," was responsible for the defenses. The key to the new model is that the psychic censor belongs to the unconscious part of the ego. In this way, the decision not to be aware does not have to be repressed, because it was never conscious in the first place. And so the paradox is resolved: one mind, after all, can be the site of both the repression and the decision to institute it.

In taking issue with Freud, Sartre (1956) develops the celebrated argument of *mauvaise foi*, which is literally translated as "bad faith," although it has also been translated as "self-deception" (see Fingarette, 1969, p. 93). Both English wordings are relevant. Sartre intends to analyze the process by which one simultaneously asserts and denies the same thing about oneself (that is, self-deception), but he also feels in the strongest way that unknowing of this sort represents a *refusal* to know, a choice, making it morally relevant and worthy of condemnation as bad faith.

Sartre claims that the solution to the problem of self-deception offered by Freud's theory of the censor is illusory. If the censor knows what is not permitted to enter consciousness, the censor must be part of consciousness, because there would be no other way to know what consciousness prohibits; but if the censor is part of consciousness, then consciousness itself, as a consequence of being able to reject anything at all, knows the very things it rejects. Such a procedure contradicts itself and defeats its own purpose.

The only way to resolve the problem is to conclude that the censor both knows and does not know. Freud, in fact, adopted just this unacceptable solution, contends Sartre, when he concluded that the ego and consciousness are not coextensive. If the censor exists outside consciousness, the censor can both know and not know, because the ego does not consciously know what its own censor-part has decreed must remain unconscious.

According to Sartre, though, this line of argument simply leads to the conclusion that the censor itself is in bad faith, like the person whose censor it is. What Freud has done, in order to explain dreams and other phenomena that seem to reveal the operation of self-deception, is to violate what for Sartre is the essential unity of psychological life, the oneness of mind that is the underlying principle of all Sartre's psychological writings. Freud first takes this falsely atomizing step, claims Sartre, by dividing the mind into geographical units (conscious and unconscious), then into functional fiefdoms (the structural theory). On top of being inaccurate, however, Sartre contends that Freud's theorizing is misleading and does not even serve the purpose for which it was devised: that is, it does not end up offering a solution to the problem of self-deception. In the process, by medicalizing what is really a moral problem, and thereby subtly excusing it, Freud distorts the true nature of the phenomenon even further. A theory of a psyche divided, claims Sartre, simply cannot avoid the implication that the mind is full of fantastical homunculi, each trying to hoodwink the others. Sartre is understandably skeptical of such a theoretical turn.

The self-deceiving person, in Sartre's model, lies to herself. While the account of how this lying takes place is subtle, the fact of the lie, Sartre believes, should be accepted simply and straightforwardly. By making bad faith into the outcome of invisible internal divisions, Freud's solution trivializes the issue of personal responsibility and falsely euphemizes people's simple refusal to accept what they know is true. Bad faith is made to appear to be a victimization of one part of the mind by another.

Sartre prefers to portray self-deception as the consistent misrecognition of the meaning of one's own behavior, while one "at some level" knows the truth. This point does not, by itself, differentiate his account from Freud's. The difference comes about in Sartre's contention that because the mind is unitary, its different levels may form a hierarchy, but a hierarchy with free traffic between levels. Freud, of course, does not agree. When Freud says that the person knows the truth "at some level," he means that the truth exists in a psychic agency or "place" that, because of a cognitive blockade, cannot be reached by the part of the mind that carries out the misrecognition.

Sartre's argument sometimes has been characterized, on both philosophical and psychological grounds, as a less powerful indictment than Sartre believed it to be. Archard (1984, pp. 44–45), for example, argues that there are ways, even within Sartre's view of psychology, that the censor *can* do its work outside awareness. Be this as it may, most psychoanalysts, even if they believe Freud's account of self-deception is contradictory, remain, for clinical reasons, sympathetic to it and incompletely convinced of the validity of Sartre's critique. We know that the phenomena we end up including in the idea we call *self-deception* occur routinely; that is not at issue. The problem for Sartre's thinking, as far as most clinicians are concerned, is that Freud's description of a psyche in which meaning can be accepted or unconsciously refused remains indispensable. It is just too useful in representing what clinicians see every day. There are too many instances of self-deception in which people cannot realistically be held to be as transparently culpable as Sartre would have it. In the clinical situation, over and over again, we see that people's unwillingness to know, and the kind of responsibility they bear for it, is more complicated than its description as simple culpability would suggest.

This is not to deny our responsibility for our experience. We are always responsible for what we wish not to know. It goes without saying, too, that we are capable of hiding from ourselves the consequences that our unwillingness to be aware have for others. There is a continuum, however, along which the degree of our culpability for the consequences of our behavior varies. A thief who absolves himself because his victim had more money than he did is nevertheless culpable in most people's eyes. In many instances of self-deception, though, establishing culpability is a hazier matter, despite the fact that the responsibility can be no one's but the self-deceiver's own. Is one culpable, for example, if one's anxiety about facing sexual feelings, an unwillingness to experience lust that can be traced to aspects of one's relationship with a parent, leads to behavior that hurts one's spouse or lover? One is certainly responsible. But is one culpable? Perhaps—and perhaps not. The answer to the question depends on the circumstances, the behavior in question, and the worldview of the one making the judgment.

These are immensely complicated issues, because our notions of right and wrong are social constructions; even inside the tiniest subgroup there may be intense differences of opinion about these constructions. In some cultural circumstances, for instance, it is justifiable to steal from the rich, depending on what one does with the stolen goods. (Robin Hood stole from the rich to give to the poor; the Marxist revolution is intended to redistribute wealth as a point of principle.) It does seem realistic to claim, though, that within the bounds of any moral system, some instances of self-deception more than others will be held to imply culpability. And as long as that point makes sense, we are implicitly rejecting Sartre's contention that consciousness is unitary and transparent. However much we may applaud the prescience and accuracy of Sartre's early corrective to the medicalizing of morality, we recognize that culpability and responsibility are not coterminous.

Psychoanalysts, though, do not necessarily even need to take issue with Sartre. Roy Schafer (1992) takes the position that the question of how it is possible to deceive oneself is basically a matter for philosophers. Analysts, because they do not have philosophical training, not only have no basis on which to give an account of how people are capable of self-deception, they do not need one. For psychoanalysts it is sufficient justification that self-deception is an undeniable, everyday clinical event. Schafer writes:

> Typical Freudian analysts [as well as analysts with other theoretical orientations] in the course of their daily practice do not concern themselves with asking "How is it possible for someone simultaneously to know something and not know it?" and "How is it possible to defend and not know that one is doing so?" They just take it for granted that it is possible to effect this split unconsciously and that the split is probably present in what they hear and see in their clinical work. They do not seek a philosophically secure account of defense, and they do not justify their doing without that account [p. 39].

SELF-DECEPTION AND UNFORMULATED EXPERIENCE

After considering Freud and Sartre, it may seem that the apparent requirement that one be able to formulate an experience in order to know *not* to formulate it (i.e., to dissociate it) is just one more version of a paradox psychoanalysts live with every day. If that were so, I could cite the willingness of most psychoanalysts to live with the paradox, and simply wash my hands of further consideration of it.

The generic problem self-deception poses for psychoanalysis, however, is not the end of the problem for defensively motivated unformulated experience. There is a further complexity, a twist in the argument that does not arise in the case of the more traditional defenses. As long as one can tolerate the paradox that one both knows and does not know, traditional notions of defense are feasible:

one simply accepts that the unconscious part of the ego somehow recognizes the dangerous experience and disguises it from the remainder of the personality.

The same is not true for unformulated experience and defensive dissociation. *No* part of the mind, it seems at first glance, is in a position to carry out the initial recognition of the dangerous experience, because any part of the mind that could carry out the recognition would have to have formulated the experience beforehand. In this case—that is, if one has formulated the experience in order to keep it unformulated—the concept of unformulated experience loses its meaningfulness. The idea of unformulated experience cannot survive the paradox of knowing and not-knowing that lies at the heart of the traditional notion of self-deception—even if, with Schafer, we are willing to ignore the contradiction. If defensively motivated unformulated experience is a matter of simultaneous knowing and not-knowing, dissociation in the strong sense is just one more variety of the traditional defensive maneuvers. Dangerous psychic content, that is, might be denied, repressed, undone—or forced to remain unformulated. Dissociation in the strong sense would have to be understood as nothing more than the refusal of experience on one level that one is capable of articulating on another, and I hope it is obvious how inconsistent with the foregoing chapters that characterization would be. We would be back to an understanding of defense in which the constitutive properties of language play no part.

And so a different theoretical account of self-deception is necessary, one in which defensively motivated unformulated experience makes sense.

SELF-DECEPTION AND FINGARETTE'S "SPELLING-OUT"

Dissociation as an Active Process

Herbert Fingarette (1969), it will be remembered from chapter 5, argues that consciousness is not the natural fate of experience, but a matter of interpretation that requires effort. The ways in which we are engaged with the world, that is, must be interpreted; they do not simply present themselves in awareness: "[G]enerally speaking, the particular features of an individual's engagement in the world need not be, and usually are not spelled-out by him" (p. 40). By "engagement in the world," Fingarette means to refer to such phenomena as an individual's aims, conduct, hopes, fears, reasons, motives, memories, attitudes, and feelings—that is, the individual's entire "understanding and 'perception' of the world and himself" (p. 41). "Engagement in the world" is a shorthand for all this: "One might (simply) have said *his world*" (p. 41).

We spell-out only some of our engagements, then. But the point goes further than that: spelling-out, because it is effortful, is the exception and not the rule. The most common state of affairs is for engagements *not* to be spelled-out. One needs a "special reason" to spell-out, "over and above the simple fact of being engaged in some specific way" (p. 41). We are selective, that is, in what we say—not only to others but to ourselves—about what we do and how we experience. "Rather than taking explicit consciousness for granted, we must come to take its absence for granted; and we must see explicit consciousness as the further exercise of a specific skill for special reason" (p. 42).

Now, to discuss spelling-out as a skill may make the activity seem merely instrumental. But to believe so would be a mistake. It *is* instrumental, of course; but that is not all it is. In chapter 5, I addressed the formulation of experience as a mystery that combined both agency and unbiddenness, and concluded that a crucial element—the creative use of language—is missing from purely instrumental accounts of formulation, such as Sullivan's "consensual validation." Fingarette is concerned only with self-deception, not with the formulation of experience, and so we do not know his views on this matter. But whereas Sullivan's operationism would actually have been contradicted by an insistence on the significance of the creative use of language, Fingarette's thinking accommodates it easily. Whether Fingarette intended it or not, we can use his concept of spelling-out as if it is nothing other than the process of formulating experience as I have described it in chapter 5; thus, for experience to be fully spelled-out is for it to be fully imagined. The fact that spelling-out is selective and partial is no contradiction of this point; it merely indicates how seldom we fully imagine what we live.

With this proviso, we can agree that spelling-out is indeed a skill. But it is a skill, Fingarette (1969) goes on, that is much more extensive than the "mere capacity to perform spelling-out."

> Exercise of the skill requires sizing up the situation in order to assess whether there is adequate reason for spelling-out the engagement. And the corollary of this is that in exercising the skill we are also assessing the situation to see whether there is reason *not* to spell-out the engagement. Where it

happens that there are both reasons for spelling-out and reasons for not spelling-out the very same thing, these are presumably weighed against one another by the individual.
Whether or not he spells-out the matter in question, or
exactly how he does so if he does spell it out, will depend not
only on his assessment but also upon his ingenuity in adapting to the conflicting considerations. All this is no more than
we allow to be the case with complex skills generally. Skill in
driving a car is not merely the ability to perform certain
movements; it is also the ability to assess the possibly conflicting considerations in a situation in order to settle which
movements to perform, when to do so, and precisely how.
Skill in speech calls for assessing just when to speak, when not
to speak, how to speak, what to say. Skill in spelling-out
requires analogous assessments [pp. 42–43].

Now, keep in mind that spelling-out is an activity. It is itself a way
of being engaged in the world: spelling-out is an engagement. And so
spelling-out is subject to the same principles as any other type of
engagement.[1] The most important of these principles is that we do
not make the activity of spelling-out explicitly conscious unless we
have that "special reason" to do so. More often than not, we do not
have such a reason. Therefore, we do not have to be aware of the activity of spelling-out; we can just do it. This idea is familiar to us from
experience. Seldom do we stop and observe ourselves bringing experience into awareness, although that otherwise rare activity is the
heart and soul of psychoanalysis.

If one is trout fishing, for example (an activity that can be quite
magical and that certainly requires imagination), and one takes note
of the swirls of current in a stream, imagining that the water will bring
food to a trout positioned just *there*, one does not spell-out the activity
of spelling-out. To do so would be an encumbrance to the activity of
fishing, and it would interrupt our pleasure. One simply attends to the
products of the spelling-out: the swirls in the water and the prediction
of the trout's location. And now consider a situation in which we
would spell-out the activity of spelling-out. If we were trying to learn to
cast a fly line, we might very well not only spell-out the details of our
performance, trying quite consciously to make it better, but, perhaps
in exasperation, we might also spell-out the activity of spelling-out, saying to ourselves something on the order of, "Can't you watch what
you're doing carefully enough to figure out what you've got to do to
keep from getting your line hung up in that bush?"

If there are powerful reasons to spell-out, it follows that there are at least equally compelling reasons *not* to spell-out. And just as spelling-out is a synonym for the formulation of experience, not-spelling-out is dissociation. When a reason arises not to spell out, Fingarette (1969) says,

> we skilfully take account of this and systematically avoid spelling-out the engagement, and . . . in turn, we refrain from spelling-out this exercise of our skill in spelling-out. In other words, we avoid becoming explicitly conscious of our engagement, and we avoid becoming explicitly conscious that we are avoiding it [p. 43].

In other words, if choosing to spell-out is an engagement, then so is choosing not to spell-out. And if not-spelling-out is an engagement, we can either be aware of it or not, depending upon whether we select it for elaboration into an explicit verbal form. We do not have to "know"—that is, articulate—our decision not to spell-out; that decision can be left unformulated.

Thus we continuously make choices about what we will articulate and what we will not, and the whole process goes smoothly, because we never spell-out those of its aspects that would disrupt it. The original reasons for not-spelling-out the engagement also serve as reasons not to spell-out the avoidance of spelling-out. One has a "cover story," in Fingarette's deft phrase, and infinite regress and homunculi are both avoided.

Is the paradox of bad faith resolved?

That is debatable, of course; Sartre would certainly say no. Even if we accept Fingarette's account, however, his theory does not yet lift me out of my quandary with unformulated experience, at least not as I have described his theory thus far. For it does seem that the knower, or the subject, in Fingarette's theory still needs to be able to formulate the experience in order to be in a position to choose not to spell it out. Have I, then, not landed right back in the middle of the problem I have been talking about? In citing Fingarette, am I just jumping out of the frying pan and into the fire?

Avowal, Disavowal, and Spelling-Out

How can we refuse to spell-out an experience without having first spelled it out? How do we know what not to spell-out? How can we refuse to know without knowing, refuse to experience without experiencing? What sense does this make?

We spell-out only those engagements that are either consistent with our cherished notions of self or that further the aims that correspond to these notions of self. Other engagements are not spelled-out.

Now consider the contents of a self: These are the stories that we use to define who we are. The experiences in our stories, and the plots that connect them, feel like they belong to us. This experience is me; I avow it; I identify with it. Other experience is *not* me; I *dis*-avow it; I do *not* identify with it. Not-me experiences, if we acknowledge having had them—that is, if circumstances conspire against us so that we are forced to avow them against our wishes, because that is the only way we would avow them—disrupt us. Although we do not recognize them as ourselves, they nevertheless seem to belong to us. Here is a simple example. To be consistent with a cherished image of ourselves in which we appear kind, we might avoid spelling-out the interpretation that we acted sadistically in a particular instance, even if that interpretation might occur right away to an observer. We might blame our unpleasant behavior on the other person in the interaction, who we then believe gave us no choice. Given the ambiguity that characterizes human experience, it is usually quite possible to select an interpretation in this way, and to end up with an unbroken story.

The worst not-me experiences are those that would disrupt our stories so thoroughly that we would be forced to ask the most basic questions about our identities, and even about what kind of place the world is and how safe it is for us to live in it. This kind of extreme not-me experience is well worth avoiding; it is frightening, even terrifying (Sullivan, 1953). Intense not-me experiences cannot break through one's characteristic patterns of formulation—the boundaries of our various self-states—without what Sullivan calls "grave consequences to the personality."

Take the example of childhood sexual abuse, a betrayal committed by someone who is supposed to take care of one and make one feel safe. (Not all frank sexual abuse may have been experienced as a betrayal by the children involved, but if the abuse seemed expectable to the child, or—God forbid—even unconflictedly pleasurable, it is hard not to imagine that the consequences for the child's future would be even more disastrous.) Disavowal of such an experience makes sense. Under those circumstances, the avowal of the experience at the time it happens—that is, the event of saying to oneself, "this is happening to *me*"—is simply too frightening and disruptive. It may require changing one's picture of the whole world, and concluding that one is living in a place one does not want to live in (e.g., Davies, 1996a). The dissociation is made all the easier because the child, if he or she is young enough, does not even have the language to symbolize what has happened. An older person, in order to disso-ciate such an episode, would have to dissociate an event that could be labeled as "sexual"; a very young child doesn't even have the word for violation. All that child knows is that something very horrible and wrong-feeling, and probably very confusing, has happened. The event may be encoded no more specifically than "something bad" that has to do with touching.

Now, keep in mind that the abuse is an engagement on victims' parts, even if it is an engagement against their wills, and even if the victims are little children. If the event is a profoundly disavowed engagement, victims do not spell it out, even if they have the cogni-tive maturity to do so. The experience is not ejected from con-sciousness, as in repression; rather, the experience never enters consciousness at all. It is never known, at least not in any clear and emotionally salient way. In most conscious respects, it is as if the experience never happened.

As a personality is built around this absence, the possibilities for articulating the experience of abuse become even more remote, until in adulthood, victims who dissociated the experience in childhood may be left with only dim, vague, unformulated shards of something that there may not even be any words for, because there were none at the time. These fragments of meaning, having no narrative context, no self-experience within which to exist, may or may not be con-structible into a viable memory. They may not be assimilable by the victim's "inner schemata" of the relation of self and world (Horowitz, 1986). And even if a memory can be constructed, it is liable to be poor in meaning, because it is bloodless and dead, lacking a meaningful emotional context. It is not fully imagined. Judith Herman (1992) reminds us that long ago Pierre Janet described normal memory as "the action of telling a story."

Traumatic memory, by contrast, is wordless and static. The survivor's initial account of the event may be repetitious, stereotyped, and emotionless. One observer describes the trauma story in its untransformed state as a "prenarrative." It does not develop or progress in time, and it does not reveal the storyteller's feelings or interpretation of events. Another therapist describes traumatic memory as a series of still snap-shots or a silent movie [p. 175].

Which is to say, this is dissociation, too. Dissociation is not necessarily limited to the absolute prevention of experience; it often merely drains experience of the feeling and the potential for narrative vigor that even the most terrible memory must have to be real. Dissociation more often drains experience of feeling by preventing it from taking its place in a story. The result is mere experiential contingency, like the experience of Mrs. Nicholson, the winner of the football pool, in chapter 5. The experience that exists in an unformulated state—that is, as opposed to being repressed or disguised—is not limited to what we usually consider cognition, or thoughts. In fact, unformulated affective experience is at least as common as the cognitions it shapes and informs—and is provoked by. Unformulated feeling may range from what would become, if articulated, subtle affective nuance all the way to the most thunderous passion. I know one man, for instance, whose detailed memories of the horrendous beatings, tortures, and humiliations he suffered as a child are accompanied by very little feeling. Like so many people who have suffered repetitive, catastrophic trauma in childhood, he has trouble being sad or angry about the way his parents treated him, or even seeing how wrong it was, despite the fact that anyone else's abuse immediately arouses his ire. He cannot even feel that what he went through was bad enough to deserve my compassion.

LANGUAGE IN FINGARETTE'S ACCOUNT

Fingarette does not explicitly discuss the degree to which language participates in the moment-to-moment shaping of experience, but, as was the practice in the late 1960s when he published his work, he seems to presume that language is simply clothing or labels for experience that already exists in cognizable form. I believe Fingarette assumes that nonlinguistically organized experience requires no interpretation in order to be spelled-out, merely a sort of "noting" in language or linguistic "pointing." For me, of course, implicit or unspelled-out engagements are a variety of unformulated experience. They are nonverbally structured unconscious experience, which suggests that the eventual reflective meaning that will be devised for them, to which language will contribute importantly, is only partially predetermined. An unconscious engagement may eventually take any one (or, conceivably, more than one) of several or many potential forms and meanings.

As it turns out, the most important parts of Fingarette's model work just as well in a psychology in which precise meanings await the explicit participation of language as they do in traditional psychology, in which language merely makes explicit reference to meanings and experiences that already exist. The point that makes possible this application to newer ways of understanding language and experience is that the activity of spelling out does not have to be an all-or-none phenomenon, as it seems to be in Fingarette's book. The activity of spelling-out can just as well be understood to be a matter of selecting one interpretation from many potential ways of understanding. If one articulates a meaning—that is, if one formulates one of the unformulated possibilities—one can avoid spelling-out the activity of that articulation, just as, in Fingarette's own work, one avoids spelling out the decision to spell-out an engagement; and if one notices an unformulated meaning that one wishes not to formulate, or spell-out, one can avoid spelling-out the decision not to spell-out that activity, too.

And thus Fingarette's work does allow me to explain how it is possible, without awareness, to formulate experience or to decide against formulating it (dissociate it), even in a world in which the ways unformulated experience might be articulated are multiple. This contribution brings me quite close to solving the problem with which I began this chapter. However, one difficulty does remain. Fingarette does not offer a description of *what it is that one recognizes* in order to set this defensive process in motion. This is no oversight for Fingarette, as I have shown, because he was not working with unformulated experience, so that he could simply suggest that one avoids spelling-out experience that is directly available to conscious inspection. His solution will not work for my purposes, of course, since it is precisely my point that the relevant experience is *not* available in articulated form and therefore cannot be recognized.

So what is it that one *can* recognize under these circumstances?

I have actually already introduced the tool I need to solve this portion of the problem, though it only becomes possible to use it for this purpose once Fingarette's argument is in place. Think of William James's (1890) "feelings of tendency," which James described as "signs of direction" in all kinds of experience—that is, in thought, feeling, perception, memory, and so on. We have momentary glimmers of where our conscious experience may go, glimmers that we may or may not be aware of, and that certainly do not require the complete formulation of a meaning or an experience. Because being aware of these glimmers or not is an activity (in Fingarette's sense of the word), we can use the spelling-out model to grasp how it is that we can be unaware of feelings of tendency for defensive reasons.

If we add to this formulation the element of anxiety, and the consequence that some of our feelings of tendency are disturbing because of their association with anxiety, Fingarette's model can be applied to show us how we can use feelings of tendency to gauge the direction our experience is taking. On the basis of that information, we can choose to develop (formulate) or avoid (dissociate) certain articulations of our experience, without ever having actually to know what articulations they would have become if we had allowed the process to reach completion—if we were, that is, to imagine the phenomenon in question more or less fully. We develop those articulations that we believe we can tolerate, or that further our purpose, or those that promise a feeling of safety, satisfaction, and the good things in life; we dissociate the meanings that we believe we will not be able to tolerate, that frighten us and seem to threaten the fulfillment of our deepest intentions.

7

Narrative Rigidity

Dissociation in the Weak Sense

AN APPROACH TO NARRATIVE

When he first left school, John Shotter (1993), who is today a social constructionist thinker, was an apprentice engineer in an aircraft factory. He remembers the thousand workers, including himself, crowding in through the single door at the back of the factory, rushing to make the 7:30 A.M. deadline for punching in. They were docked 15 minutes pay for every minute they were late. Management and administrative staff, on the other hand, "strolled in" at 9:00 "through big double doors in the front." The management staff, served on white tablecloths by waitresses, were seated for lunch on a mezzanine raised five feet above the floor of the workers' lunchroom. The workers had no service, but "buttered sliced bread straight from the paper packet on the formica top of the table" (p. xi). The list of major and minor indignities goes on. The workers were treated like "about-to-be-naughty children." Many years later, it intrigued Shotter that,

> when workers had returned to the floor, seething, after a brush with management, and everyone had said "Oh, you've just got to complain about that," no one ever did. In the end, it seemed too trivial, and one knew it would be useless. To complain, for instance, about the windows in the men's toilets—put there so that the foreman could see that what was being done there was being done properly, and not wasting time—to complain just by saying "Well, I don't like being

129

watched at those times," seemed both inadequate to the anger and unlikely to be effective. But what else could one say? Our rage was impotent rage; we didn't even know where our anger came from, so to speak. There seemed to be no adequate language within which to express why we had become so angry, to explain why these little degradations mattered so much to us [p. xii].

Similar stories could be told about any number of situations in which people are treated differently according to class (power) distinctions. But the point I want to make is not about oppression. It is about the telling of stories.

When and why does a situation like the one Shotter describes begin to change? Only when someone sees the parts everyone is enacting in a new moral relation to one another. Someone tells a story that brings into the light of reflective awareness a new and convincing picture of the social context. The story, of course, must be told from a perspective; that is, the story told by most members of management would not be the story told by the workers. Power relations being what they are, the creation of an opportunity for change in the distribution of power, or even for the perception of the social relations of the factory in the terms of unacceptable, entrenched power relations, would probably require that the new story be told by a worker, or a group of workers. Prior to that, all the workers can do is complain about individual incidents. One can easily imagine how management might perceive such complaints as selfish whines ("Here we're building planes to defend our country and you're worried about a window in the john?"). In fact, isolated complaints of this sort—that is, complaints not embedded in a coherent narrative context—might even have seemed whiny to the workers themselves, because isolated complaints miss the point. And even if someone could have told a plausible story rejecting power and class, of course, he or she may not have been able to convince other workers, much less management, of the validity of the account, or of its significance. That a new story is conceivable is not enough. It must fall on fertile social ground. A new perception will die unless it occurs in an atmosphere of readiness (of course, in a social context inhospitable to it the new perception is less likely to occur to anyone in the first place), just as psychoanalytic interpretations carry an affective, mutative charge only if they concern what is accessible to awareness, what can be experienced directly.

It is easy enough to see the advantage for the management staff of telling the story of the "just-about-to-be-naughty children" who need constant supervision. The state of these "children" probably seems to management to justify its self-perception of benevolence and superiority. But why do the workers not see the master-slave story? (Or why do they not see it as unacceptable?) Why is there "no adequate language within which to express why we had become so angry, to explain why these little degradations mattered so much to us"? Why, in other words, are the alternatives dissociated? Why can no one see the situation imaginatively and use language creatively to redescribe it?

We know from Shotter's description that none of the workers, as far as he was aware, could tell a story that managed to contain the abuses of authority and the details of degradation in a single narrative. We can guess that they did tell themselves stories, but that these stories justified the status quo. "That's just the way managers are. Let it roll off your back"; or "We've got no time for petty bickering. There's a war on!"; or (with a sneer) "You've got to have education to get those jobs. Go to school and come back; and then you'll end up just like they are." Or even something angrier, but no more innovative, such as "They're bastards and I won't let them push me around." None of these stories is untrue; they are just selective. Many of them, as a matter of fact, would probably still be told in an environment more consciously organized around themes of class. As stories, though, they are not as good as class-based narratives because, while they may be coherent, they do not account for as much of the available data.[1]

Why could these people not construct a better, more inclusive story? The closest Shotter comes to answering this question is to say that "we still do not quite understand how to articulate the way these small things work to influence us in our feelings as to 'who' we are, that is, to influence us 'in' our identities" (p. xii). But in a different context, he offers what I am sure he intends his answer to be. The answer is simply that the people, in that particular place and time, could not envision a way of asking the question, "Could it be otherwise?" The class distinctions seemed to the workers (and no doubt to management as well) so much a feature of the natural world—they were so thoroughly taken for granted—that they could be questioned only in particular instances, and those specific instances could not be held together in a single, coherent story that accounted for them all. The workers did not—could not—imagine a different system. We shall see later that Foucault offers a reason why.

Shotter's aim is philosophical and social-psychological. He approaches that-which-we-do-not-know as a broad social phenomenon, not as the unexpressed implication of the individual consciousness. A psychoanalyst would ask what stories each worker tells about work, how that worker's life up to that time predisposed the telling of those particular stories, and what place the stories hold in the worker's psychic life in the here and now. An analyst would expect, of course, a good deal of overlap from the account of one worker to the account of another, because the workers all face the same situation. It is in this overlap that sociological interest lies. But there would be important differences, too, depending on individual perceptions of emotional safety and security, danger and insecurity, hopes and fears and cherished beliefs.

In this case, we do not have to posit that the workers refused to be aware of a story they actually unconsciously knew. Instead, we can take the much more economical position that the workers actually did not know, and had never experienced, a class-distinction story of their working conditions. They had never formulated it, because they were too attached to whatever stories they did tell to see any alternative to them. From this point of view, people do not construct life stories only to avoid something (sometimes the truth), but often to accomplish something else (tell the story a certain way). The class-distinction story must remain unformulated until someone can ask the question, "Could it be otherwise?"

This kind of not-knowing—a passive sort of dissociation—is based in selective attention, not in the selective *in*attention that we could invoke, if we wished, to characterize the active, defensive dissociation discussed in chapter 6. Passive dissociation, or "dissociation in the weak sense," is indirect, because it is the consequence of so insistently turning our attention elsewhere that we never even notice alternative understandings. Focal attention under these conditions is controlled by the intention to enforce narrative rigidity. One sees and participates in the ways one wishes to do so, and in ways that are familiar.

The very familiarity of a story line can be quite comfortable. It is not necessarily the need to avoid anxiety about specific content that motivates a story, but the desire to tell the story a particular way, the desire to live a particular way, the intention to maintain predictability and not to slip the traces. The more rigid that desire, the less interpretive freedom one has.

NARRATIVE RIGIDITY IN PSYCHOANALYSIS

This inverse relationship between narrative rigidity and interpretive freedom is important, not only for the kind of sociological example I have been considering but for individual experience as well. It often really is not clear what interpretation will fall into place when the hold of an old narrative relaxes. Narrative rigidity is not simply a way to distract attention from a single denied and preexisting psychic content.

The continuous construction of a story of the self (or multiple stories of selves) requires the equally continuous activity of selective attention. The various previously established directions and urgencies of one's life story define a few categories of experience as virtually irrelevant, a few others as essential, and most as variably salient, depending on context and circumstances. Telling a story—and listening to one—requires a "drawing in of awareness to a (relatively) small mental content, leaving . . . important, but to-be-unattended-to, events sort of in a marginal, shadowy, not-quite-complete condition" (Sullivan, 1956, pp. 55–56. Ironically, Sullivan means to refer here, not to selective attention, as I do, but to selective inattention).

That "marginal, shadowy, not-quite-complete" byproduct of telling a story is unformulated experience. Unformulated experience is the continuously accumulating byproduct of our evolving autobiographies. This kind of unformulated experience, however, unlike uninterpreted but structured unconscious organizing activity, is genuinely vague and unstructured, even at a prereflective level; it is the implicit unconscious. It exists relative to the stories we tell, and thus relative to language. It is composed of all those stories that fall within our grasp, all those narrative roads we could have taken but did not, all the potential interpretations that might have been articulated—and, in many cases, still might be. Because the stories of a life change in subtle ways from month to month, from day to day, and even from one moment to the next, the nature and content of this relative and implicit part of unformulated experience does as well. The stories of a life and the unformulated alternatives implicit to them are each "visible" and meaningful only against the backdrop of the other. As one changes, so does the other, so that they continuously re-create one another, like M. C. Escher's image of two hands in the process of drawing one another. The relationship between the life stories we tell and those we don't—between reflective consciousness and unformulated experience—is dialectical, each pole both outcome and determinant. The implicit and the story that sloughs it off are both meaningfully apprehended only in the present tense. The swarm of potential meanings that exist in any one moment, available for articulation, belongs to that moment alone. But because what we are in the present is heavily influenced by what we were in the past, certain implicit unformulated experience may exist over long periods of time, recreated in each passing moment by the ongoing retellings of our most stable narratives of self.

STEREOTYPED NARRATIVES OF SELF

We take for granted in psychoanalysis that stories more specific to the patient's particular context replace stereotyped stories of much wider applicability as treatment progresses. One can see this kind of increasing specificity in the forward movement of every single successful case. It is so common in psychoanalytic treatment that we hardly pay attention to it. Loewald (1980) tells us over and over again and in many different ways that insight is the evolution of a greater articulation and differentiation in our understanding. Our new understandings therefore tend to be increasingly tailored to our lives and our defenses to be relatively more generic. Analogous to the the "layering" of the "psychic apparatus" proposed long ago by Merton Gill (1963), each level of the articulation of meaning, depending upon context, may serve either to prevent levels of articulation finer than itself (that is, it may function as narrative rigidity) or, if one comes upon it from a less well-articulated understanding, may qualify as new understanding.

Our embeddedness in the various overlapping cultures and subcultures to which we belong is a significant source of narrative rigidity. We are drawn to narrate events in familiar ways, according to familiar plots, and starring familiar characters. Even when narrative rigidity is specifically motivated (that is, when the reason for telling a story rigidly is dynamically meaningful and not merely the unwitting assumption of the categories and expectations of one of one's cultures), the ease of adopting a particular motivated narrative is often due to its relative conventionality. The availability of narratives—what we might call the "vocabulary" of narrative—is the province of the social discourses, or cultural contexts, in which we live, and which shape us. One might even say that cultures *are* vocabularies of narrative (Bruner, 1986, 1990).[1]

"THE WAR OF THE GHOSTS"

Frederic Bartlett's (1932) classic memory experiments established schema theory as a convincing account of remembering and, along with the very different work of Freud, forever banished our easy confidence that memory requires nothing more than drawing attention to experience stored in the form of copies. Although the implications of Bartlett's work are still being explored, the overall accuracy and utility of his observations (ingeniously replicated by I. H. Paul, 1957) are not seriously questioned. Bartlett's description of memory as "imaginative reconstruction" is especially compatible with the various general psychological theories of narrative that have become influential in recent years, all of which center on the observation that human beings construct experience by telling stories (e.g., Bruner, 1986, 1990; Sarbin, 1986a, b; Polkinghorne, 1988; Shotter and Gergen, 1989). I. H. Paul (1967) summarizes as follows:

> Remembering by turning upon one's schemata consists not in the direct recall of the past (however that may be conceived), but in the imaginative reconstruction of the situation at any given moment in the past by inferring (unconsciously or preconsciously) from the present form of the schema what ingredients must have gone into it and when [p. 228].

That is, we tell stories from our position in the present. We are hardly restricted to a recitation of the "facts"; we often actually select the "facts" to make the past conform to our present view of it (see also Hirshberg, 1989). Of course, we cannot simply have our cake and eat it too. We cannot remember at all if we violate the past too seriously. If we try to remember a picnic on the basis of a "set" or a schema developed for a visit to the theater, for example, we will remember nothing at all.

How much variation from the past is too much? How different is too different? What Bartlett showed is that there is an enormous amount of "give." Memory has a great deal of room for variation before "too different" is reached. Take Bartlett's famous experiments on Cambridge University undergraduates' memory of "The War of the Ghosts," a Native American tale told (in easily comprehended English) by a member of that culture. Each subject read the story several times at his regular reading pace and was then asked, at various intervals, to write down his memory of exactly what he had read.[2]

The remembered versions were startlingly different from the original. Bartlett uses the word "rationalisation" to describe the process by which the story was changed. "Rationalisation" is primarily a matter of "conventionalisation"; that is, the stories remembered by the undergraduates were uniformly more conventional than the story they had read. In reading Bartlett's (1932) description of "rationalisation" that follows, consider how easily this process might come to the service of narrative rigidity. Think back to the aircraft plant, for instance, and consider the role conventionalization played in establishing the various story lines Shotter's fellow workers told about the relations between themselves and management—and, for that matter, the stories management personnel must have told about the same situation.

> The general function of rationalisation is in all the instances the same. It is to render material acceptable, understandable, comfortable, straightforward; to rob it of all puzzling elements. As such it is a powerful factor in all perceptual and in all reproductive [i.e., memorial] processes. The forms it takes are often directly social in significance [p. 89].

Was the more specific and highly unconventional original material in Bartlett's experiment—the original form of "The War of Ghosts"—*repressed* by the subjects and therefore still somehow available in some recess of their minds? There is certainly no reason to think so. Each recall of the material seemed to proceed on the combined bases of those that came before, so that recall became less like the original and more conventional with each retelling. The most convincing interpretation of these findings is that these undergraduates had no idea (no idea "at any level") that they were fabricating. They did not suspect their errors. Their stories seemed to them to be the altogether "natural" forms of their memories; the subjects just did what came "naturally." Apart from the fulfillment of the expectations of their cultures, there was no conceivable intrapsychic or interpersonal advantage for them (and each and every one of them did it) to press their stories into a conventional mold.

Fascinatingly enough, the single most potent influence on the memories was the general affective attitude the subjects had toward their memories. Bartlett concluded that we do not carefully reflect on or think about the source of what we remember. "We rely rather upon a general impression, obtained at the first glance, and issuing in immediate like or dislike, of confidence or suspicion, of amusement or gravity" (p. 53). When we remember, what comes back to us first is that affective attitude, and we then use the materials available to us to construct a memory that will justify the attitude. The result feels accurate and natural; and "naturalness," of course, is the hallmark of convention.

FOUCAULT AND POWER

But *why* did the undergraduates reshape their stories? And why were the inequalities in Shotter's aircraft factory so hard for the workers to conceive as a story of power and class? We know that no one could find a way to ask the question, "Could it be otherwise?" But what accounts for this cognitive mire?

Michel Foucault's (1980) understanding of decentered power relations has much to offer here. Foucault argues that the way we usually conceive power is inadequate. The idea that power is the domination of one person or group by another, accomplished by an imposition of will, is ponderous and incomplete. Especially today, that kind of domination is not even the most significant form of power. Rather, power is a *productive* force.

Power is decentered; it does not issue from a particular place or person. It is not exercised by anyone in particular, but by everyone; it is the shaping activity wielded by cultures themselves. It exists in and through its effects, and it is felt in the local contexts to which it happens to apply. For Foucault, power is effective to the extent that it is not perceived. To just that extent, it shapes individual experience, and it does so while obviating the necessity to explain the exclusion of alternatives. Alternatives are simply unformulated. Power is a positive force, a shaping force, as opposed to the negative forces—forces that delete experience, such as repression—that we tend to cite more often in psychoanalysis.

Power, in fact, is entirely consistent with the constructivist understanding of consciousness as an interpreter, rather than as the passive recipient of whatever insurgent unconscious content can slip past the censor. In the following passage, Foucault (1980) lays out his understanding of power and contrasts it with repression.

> But it seems to me now that the notion of repression is quite inadequate for capturing what is precisely the productive aspect of power. In defining the effects of power as repres-

sion, one adopts a purely juridical conception of such power; one identifies power with a law which says no; power is taken above all as carrying the force of a prohibition. Now I believe that this is a wholly negative, narrow, skeletal conception of power, one which has been curiously widespread. If power were never anything but repressive, if it never did anything but to say no, do you really think one would be brought to obey it? What makes power hold good, what makes it accepted, is simply the fact that it doesn't only weigh on us as a force that says no, but that it traverses and produces things, it induces pleasure, forms knowledge, produces discourse. It needs to be considered as a productive network which runs through the whole social body, much more than as a negative instance whose function is repression [pp. 60–61].

All people are caught in the grip of power, not only those who have the least prestige and raw social muscle. A Foucauldian analysis of power relations is an analysis of systems, not simply the revelation of purposeful (even if unconscious) abuses of influence. In such an analysis of Shotter's aircraft factory, the behavior of the management *and* the workers would be understood as a set of roles dictated by *all* these persons' positions in the discourses of class relations. Neither management nor workers are necessarily to blame for the class inequities; contrary to Marx's totalizing philosophy of revolution, the solution to the injustices (that is, once an injustice is widely perceived) would not necessarily be the same at the aircraft factory as it might be in another instance of class inequities in a different place, a different time, or both. Politics and thought in Foucault's frame of reference are insistently local and nontotalizing.

There is really no reason that decentered power relations must be limited to molar events—which is why I have brought up the topic. The interpersonal field, too, can be conceived as a social context structured by power relations. Many contemporary psychoanalysts are well prepared for this kind of analysis, because we have today transcended simple models of the therapeutic situation in which countertransference enactments are inevitably collusive and exploitative. Like social constructionists (in at least this one respect), many modern analysts do not consider blameworthy the countertransference of a competently functioning analyst, but see it instead as part of a wider transference-countertransference system. It will no longer do simply to analyze the patient's transference, as if it were a distortion that could exist apart from the analyst; neither is it adequate for the analyst to think about his involvement with the patient as nothing more than a manifestion of his own, internally contained neurosis.[3] Contemporary psychoanalysts are responsible for trying to see the positions they occupy in the discourses that structure the therapeutic situation.

POWER AND CONVENTION

Now consider Bartlett's findings in the light of Foucault. The alternative ways that the undergraduates might have remembered "The War of the Ghosts" include many that would have been more exact reproductions of the original, and others that would have been inconsistent with the subjects' affective attitude toward the story (which, incidentally, would no doubt include discomfort with its lack of familiarity). It is clear enough that Bartlett's subjects *constructed* their versions of the foreign story. They did not merely delete the parts they did not grasp; that is, they did not merely ignore or "repress" the most foreign parts of the material. They reformulated the entire story into one that could be more easily understood in the terms by which they lived their everyday lives. Their retellings of "The War of the Ghosts" were an expression of the invisible operation of powers of the unconscious imposition of the patterns of dominance and submission, of inclusion and exclusion, that defined the Cambridge undergraduates' cultural world.

Through no particular exercise of anyone's will, and without pressure from any particular interest, Native American culture has no place to "be" in 1930s uppercrust England; it falls outside the "horizon" or the "clearing," and it therefore simply cannot be perceived or remembered; it is not "natural." In the absence of a much more detailed and sympathetic acquaintance with the alien ways Native Americans constructed experience, which would have required an interest in such things and the availability of the material (which, in turn, probably would have required that 1930s uppercrust England not *be* 1930s uppercrust England), much of what constitutes one of these worlds must simply remain unformulated in the terms of the other.[4]

My intention in taking this digression into power, memory, and convention is to provoke a further appreciation of the nature of narrative rigidity. From Bartlett we learn that closely tailored, particularized, and original narratives are the exception and that convention is the rule. Conventional narratives are easy to adopt; we tend to slip into the simplest account of the events at hand (or in memory), and the simplest account is the conventional account—the "natural" one. We are in the midst of living conventional narratives virtually all the time, as Ernest Schachtel (1959), a psychoanalyst and one of the most important of the early schema theorists, conveys in his conception of "secondary autocentricity."[5] Schachtel also saw that conventionalization is not only a disadvantage, but is, in fact, a necessity. We must have shorthand methods of negotiating life. A great deal of what we do and perceive and remember must be done without a second thought, or we could never do anything at all; the least important task would command endless fascination. Nevertheless, there is a price to be paid: conventional narratives, always the paths of least resistance, are so seductively easy to slip into that we are seldom even aware of having chosen them. It is dismayingly easy, when one has some reason to reflect on one's experience in any particular moment, to find oneself hovering around the cultural mean, around the predigested perceptions that probably would occur to a substantial portion of the populace (those who share with one the relevant cultural niches). One's own lack of originality can actually be quite shocking at such moments.

Original narratives are difficult to formulate; we have to think carefully, explicitly, imaginatively, and feel deeply, to come up with a story that includes all the details and still ends up saying what we really mean. To do anything more than unwittingly slip into the most "natural," stereotyped narrative, we have to give explicit consideration to the need for an account; and we usually just do not attend to our experience in that self-consciously reflective way, even under circumstances in which it would be fair to say that our interests would be best served by doing so. Even when, in a particular situation, we actually transcend the effects of convention enough to perceive our opportunity to tell our story a different way, we still cannot count on ourselves to come up with what we need. As I have already quoted Paul Valéry (1952), "we must simply wait until what we desire appears, because that is all we can do. *We have no means of getting exactly what we wish from ourselves*" (p. 102). We can add to that the wisdom of Heraclitus, who tells us that, "If you do not expect it, you will not find the unexpected, for it is hard to find and difficult" (cited by Eiseley, 1969). Recognizing one's need for a tailored narrative, that is, is a necessary but not sufficient impetus to the creation of such a thing. Ask any writer up against an unproductive afternoon. We can be sure, though, that *without* recognition of a need, we will always end up unthinkingly adopting a conventional route.

The purposes of defense, or the prevention of alternative formulation, are therefore well served by the processes of decentered power. It is decentered power that is behind the availability of conventional narratives, and the unreflective adoption of convention results in narrative rigidity.

THE MORALITY OF PSYCHOANALYSIS

Psychoanalysis is a morally saturated endeavor. Our theories are cultural products, heir to the same conventionalizations we see in the undergraduates' attempts to remember "The War of the Ghosts." And all of us, to the extent that we unthinkingly constitute the events of our everyday lives with the conventional narratives available to us, are captives and unconscious exponents of various decentered power relations. Clinical psychoanalysis, with its commitment to tell stories that are increasingly well tailored to the lives they describe, and to freedom and flexibility in thought, inevitably crosses swords, not only with narrative rigidity, but with unconsciously adopted convention and entrenched unconscious power relations. If conventional narratives are essentially prescriptions for how we ought to live—and what else could they be?—then clinical psychoanalysis, because these conventional narratives tend to be used defensively, routinely takes issue with them; that means that psychoanalysis, too, is always concerned with how people ought to live. To be a psychoanalyst is inevitably to take a political and moral stand. Psychoanalysts have no choice but to be critics of the cultures within which they move and work—critics of any unthinkingly adopted prescription or proscription, of any unconsidered inflexibility of thought—even if they are not aware of functioning that way. I do not mean to gild or romanticize the analyst's role in making this point, though. Being a critic is not the same as succeeding as one. Analysts have the same trouble locating interpretive inflexibility in their own experience that anyone else does.

CLINICAL ILLUSTRATION

I turn to the clinical setting to illustrate the way conventionalization supports narrative rigidity and the consequent unintentional cloaking of alternative interpretations. The example I consider concerns a dream reported to me by a professional woman in her middle 30s. This patient had just become pregnant after many years of treatment devoted to her terrible fear of having children. She had always been afraid that she was too narcissistic to be able to offer a child good mothering. She was afraid she would resent a baby's neediness and the sacrifices that that neediness would require of her. It will come as no surprise that this woman had grown up with a highly narcissistic mother who had given the patient every reason to believe she (the mother) felt just as resentful of the patient's needs as the patient was so frightened she herself would feel with her own baby. The transference-countertransference had been focused around generosity, hoarding, and resentful giving. By the time the patient finally met a man, fell in love, and married, enough of the relatedness around giving and resentment had been worked through that she felt she could go ahead with having children. She became pregnant, but remained worried.

In the dream, the patient was with a man she thought was her husband, and the two of them were caring for a baby. Unremarkably (so it felt), the baby was in separate parts: legs, arms, body, head. This state of affairs seemed to be fine; the parents just kept making sure all the pieces were there. They knew that as long as they had all the pieces, the baby would be fine whenever it was put back together. Then, suddenly, the patient realized they didn't have the baby's head. Something had happened to the baby's head, and she knew it was her fault. She searched frantically, because she knew the baby could not possibly survive without a head. It seemed to her that the head was the seat of this baby's personhood, and that without that, the baby was incomplete and dead.

The patient awoke distraught from the dream, and arrived at my office later that day in great distress. She knew perfectly well, she said, what this dream meant. It meant she had been right all along, and she didn't want a baby. She must wish this baby dead. She must wish to tear the baby to pieces.

It turned out, on my questioning about possible day residues, that the patient had seen a TV documentary the night before in which surgery on children with certain physical problems had played a peripheral role. She was worried about the possibility of her own baby being born with physical problems, or of the pregnancy (which was nearing the three-month mark) ending in a miscarriage, and so this program had scared her. The idea of surgery had also made her think about abortion, which she had long since ceased considering. The pregnancy had been planned. Nevertheless, the program made her think once again that she would soon not be legally entitled to an abortion, which meant that her decision to have a baby was becoming final in a whole new way. She felt sure that the program had been the immediate impetus for the dream; but she felt just as sure that her death wishes toward the baby were the more important, underlying reason.

I really was not sure what to make of her interpretation. It seemed superficially reasonable, I thought; but we had seemed to make more headway on the issue than that interpretation would suggest. It was too raw and destructive to fit the ongoing context of what we were doing; its tone was out of the blue. Its bald reference to destructiveness also did not ring true in my experience of the patient.

The patient had not yet, in this session, talked about her actual feelings about the dream-baby, but only about what she *must* feel in order to have such a dream. I asked her if she was aware of any feelings that would make sense of her interpretation that she had "intentionally" lost the baby's head. She said she was not, but that perhaps that was irrelevant. She went on for a time, quite miserably, discussing whether she really had to accept that she felt the way the dream portrayed.

In the meantime I was thinking along a different line.[6] Eventually I told her that I agreed; we *could* certainly look at this dream as an expression of her conflict, as she said it was, with one side feeling protective of the baby and the other side destructive; but (I continued) it seemed to me another interpretation might fit the dream at least as well. I suggested that she had seemed to come into the session that day terribly afraid that she felt destructively toward the baby. Why couldn't the dream be saying exactly that—and nothing more? She is afraid she wants to destroy the baby; she is afraid that she doesn't want the baby; she is afraid that her recognition, during the TV program, of the three-month mark means that she wants to abort; and she desperately wants not to feel any of these things. Why did we have to conclude, in other words, that the dream was actually telling us about a feeling she cannot otherwise identify? Why did the dream necessarily concern anything more than her *fear* of what she felt?

This woman does not easily give up a criticism of herself, because to do so would be (she fears) to take the easy way out, to deny about herself what she wants least to know. She suffers at her own hands more than she needs to. Nevertheless, her relief at my interpretation and her sense of conviction about its rightness were immediate.

In this particular instance, the patient made a conventionalized interpretation on the basis of a convention contributed by psychoanalysis itself. It has become a commonplace in the culture at large that dreams are wishes, and this patient was well aware of the idea. One of the reasons she did not formulate on her own the interpretation I offered her is that she reacted quite automatically to the interpretation she was led to "naturally" (and ironically) by a convention that arose from the very field that made it possible for her to take an interpretive stance toward her dreams in the first place. The idea of the wish-fulfilling dream, in concert with her masochistic characterological trends, was enough to convince her that the self-blaming interpretation was good enough to accept. Defense, that is, was well served by convention. Note that the new understanding was more highly differentiated than the old one.

CONCLUSION

Telling one story means not telling another. The world is heterogeneous, and any account of it, or of its parts, appears orderly, regular, and seamless only at the cost of excluding from consideration other, conflicting ways of seeing and understanding. Narrative coherence is the result of invisible underlying assumptions that shear off some parts of life and corral others. Any interpretation or story line is as much a set of blinkers as it is a way of seeing.

We seem to be narrative creatures (Bruner, 1986, 1990; Sarbin, 1986a, b; Polkinghorne, 1988). Coherent stories, those that seem to us ineluctably accurate, inescapable, as if they were the only possible ways to describe and order events, are the only stories that make sense to us. From Bartlett we have learned that, if a story is less than coherent, we force it to conform to our standards of coherence, even if doing so requires us to change dramatically our descriptions of events. And so the world's heterogeneity and multiplicity tend to be invisible to us. We sacrifice them for the sake of constructing good stories. We can only hope we gain in comprehension what we lose in comprehensiveness.

It is worth reminding ourselves of the truism that the past can be told only in retrospect. The classic example is that the birthdate of a famous person becomes significant only after achievements that occur later in his or her life. One's "place" in history, whether that history is the description of a whole society or of our individual lives, can be determined only by telling stories while looking backward in time. In the words of English historian C. V. Wedgwood (quoted by

Atlas, 1995), "We know the end before we know the beginning and we can never recapture what it was to know the beginning only" (p. 1). Life, therefore, does not unfold from beginning to end, as it seems to us, at least not in any simple way. There is a certain truth to the idea that life is a matter of retelling, and that it actually takes place from end to beginning.

Since the beginnings of psychoanalysis, and throughout its history, the avoidance of anxiety or other noxious affect has virtually always been the sole and unquestioned basis of motivated lack of awareness. We have assumed that the stories of our patients' lives need to be told from beginning to end, and we have given short shrift, in our attempts to understand how our reflective experience comes into being, to the formative significance of interpretation and narration and the shaping influence of convention. From the vantage point of psychoanalysis, it often seems that the stories we would tell, if we were capable of being absolutely truthful in some impossibly literal sense, are already in us. That way of looking at life has left us with a burdensome and contradictory notion of self-deception, so that we have believed for generations that we must somehow come to terms with the idea that we both know and don't know. If these last three chapters have served their purpose, they raise a single question.

Could it be otherwise?

8

The Problem of the Private Self

Unformulated Experience, the Interpersonal Field, and Multiplicity

As Harry Stack Sullivan was the first to see, the smallest meaningful unit of human experience is not the individual human being, but the interpersonal field. In arguing to reject the traditional notion of a unitary, interior, unique self, Sullivan portrayed the psychic life of the individual as a collection of what today we might very well call multiple and discontinuous selves or states of self. A number of today's theorists of the multiple self (e.g., Mitchell, 1991, 1993; Bromberg, 1993, 1994, 1996a, b) acknowledge Sullivan's work as an important inspiration. Even among those multiple-self theorists who do not embed their ideas in the interpersonal tradition, ideas similar to Sullivan's are in common usage, most particularly the idea that a self or self-state can be understood as "the crystallization of different interactional schemes" (Slavin and Kriegman, 1992, p. 204).

In what is arguably his single most mature and seminal paper, "The Illusion of Personal Individuality" (published in 1950, but orally presented six years earlier), Sullivan made his position crystal clear: the feeling of being a unique individual, and of having a uniquely individual self, is nothing more than a narcissistically invested fiction—a useful fiction for most people to have, perhaps, but one that clinicians should be knowledgeable enough to see through. What he called the "self" (or self-system) was not connected with the sense of identity, as it was for Erikson, and had nothing to do with shaping life in the pursuit of ambitions or ideals, as in Kohut, but was instead that part of the personality central in the avoidance of anxiety—and

147

anxiety was everything to Sullivan. According to Sullivan (1950), people cannot exist outside the interpersonal field; hence, this psychic, adjustive mechanism, this "self-system," can never be understood in isolation from others. Therefore,

> one of the greatest difficulties encountered in bringing about favorable change is this almost inescapable illusion that there is a perduring, unique, simple, existent self, called variously "me" or "I," and in some strange fashion, the patient's, or the subject person's, private property [p. 220].

And again:

> You will find that it makes no sense to think of ourselves as "individual," "separate," capable of anything like definitive description in isolation, that the notion is just beside the point. No great progress in this field of study can be made until it is realized that the field of observation is what people do with each other, what they can communicate to each other about what they do with each other. When that is done, no such thing as the durable, unique, individual personality is ever clearly justified. For all I know every human being has as many personalities as he has interpersonal relations; and as a great many of our interpersonal relations are actual operations with imaginary people—that is, in-no-sense-materially-embodied people—and as they may have the same or greater validity and importance in life as have our operations with many materially-embodied people like the clerks in the corner store, you can see that even though "the illusion of personal individuality" sounds quite lunatic when first heard, there is at least food for thought in it [pp. 219–220].

These were not Sullivan's only descriptions of this view. Earlier, he had referred to "the overweening conviction of authentic individual selfhood" that "amounts to a delusion of unique individuality" (1936–1937, p. 16). Later (1938), again mentioning "delusions of unique individuality," he went so far as to label such beliefs as "the very mother of illusions, the ever pregnant source of preconceptions that invalidate almost all our efforts to understand other people" (p. 33). Sullivan recommended, in the strongest terms, that we give up the attempt to characterize unique, defining "selves" and instead try to grasp what is going on at any particular time in the interpersonal field. In such an inquiry, the place of history remained secure, because the way the field operated was a combinatorial function of one's past and one's perception of the present.

Here we have Sullivan on one side and all of the psychoanalysts of his day on the other. No wonder classical analysts have sometimes misunderstood the work of interpersonal psychoanalysts as radically environmental (though there was an important political agenda in this rejection as well). And no wonder some of those very interpersonal psychoanalysts who were inspired by Sullivan's work have argued that he didn't *really* mean to exclude the uniquely individual self, that he was only following the dictates of his operationist principles, and that there actually is room in his theory for a self and an internal world.

But he *did* mean to exclude the unique, individual self. He meant just what he said. I cannot read the passages I have just quoted any other way than as a straightforward rejection of the traditional unitary, unique self and its contained inner world. Sullivan means to define the personality as the sum total of one's interpersonal relations, and the self-system as the anxiety-gating processes of the personality. We are nothing more, he says, than agglomerations of interpersonal relations, although many of those relations may go on privately (that is, with a symbolic or fantasized other) after an origin in the external world.

The argument is brave, brilliant, and prescient; but it is too extreme. Sullivan sought a remedy for the exaggerated internality of the psychoanalysis of his day, and he found one. Like many who propose correctives, though, he rode the pendulum too far in the other direction. We do not have to do away with the inner world to preserve what is most important about his insight.

I should add, whereas Sullivan intended to explode the unitary self, he was certainly not arguing in favor of a theory of multiple, discontinuous selves. Multiple-self theory was, at the time, no more than a novelty, written to deal with certain rather bizarre cases (multiple personality), the reality of which was in question to most clinicians. It is also important that Sullivan understood dissociation as a defensive process, the one used in the most severe instances of anxiety. He did seem to imply the possibility of a multiple self, but he did not explicitly conceive the idea; he did not get to the point of thinking through the notion that various selves or self-states might interact, or that dissociation was a concept that described such a phenomenon. Those meanings, however, are among the most important meanings of dissociation in today's literature.

What, then, does Sullivan mean when he says that "every human being has as many personalities as he has interpersonal relations"? He means that each relationship creates a certain kind of interpersonal field, and that as long as we limit our frame of reference to the confines of that field, it is fair to say that a human being has a certain "personality" or "self." From a more contemporary perspective, we would add that the field is not an objectivistic concept; it is not construed on the basis of data or essences to which we somehow all have access in just the same way. (Sullivan's attitude toward this point would have been highly ambivalent, and perhaps more negative than positive.[1]) It is constructed, rather, according to the interaction of the conscious and unconscious psychic realities of the participants.

How does an interpersonal field come into being in any particular instance? For instance, what happens when the telephone interrupts me while I am talking to my spouse? How do I suddenly become the person I am with the salesperson on the other end of the line, or with Aunt Bess, or with my best friend? How do we move from one "personality" to another? Part of the answer here depends on Sullivan's notion of what a "personality" is. Each person we know (or think we know, as when we make assumptions about a new acquaintance) calls out in us a set of operations that have been effective in the past with this person, or with a person we take to be similar, in managing the regulation of security and insecurity. Thus, for Sullivan, each "personality" is no more or less than a set of security operations; these, however, can be immensely complex. These various individual "personalities" we "have" can be linked in groups. Some people somehow remind us of our fathers, for instance, or make us feel like the son or daughter of our fathers, and therefore tend to call out the repertoire of security operations related to the expectations, perceptions, and so on, that we bring from that relationship.

What are security operations? Very simply, they are ways of constructing and constricting experience in order to avoid anxiety and encourage its opposite, security. To refer to security operations is to refer to the shapes and limits of the experience that we allow, prohibit, or encourage ourselves to formulate with particular individuals. This shaping and limiting is carried out by means of a process Sullivan describes, in self-explanatory fashion, as selective inattention. In Sullivan's frame of reference, then, it is the interpersonal field, by means of the security operations deployed by the self-system, that determines the moment-to-moment content of consciousness—for both participants. This is very important, crucial even, because it means that the interpersonal field determines what unformulated experience is articulated, and how; similarly, it is the field that determines what unformulated experience remains unarticulated.

BEYOND ANXIETY

At this point in the argument, however, Sullivan and I part company, because he was really interested only in helping people to become functional members of their society. Although psychoanalytic ideas have been partially inspired by some of his ideas, Sullivan was not a psycho-analyst, and did not pretend to be. He did not even wish to be.[2]

Contrary to Sullivan, I (along with most contemporary analysts who have been influenced by Sullivan) hold that the configuration of anxiety and security operations are only part of what defines any particular interpersonal field (e.g., Lionells et al., 1995). The conception of the field I favor is something broader than that, something that better suits psychoanalytic purposes. The field should be defined in terms that include anxiety and its avoidance, but that also go beyond them, terms that refer to the other aims and purposes the field's participants try to fulfill with one another, and especially unconscious aims and purposes.

Each of us continuously and unconsciously casts about for other people to play roles reciprocal to our own in various fantasied interpersonal events that we actually want to create in the outside world. These key events have to do with intrapsychic dynamics and early history, which are represented in our minds by internal object relations. We are searching, therefore, for ways of actualizing our wishes by means of bringing certain internal object relations to life in the outside world. We "cast about" by means of unconscious behavioral invitations for partners in various interpersonal ventures (cf. Sandler, 1976). The field that is constituted depends on the other person's generally unconscious response to these invitations. That is, we continuously treat other people in ways unconsciously designed to have certain effects. Each of us, then, is not only ceaselessly issuing invitations, but just as ceaselessly and unwittingly responding to the invitations of others. This is interpersonal life.

It seems unlikely, though, that we simply issue the same invitations to everyone we meet. It makes more sense to imagine that we unconsciously test the waters first, so that we issue only those invitations (that is, we "inhabit" only those self-states) that have some chance of being accepted and eventually fulfilled by the other person. We seek out safety and avoid putting ourselves in the position of being turned down flat and made to feel foolish, humiliated, or worse. Such an addition makes interaction more complicated, but by making it possible to understand how different selves or self-states come into play in different environments, this revised version is a better fit to the world we live in. All of us are continuously and unconsciously testing the water, issuing what seem like the appropriate invitations, responding to invitations, revising the invitations we send on the basis of the responses and invitations we have received, and so on.

Heinrich Racker's (1968) theory of transference and countertransference (see especially pp. 134–136 and 175–176) is a good way to conceptualize this testing of the waters, because Racker suggests that analyst and patient inevitably adopt crucial unconscious parts in one another's intrapsychic dramas, played out and possibly solved anew in the therapeutic relationship. When we approach another person with the intention to understand him—as we do in the analytic relationship, of course, but as we also do in "testing the waters" or in any part of life when a grasp of the other's experience has some personal import—we tend to identify with that person. We learn about people by experiencing ourselves as if we were them. Racker proposes two kinds of identifications. In *concordant* (or *homologous*) *identifications,* each "part of our personality" may identify with the corresponding "part" of the other person's personality. Ego identifies with ego, id with id, superego with superego. This kind of identification might feel like, "I can understand that kind of wish easily enough, because I would wish it myself," or, "I would criticize her husband just the way she does." On the other hand, in *complementary identifications* (a term Racker adopted from Helene Deutsch), the analyst's ego identifies with some internal object of the analysand's, such as the superego. In this kind of identification, the analyst actually feels like one of the other person's internal objects, or like one of the important people in the patient's life, something on the order of, "This guy is so provocative that he's really asking for it," or, "I am deeply moved by her generosity." Concordant identification is "feeling with"; complementary identification is "feeling toward."

Now widen the range of application of these two kinds of identifications from the analytic situation to the continual everyday activity of "testing the waters." For "parts of the personality" or psychic agencies, substitute aspects of the self, or multiple selves. And think of identification as the conscious or unconscious attempt to *imagine* another person's state of mind, doing away with all traces of direct knowing. We then have a situation in which each of us continuously identifies with those around us, trying to develop concordant identifications in order to know who will respond favorably to the invitations we want to distribute (who will feel well disposed toward the kind of interaction we seek?), and who will not. We try to develop complementary identifications, on the other hand, so that we may know whose invitations we want to respond to favorably and whose we want to reject (how would we feel about responding to the kind of interaction offered by this one or that one?). Through our different self-states, or selves—each the sedimentation of a bit of history and a clutch of hopes and fears for the future, each called out by the invitations we receive and those we want to give—we imagine how other people will respond to us and how we will feel about them. The resulting sets of interactions between our various selves and everyone else's begin to seem quick, evanescent, and enormously complicated, a kind of crowd of selves whizzing hither and thither like fireflies on a summer night. This is the interpersonal field, and if it is not blooming and buzzing, it is close. To see human interaction this way is to gain a great deal of respect for the difficulty of formulating it, and an equal degree of certainty that what we do formulate is a tiny proportion of the events that make it up. Each of us seems to be so much more—and perhaps so *many* more—than we can ever know. Many different experiences, it seems, many selves, can be simultaneously represented in the codes of practice or action (see chapter 1). Interpersonal life, that is, can be processed in parallel. But verbal reflection is linear, and therefore clumsy by comparison. We can "act" many things at once, but we can "know" only one at a time.

THE FIELD AND PERSONAL AGENCY

The field that emerges from the invitations and responses thus unconsciously issued and unconsciously received should not be understood as one's simple choice, not at any level of awareness, but as unformulated experience or an ongoing "crowd" of (in Fingarette's terms) implicit engagements—that is, as activities we participate in, but that we do not "know" we participate in. (And as always, our not-knowing in this case may be either implicit to language or structured and nonlinguistic.) We do not have to take the action of "not-spelling-out" (chapter 6) for the field to be an implicit engagement. An engagement may remain implicit for reasons not connected to defense, but to other factors—narrative rigidity, for example, and the role of convention in supporting it (chapter 7). The implicitness of an engagement certainly *may* be unconsciously purposeful, of course; but it may also be that we simply have not had a sufficiently compelling reason to articulate it.

In either case (that is, whether our unawareness of the field is motivated or not), we do not and cannot "plan" or "intend" the eventual shape of the field, at least not in the strongest sense of those words. We cannot plan the field on any level, conscious or unconscious, because we do not control it. We can plan what we *desire* the field to be, of course, and routinely we do; and we act on the resulting wishes by exerting unconscious influence. But we have no way of ensuring that the field will *become* exactly what we desire it to be. Each person we are with, and sometimes even a particular kind of interaction with the same person, "calls out" a different interpersonal atmosphere, which makes possible and appropriate, in our own frame of reference, a certain set of invitations and responses. Each field, that is, calls out our capacity to formulate experience in a particular way. What we can imagine fully, and what remains dissociated, is a function of the field we are inhabiting at the moment; which is to say that even on an unconscious level, and even if we broaden the scope of our responsibility to enclose what we intend without knowing we intend, we cannot be held fully responsible for the limits of what we are capable of formulating in any particular interpersonal field.

In contemporary psychoanalytic thought, we are becoming used to the idea that we move in and out of self-states on the basis of our perceptions of the interpersonal world that faces us. But we are less used to the thought that we also *are moved* in and out of self-states. The degree of personal responsibility we have for the exact shape of the interpersonal field, I suggest, lies somewhere between these active and passive poles. We do not move or purposively "stride" in and out of self-states, nor are we simply transported. It is the interactive combination of we ourselves and the influence on us of each person we encounter that calls out a particular interpersonal field. The influence of another person on us, of course, can be shaped and dominated by our autistic perception of that person; but unless we are flagrantly psychotic (and probably even then), our perception of the other is always at least partially shaped by what the other actually brings to the situation, and this contribution is beyond our control.

The field, therefore, is neither simply the result of our own unconscious internal choices nor a force or filter imposed on us by others. It is both simultaneously. I am looking here for a degree of responsibility somewhere in the middle of the continuum, suspended between undiluted personal agency and absolute destiny. Somewhere between activity and passivity, the field continuously reconstitutes itself. Its shape changes; its atmosphere changes; the selves and motives it brings to relevance change. The limits it places on what can and cannot be imagined within it change.

We take advantage of whatever freedom we sense in the field at any particular moment (as we test the waters and note the invitations and responses we receive), but we neither observe nor go beyond the limits that determine that freedom. Unless we have some very special reason to do so, we do not spell out content outside the field's boundaries, nor do we issue or respond to what we sense are dangerous invitations. In this way, the engagements that make up the field generally remain as implicit as they begin. A reason that is good enough to encourage us to take a risk (that is, to stretch the freedom offered by the field) does two things: it draws our attention to the relevant aspects of the field, making it possible for us to reflect on these heretofore implicit parts of our experience; and it makes us feel safe enough, or gives us a reason to be courageous enough, to formulate those aspects in language. Analytic curiosity is designed, among other things, to draw attention to just this kind of dangerous content, and the analytic situation itself is intended to create enough new safety, or courage, or both to increase the patient's freedom to render it in creative language.

Under most of the rest of life's circumstances, however, it is only when the field itself allows certain formulations that those formulations are articulated. If a particular formulation would violate the limits of the field, that content simply goes unarticulated. Prime examples of formulations that would violate the limits of the field are explicit descriptions of the field itself. Fields, then, are not only defined by the experience they make possible for their participants to formulate; they are also defined by the experience that may not, and sometimes must not, be formulated within them. Each interpersonal field is defined by both dissociation and imagination, by what it illuminates and what it keeps in the darkness.

I am proposing that the outer world plays an *independent* role in establishing which parts of the inner one—which selves—are relevant at any particular moment. The influence cuts both ways, in other words. The outer world, by setting the limits on what the field can be, helps to determine what parts of the inner world are relevant. The inner world influences what parts of the outer world we select and try to encounter, and what parts of those selected aspects of the outer world we try to bring into active relatedness with us. The relationship of the inner and outer worlds is dialectical, with each the primary ingredient in the recipe for the other.

We can use this point to broaden Fingarette's (1969) perspective. We do not simply decide, all by ourselves (as Fingarette seems to imply), which experience to formulate and which to perpetuate in its unformulated state. It is the field that sets these parameters; it is the field that determines what will be worthy of our actualization, what is relevant, safe, and so on. And the field is only partially our own creation. It is, to an important degree, imposed on us.

MULTIPLICITY AND EMBEDDEDNESS

I want to return now to the general orientation of postmodernism, that set of ideas that asserts that not only our knowledge of our experience, but our experience itself is continuously and necessarily shaped by our embeddedness in various social and cultural phenomena. One of the things most of these theories have in common is their rejection of the private, unique, interior, unitary, and masterful (that is, self-directing) self, in favor of a recognition of ourselves as socially constituted, as the products of cultures. We are not only the result of our own decisions, inner workings, and individual histories, but are the creatures of our time and place; our picture of the self is not the "natural" or necessary phenomenon we take it to be on an everyday basis, but a construction—and a construction of the West, at that. Anthropologist Clifford Geertz (1974) says it this way.

> The Western conception of the person as a bounded, unique, more or less integrated motivational and cognitive universe, a dynamic center of awareness, emotion, judgment, and action organized into a distinctive whole and set contrastively both against other such wholes and against its social and natural background, is, however incorrigible it may seem to us, a rather peculiar idea within the context of the world's cultures [p. 59].

In our notion, the self is the captain of its own ship, the undisputed master of its own destiny; it has control over everything about its own experience—even if that control is unconscious. It is *I*, and *only* I, who decides what experience I will be aware of; and it is *only* I who decides what experience I will not acknowledge.

This set of assumptions is under increasing scrutiny, and sometimes downright attack,[3] though the ramifications are just beginning to be felt in American psychoanalysis (Europeans have been dealing with them for years). Although psychoanalysis, because it is an individual psychology, will never be social constructionism, and should not be, psychoanalysis does need to take account of the social-constructionist critique if it is to continue the creative reinvention of itself that has been reinvigorating it since the first dissident analysts broke with Freud. Psychoanalysts must begin to imagine the ramifications of the fact that consciousness is a much more social phenomenon than we have characterized it to be. We need to think through what it means for theory and clinical work that we are so much more thoroughly embedded in the world around us than we experience ourselves to be. Our theories must come to grips with the reality that cultures set the ground rules according to which experience can mean anything at all, and that psychoanalysis is therefore a cultural product, not the description of eternal essence. With the rest of the contemporary intellectual world, psychoanalysis must turn back on itself and find a way of bringing into explicit reflection the tools we use automatically and unthinkingly to grasp our experience in the first place.

If we take seriously the embeddedness of our experience in cultures, as claimed by the postmodern critique, we must also accept our embeddedness in relationships, because it is only by means of relationships that the broader discourses of the cultures we live in have their effects on individual human beings.[4] And if we take this smaller-scale, personal embeddedness seriously, we must question the dictum that people originate, by means of potentially identifiable unconscious intentions, all the engagements in which they are involved. It is not just other people's participation we do not control or intend; it is the very field itself. Our participation may be motivated, but its result is only partially so.

The fields we attempt to construct, in the same way over and over again throughout our lives, are the ground of our being, the warp and weft upon which we weave the patterns of our experience. It is as true to say that the interpersonal field structures us as it is to say that we structure it. The horizons that define the shape and lim-

its of that which can have meaning for us are inevitably social constructions, whether those horizons are the massive and (relatively)
static experiential clearings that define what it is to participate in a
culture, or the tiny, quicksilver clearings that two people create
between them to define what is relevant to one another about each
other's inner worlds and outer behavior. I mean to describe the
interpersonal field, as a matter of fact, as a small-scale analogue of
the horizon or the clearing discussed by hermeneuticist Hans-Georg
Gadamer (who, in turn, took the idea from his mentor, Heidegger;
see chapter 11).

The field is the very epitome of what Fingarette (1969) means by
an implicit engagement. It is, in the metaphor I used in introducing
Fingarette's views in chapter 5, one of those "rocks" we do not "lift
from the bottom" unless we have a special reason to do so. As long as
we do not formulate it, the field exists in dissociation. It is a consoli-
dation of experience in the mode of action. And until we do formulate the field, we blindly follow its dictates; that is what a field is; that is
what "field" means.

Among the actions the field leads us to take are episodes of
spelling-out and not-spelling-out; and to say that is also to say that the
field shapes and contains our motives, which therefore always exist
relative to the interpersonal surround and never in some kind of
intrapsychically pure state.[5] And that idea, in turn, is tantamount to
saying that the field is the greatest influence on the selection of the
self-state(s) in which we experience at any given moment. The concept of the field, then, when married to the idea of unformulated
experience, leads virtually inexorably to both dissociation and the
multiple self. Because we are always caught in the grip of the field,
the upshot for clinical purposes is that we face the endless task of trying to see the field and climb out of it—and into another one, for
there is nowhere else to go.

DISSOCIATION AND SELF-DECEPTION

The problem of self-deception disappears, just as Fingarette claimed,
when we reconceptualize the entire question; but Fingarette did not
sufficiently justify his rejection of self-deception, because he did not
go far enough in his reconceptualization. We need to realize that the
humanism of Sartre, with its transparent consciousness and valoriza-
tion of absolute personal agency, is no longer viable.[6] Our experience

is partitioned, selected, made relevant, and banished by a process of social construction in which we participate—in which we are, of course, the most important participants—but which is by no means wholy our own. In that sense, we are always at least partially strangers to ourselves, inhabited and influenced by others, and by interactions with others. Our embeddedness in the people and influences of our histories is a socially constructed "other" in our psychic lives, potential experience that exists "within" us, in the sense that it is unconscious meaning, part of our unrealized verbal and nonverbal subjectivity. But while this potentially explicable experience is unquestionably our own, it may not exist within the horizons of a self-state that the interpersonal field ever manages to make safe enough for self-reflection— though, with analysis, we may accomplish such reflection.

And so we are not masters of our own destinies in any simple way. We are not even masters of that part of our destinies unaffected by accidents, natural disasters, wars, and so on. Sartre's objection to self-deception as bad faith therefore can be answered.

On the other hand, we can also say, on the basis of this conception of the field, that the inner world is not the unique creation of an isolated consciousness deploying individually determined motives, as Freud's model of self-deception would have it. Self-deception, that is, is not a matter of a house mechanistically divided against itself, at least not in the way Freud proposed.

We are neither in bad faith nor operating like machines. We are, instead, participants in interpersonal relations that structure our experience in the same way that the larger social configurations of cultures and subcultures do, and according to the same discursive formations. Simultaneously, we are agents pursuing our own courses, influencing the interpersonal relations in which we are involved in ways we fully intend and for which we are responsible. Self-deception, because it assumes absolute personal agency, is an incomplete description of the processes involved. It seems that the problem of what to do with self-deception, in the end, is really the problem of what to do about the private, self-contained, uncompromisingly agentic Western self. Self-deception disappears right along with that vision of what we are. We do not have to deceive ourselves; we do not have to refuse to know what we know. To dissociate, we have only to accept the limitations of the field in which, with the other, we are mutually embedded. We have only to take the path of least resistance and leave the rock on the bottom. We have only to be less than fully imaginative and curious. Paraphrasing Merleau-Ponty (see chapter 5), we have only to refuse to lend ourselves to the life of language.

COURAGE AND CURIOSITY

Since we coestablish the field, we are only partially responsible for the shape it takes. But in psychoanalytic terms, we *are* responsible for being curious about it. Both analyst and analysand are responsible in this way; this is psychoanalytic morality. We are responsible for turning back on our own experience and reflecting on the fields we have cocreated and in which we live.

It is true that there are some parts of experience we could not avoid formulating if we wanted to (how could one not be explicitly aware of going grocery shopping?). It is equally true that we need someone else's help to formulate other aspects, in which we are so thoroughly buried that our capacity for self-reflection is hopelessly occluded. But there is a range of experience in between, and in this range, it is possible to be effectively curious about ourselves, though it may be difficult. We may not characteristically deploy curiosity about these things; we may even prefer not to know them; we may not understand *why* we prefer not to know them. But it is *possible* to know them, or at least we are capable of knowing that there is *something* "there" to know, if we are but willing to transgress our own most natural inclinations to leave the experience unformulated. We have this choice. We have choice, too, about how openly or defensively we respond to another person's attempt to draw our attention to something we would rather not see. The choice of what to do about the other's call to curiosity is seldom made simply on the basis of the presence or absence of automatically deployed defense mechanisms.

The specifically psychoanalytic kind of courage is the willingness to be curious about oneself, even at those times when one knows, or has a sense, that the outcome may be distressing. Here I return to Sartre's *mauvaise foi.* Because of our embeddedness in cultures and in personal relations, I cannot accept the transparency of the self Sartre believed in; but I nevertheless believe that the courage to bear curiosity about what is not immediately knowable has the same moral authority as Sartre's ideal of the person who refuses to look away from what is plain to see.

PART III

Unformulated Experience
in the Work of the Analyst

9

Interpretation and Subjectivity

A Phenomenology of Resistance

INTERPRETING THE ABSOLUTE UNCONSCIOUS: SCIENCE AND OBJECTIVITY

If unconscious experience does not have a single, predetermined meaning, but remains to be interpreted in reflective awareness, the effect of clinical interpretation does not depend on objective accuracy and cannot be judged on that basis. This is a clinical stance about the nature of the unconscious and the interpretive qualities of reflective consciousness, but it is also a philosophical position on matters of mind and experience, and so it should come as no surprise that philosophers have given their explicit attention to it. In independent proposals, hermeneuticists Paul Ricoeur (1970, 1977), Karl-Otto Apel (see Warnke, 1987), and Jürgen Habermas (1971) have taken the position that, though consciousness is phenomenological, so that we are correct to understand it to be constituted socially and linguistically, the unconscious is just as thoroughly nonsocial, nonlinguistic, and nonphenomenological. In fact, they argue, the quality of unconsciousness is actually the result of the complete removal of experience from a social context; such contents have been "delinguisticized" and now exist in an "absolute" realm, a realm with a real, objective existence outside the range of phenomenology and social construction. This absolute unconscious (Ricoeur's term) acts on consciousness with (invisible) objective force, a force no less real and concrete than those operative in chemistry and physics.

All three of these hermeneutic writers consider psychoanalysis and Freud to be synonymous, and so they do not question the concept of drive, a stance that perhaps makes it more natural for them than it is for psychoanalysts today to attribute objective force to the unconscious. Perhaps, however, we can do away with the notion of objective force and still maintain some of their argument. It is at least barely possible to conceive an objective existence for even the socially constructed unconscious posited in "relational-conflict theories" (Greenberg and Mitchell, 1983) ever since the work of Fairbairn. That is, perhaps a socially constructed unconscious can still be conceived to cause its effects directly, by means of such sub rosa phenomena as fantasies, feelings, and wishes, all of which we have to conceptualize, in this case, as having objective existence (cf. Schafer, 1976). To understand fantasies, feelings, and wishes as objective, of course, would contradict the thesis of this book. But even if we were willing to stretch that far to accommodate the views of Ricoeur and others, it would be impossible to align them to the phenomenology of clinical interpretation.

If unconscious meaning is an objective fact, and the clinical function of language is to label it, then the purpose of interpretation is the accurate matching of facts and labels. The only interpretations we can possibly make of objectively existing unconscious content must be—like their objects—objective, scientific, and nonphenomenological. Under these conditions, the analyst would be expected to explain the patient's conduct and experience on the basis of nonintrospectible, but theoretically conceivable, absolute unconscious phenomena. The analyst would then be expected to convey these explanations to the patient in the form of objectively accurate interpretations. We might imagine, as a very rough example, that the only way a certain patient will ever learn that his problems with women have to do with his mother, because he cannot observe his own unconscious, is for the analyst to make some kind of objective statement about the matter. Or, to be (a bit) more subtle, we might cite the analyst's objective interpretation of the patient's resistance to knowing the relevant pathogenic experience. Fourcher (1992) calls these interpretations of the absolute unconscious "shovels" to distinguish them from the "lens" interpretations that formulate or "focus" what is implicit. Approvingly citing Ricoeur, Fourcher goes on to say that objective interpretations themselves, once offered, may go on to become causative agents in the unfolding of events in the treatment.

INTERPRETING UNFORMULATED EXPERIENCE:
SUBJECTIVITY AND PHENOMENOLOGY

What is the alternative?

One can usually sense whether the verbal meaning one selects or constructs is adequate, that is, whether it is at least a barely satisfying answer to certain vague expectations one has developed prior to the appearance of the interpretation. But one cannot say whether that verbal meaning is the single best answer to one's expectations. One often knows quite clearly, in other words, when an interpretation is *ina*dequate, but it is not similarly possible to know when one has arrived at the understanding that best suits one's purpose.[1]

This is an important difference between the formulation of unformulated experience and the traditional psychoanalytic understanding of interpretation. In most traditional views, the goodness of an interpretation is judged by a correspondence between the verbal description and the nonverbal, unconscious material it encompasses. Consider Freud's (1913) metaphor of the landscape outside the moving train window, a metaphor he devised to capture the nature of free association, and which Donald Spence (1982) offers, approvingly, as a description of what free association should be. The analysand in this model is not to select what to say, but simply to describe passively the contents passing through her mind, as a passenger on the train would describe the passing view. Language is used as a set of labels in this view, and accuracy is the criterion of truth.

Psychoanalysts and analysands do judge the goodness of their interpretations, of course. They do that continuously. But the accuracy of our portrayals of unconscious meaning is virtually irrelevant as a truth criterion. "Accuracy" is not really even a meaningful term in discussing the interpretation of unformulated experience, because the term cannot be defined by reference to an observable relation between itself and its object. We know the object (to repeat the essential point) only *by means* of our interpretation of it. That means clinical interpretation is not objective and scientific, as Ricoeur and his colleagues claim, but subjective and phenomenological. And it spells the end of correspondence theory in psychoanalysis. We can no longer hold that the nonverbal unconscious meaning is the "real" one that our words simply clothe or represent, or to which they correspond.

CORRESPONDENCE THEORISTS IN PSYCHOANALYSIS

Two notable contemporary articulators of psychoanalytic correspondence theory are Wilma Bucci (1985), who proposes a dual coding model for psychoanalytic research, basing her thinking in the work of Paivio (1986, 1991), and Donald Spence (1982, 1987, 1988a, 1990, 1993), whose approving citation of Freud's train window metaphor I have already mentioned. Spence, though he has done so much to bring hermeneutics into psychoanalysis, claims nevertheless that the ideal of clinical interpretation is still the accurate, passive verbal representation of the nonverbal, as if a noninterpretive registration of the view outside the train window were actually possible—as if the view itself were not *already* an interpretation. Despite his hermeneutics, then, Spence is an objectivist. He does accept that we have no choice but to couch our reflective thoughts in language, and he accepts that language can have constitutive properties; this much of his position is hermeneutic. But he laments these properties, claiming that because of them language almost inevitably distorts what it represents. Here, in the assumption that language is most properly used to represent accurately what is already there, he deserts hermeneutics and lapses into objectivism.[2]

In her influential 1985 article, Bucci makes no bones about rejecting hermeneutics, calling it "both an incorporation of and a backlash to verbal dominance theory and the associated behaviorist position" (p. 600). Bucci argues for a cognitive science model that will allow experimentation and quantifiable results on psychoanalytic propositions. Since I am basing my thinking not in science at all, but in a hermeneutic approach to language, it is odd that Bucci's position is in some ways closer to my own than Spence's.

In Bucci's view, experience is coded in two separate systems, one verbal and the other nonverbal and imagistic. For the most part, language is what makes experience conscious. To be mutative, language must connect with something in the patient's mind that is already there: a nonverbal representation. And yet the nonverbal representation, because it can only become conscious by means of language, cannot be directly accessed to check the degree of correspondence between itself and the language used to represent it. To this point, Bucci and I think along a similar path, except that I also make room for unconscious meaning implicit to language and she seems not to. It is when we consider the *kind* of connection that must be made between language and nonverbal representations that differences emerge.

Here Bucci's theory becomes a classical objectivist theory of correspondence, for Bucci explicitly eschews truth criteria of aesthetic appeal and pragmatic effectiveness, and insists instead that the connection between language and nonverbal representations must be evaluated only by an assessment of representational accuracy. She writes that "the issue of verification concerns the extent to which the language spoken by the patient and heard by the analyst, and the interpretations with which the analyst responds, correspond to the mental representations—memories of the past, images, fantasies, and beliefs—registered in the patient's mind" (p. 601). The means by which Bucci proposes to conduct this assessment of validity are somewhat novel. They have to be, because she grants that the nonverbal representations are not accessible. But, in the end, the view is traditional.

Bucci decries any way of thinking that takes psychoanalysis away from science. "If language determines thought, then we cannot look beyond language to any independent level of representation. Furthermore, if it is the case that a scientific theory can refer entirely and only to observables, then indeed we must despair of setting psychoanalytic theory in scientific form" (p. 600). Well, as I have tried to say, granting language constitutive properties does not have to amount to the claim that language *determines* thought, only that it *cocreates* it—that is, that language operates constructively, but within constraints. When we maintain experience in an unformulated state for defensive reasons, we are avoiding making an interpretation; we are not preventing an uncontrolled "appearance" of experience in consciousness. But with that caveat, Bucci's assessment seems correct to me. We *do* need to stop insisting on setting psychoanalytic theory in scientific form; but first, we need to stop seeing that alternative as the embrace of despair.

THE VALIDITY OF THE VERBAL

In making sure to give nonverbal patterning in experience its due, it is possible to bend over backwards and go too far. We need to remember that verbally structured experience also has an integrity of its own. In any particular instance, what we come up with when we develop a convincing reflective understanding of ourselves is not a pale form of a more full-bodied and basic nonverbal truth, but the certain *kind* of truth that verbal language makes available to us, and that is available to us in no other way. To understand in any terms, verbal or nonverbal, takes interpretation; but to understand in a way we can reflect on explicitly takes the particular kind of interpretation offered by verbal language—not in spite of its constitutive properties, but because of them.

Thus there is no reason to believe that the reality analyst and patient so painstakingly construct, however specific it is to their work together, is either arbitrary or frivolous. Postmodern views, for obvious reasons, encourage the preservation of whatever uncertainty we can manage; but in directing our attention to what we *don't* know, they do not necessarily threaten the conviction with which we defend the thoughtfully considered clinical constructions we *do* know. Analysts in these postmodern days remain just as passionate as analysts have always been in searching for what is most true and useful, and they maintain the strongest kind of feelings that one thing is more true and useful than another. Giving choice and conviction their due in the process of thought, as postmodernism does, is not at all the same thing as saying that we can conclude anything we please and still claim to be carrying out our work responsibly. We still have to choose the point of view that works the best, that is most complete and satisfying in its account of the phenomena in question. And we do not have to accept that reality itself has no structure other than that which we impose upon it. There are many ways of understanding "what is," and some of them—the ones that are most appealing and convincing to me, as a matter of fact—argue that each human being and the world around him or her are a unity, that person and world both participate in the creation of experience (e.g., Feffer, 1982, 1988).

INTERPRETATION FROM THE PATIENT'S PERSPECTIVE

The phenomenological contradictions in the concept of the objective interpretation come from both the analyst's perspective and the patient's. Even if it were feasible for analysts to be objective in their private thoughts about the patient (and even that limited goal is not realistic), it is utterly impossible for the patient to experience the analyst's spoken interpretations in an objective mode. No patient accepts or rejects an interpretation because it is "objectively" true or false, but because it is or is not *subjectively* convincing. The successful interpretation touches the patient in a way that the patient can identify in her own experience. Therefore, even in a world in which the analyst's observations could be objective, "scientific" (third-person) accuracy would be a futile goal for interpretation. We use no shovels.

It certainly is a common enough occurrence for the analyst to think she is right and the patient to think the analyst is wrong (or vice versa). We might cite these disagreements as evidence that the patient's sense of conviction is not always the determining factor in how the analyst makes interventions, and we would be correct. At times, patients and analysts may even argue about whether a particular interpretation is accurate, or whether one is better than another (e.g., Hoffman, 1992b). The psychoanalyst, too, after all, develops subjective convictions about the best way to understand.

But if the disagreement provokes strong feelings on the part of either or both participants, we expect something to "give" before too long. Either the analyst finds a better way to make the point (or to help the patient see why she avoids it); or the analyst decides, on the basis of what the patient has to say, that she (the analyst) was wrong; or the patient, because of the depth of the collaboration, accepts that the analyst may be on to something and keeps chewing over the analyst's point, until finding a way to link it to her (the patient's) own experience and develop conviction about it. The analyst and patient may also decide to maintain a mutually respectful disagreement until (or unless) an agreement becomes possible.

But if the disagreement does not progress in any of these ways, and patient and analyst stay at loggerheads with one another for more than a brief period of time, it is not our inclination to say that one of the two is right and the other wrong. At least, even if this statement were true, it would not be the focus of our clinical interest. We would instead begin to think in terms of a transference-countertransference bind.

I intend this little digression to be an illustration of the fact that analysts do not—cannot—depend on being "right." Rather, they think about how to account for the patient's experience from within the patient's perspective. Because they know that only those observations that arouse the patient's recognition will be useful, analysts try to observe from within what they imagine the patient's frame of reference to be. And even when analysts do make observations from a different perspective (on the basis of their own theoretical leanings, experience, or emotional reactions), they ask themselves how such observations would be framed from within the patient's point of view, and even use their capacity to frame their observations in those terms as a test of the observations' accuracy and utility.

Objectivists might argue that third-person, scientific interpretive accuracy *would* be effective if it weren't for the patient's resistance, that it is only resistance that keeps the patient from accepting the analyst's objectively correct observation. With even greater justification, it might be claimed that resistance *must* be interpreted in the third person. Because the patient obviously cannot observe her own unconscious reasons for defending against a particular kind of experience, the analyst must suggest it by way of interpretation. Such an interpretation, if it really does have nothing to do with the patient's conscious experience, must be couched in the third person, and therefore qualifies as an objective observation by the analyst of an unconscious fact about the patient. The analyst's objective interpretation of resistance is perhaps the epitome of the shovel interpretation. It cannot possibly be couched in phenomenological terms—or so the argument goes. This is the key issue here, because unless we can understand some way that the patient develops a phenomenological appreciation of the analyst's interpretation of material that is (for the patient) unconscious, we have little choice, from a purely logical perspective, but to fall back on the idea of third-person, objective interpretation.

"FIT" AND RECOGNITION

The patient always has a sense of whether or not the analyst's interpretation "fits." Without the feeling of fit, the patient can develop no sense of conviction. And without conviction, the interpretation may as well have appeared in the patient's morning newspaper, for all the good it will do.

Usually, and always in the case of unconscious material, the judgment of fit the patient makes about what the analyst has to say is not as simple as the evaluation of whether or not the interpretation "matches" some preexisting content in the patient's mind. The judgment of fit in psychoanalysis is much more complicated than the judgments we make about the physical world. Because preexisting nonlinguistic representations must be interpreted in language before they can be reflected on, there is no such thing as pristine "preexisting content" that exists in the patient's mind, and against which the "accuracy" of the verbal interpretation can be tested. In a very real sense, the interpretations we make of nonlinguistic unconscious representations *are* those representations—because they are as close as we can get to thinking about them. In fact, we can say not only that evaluating fit *is* not a matter of judging brute accuracy, we can actually say that it *cannot* be. As Loewald (1960) taught years ago, interpretation has an *organizing* function. It is not a set of correct labels, but a redescription of the patient's experience at a level of differentation and articulation higher than the patient had heretofore reached. In this process of redescribing, an interpretation may bring together pieces of experience, or even of logic or emotional argumentation, that have never before appeared in the patient's mind in a single configuration. An interpretation is a new *Gestalt.*

What, then, accounts for the patient's feeling of fit? In certain instances that tend to be rare and dramatic, the perception of fit follows the patient's sudden feeling of always having known, in some vague way, what the analyst is trying to say. More commonly, the patient feels that what the analyst says has "pulled something together," and is correct (or better, useful) in that respect. (But note, although the patient judges the analyst to have made a good integration, this does not necessarily imply that the particular integration is the only one that could have been made.)

It is interesting and heuristically useful to realize that, at least in this account, the patient judges the fit of the analyst's interpretation in the same way we all judge whether or not *we ourselves* have said what we set out to say. When we speak, our words either satisfy us or they do not; they either give us the sense that something has been expressed, has been grasped in words, or they do not. We often say, about our own descriptions, "No, that's not exactly right. That's not exactly what I want to say." Or, in more fortunate circumstances (and these are deeply satisfying), we say "Yes, that's it *exactly.* That is *exactly* what I meant." When we are trying to capture a thought in speech or writing, most often we feel something like, "That's close. It's the best I can do for the time being, but there may be something more that I can't grasp yet."

We seem to know when we have fit our words to a preexisting meaning—or perhaps better, a preexisting *absence.* The fact that we are capable of sensing such a thing, and that patients invariably evaluate and use (or discard) their analysts' interpretations on such a basis, means that there can be no such thing as an effective shovel interpretation, because shovel interpretations are themselves understood to be the "causes" of patients' reactions to them. The judgments patients make about their analysts' interpretations are not whether they are scientifically accurate, but whether the interpretations *speak* to them. Has the analyst said something that the patient recognizes as something she herself would have said, if she could have? If an interpretation is useful, it can only be because the patient has grasped it phenomenologically—which is exactly how shovel interpretations cannot be grasped.

THE PATIENT'S FEELING OF SAFETY

There is in psychoanalysis a long history of conceptualizing the interventions that "lead up" to interpretation (see, for instance, Bibring's classic 1954 contribution). One of the subliminal reasons this literature had to exist—one of the reasons psychoanalysis needed descriptions of interventions like Bibring's "suggestion," "abreaction," "manipulation," and "clarification"—was that there had to be some way to explain why the patient accepted interpretations of resistance. With preparation over time, the relevant material could be brought slowly into the patient's preconscious via the noninterpretive interventions until eventually, at just the right moment, the analyst could make the mutative interpretation, finally freeing the patient from unconscious tyranny.

But this literature really only moved the problem of how patients recognize the utility of an interpretation of unconscious processes farther back from the moment of the interpretation, much the way Mitchell (1984) shows that certain theorists have explained difficult clinical problems by assigning them ever earlier developmental origins. Even if we admit kinds of interventions other than interpretation itself, the analyst must still make an initial foray into unconscious material at *some* point in the treatment; and even if that foray is not formally categorized as an interpretation, the patient must have some kind of reason to consider it.

It was Freud (1913) who offered the beginning of an answer to the problem. He wrote that, although the positive transference should not be used for the purpose of suggestion in psychoanalysis, a treatment should *only* be called psychoanalysis "if the intensity of the transference has been utilized for the overcoming of resistances" (p. 143). This observation (which has not been elaborated as much as might be expected[3]) acknowledges that, if the patient is to recognize the truth of the analyst's interpretation of the unconscious, the patient must have some awfully good reason to *care* about the analyst's interpretation. The patient, that is, must harbor the strange and seemingly paradoxical willingness to work toward the acceptance of understanding she otherwise wants to avoid. What emotional or esthetic purchase is the patient supposed to get on an interpretation that is wholly unfamiliar to her conscious experience, but that the analyst claims is objectively true? What is the patient to *do* with such an interpretation? And if objective interpretation is not the royal road to unconscious material, what is?

In the case of an interpretation that is uncontroversial, one that integrates without challenging dynamic equilibrium, what I have already said about "fit" is not terribly difficult to accept. But where does what I have said leave us in the case of resistance? What can a phenomenological recognition of resistance possibly mean? Is the phrase not an oxymoron?

It is in most of life. But there is a crucial ingredient in the analytic situation that appears in no other relationship, and it is not mere suggestion. It is rather the collaboration between analyst and patient, initially undertaken as a result of a mutual decision to begin treatment, but eventually deepened and widened because of the patient's trust in the analyst—which is, in turn, born of the atmosphere of safety the analyst provides.[4]

"Trust" is a terribly overused word, one that has been applied in the field of psychotherapy with appalling naiveté. In referring to the patient's trust in the analyst, I certainly do not mean to suggest what has so often been implied in nonpsychoanalytic accounts of therapeutic practice: that the therapist is somehow to persuade the patient, or provide some convincing demonstration, that she is worthy of trust, so that the patient will "open up." No transference worthy of the name could possibly be breached by this kind of frontal attack, which is more accurately described as a reaction formation against the therapist's aggression than a genuine attempt to establish trustworthiness. In this scenario, trust is equivalent to being accepting, uncritical, and nonretaliative. All of these characteristics, if they are not assumed in too thorough or hidebound a fashion, are certainly worthy. But none of them is what I am referring to in using the word "trust."

Acceptance that the analyst intends for its own sake is useless. Unconditional positive regard is ultimately ingenuine. Real acceptance does not preclude the analyst's rejecting internal reactions; it only precludes making the patient responsible for alleviating them. Therefore, acceptance that is a contribution to the patient's feeling of safety and the establishment and growth of a therapeutic collaboration can only be the acceptance inherent in the analyst's genuine curiosity—compassionate curiosity, to be sure, but curiosity nonetheless. To claim the presence of a collaboration, as a matter of fact, is just another way of saying that the patient has accepted the analyst's curiosity about her and has developed the capacity to be curious about herself, free (or relatively so) of reflexive self-hatred.

And what is the analyst's curiosity? It is not merely the conscious application of inquisitiveness, the asking of questions. It is the more basic capacity to become aware of questions, of gaps in the material, to sense that there is something there to be curious *about.* Curiosity is the sensitivity to the possibility of a question. It is the means by which the analyst gains self-reflective access to experience, the means by which she disembeds herself from immediate circumstance and unconscious assumptions, especially those that structure the interpersonal field of the analytic situation. The analyst's accepting attitude toward her inevitable involvement in enactments with the patient, and the curiosity that this acceptance allows about, not only the patient's experience, but her own, is the only means at the analyst's disposal to provoke this crucial process of disembedding. And each time she is successful in provoking it (though she never knows quite how it has been accomplished), she is able to refrain from the enactment in question and instead interpret the patient's transference. Thus, transference interpretations are the only evidence the patient can really depend on that the analyst is not "drowning in the countertransference" (Racker, 1968), the only authentic indication that the analyst is able to know and tolerate the countertransference and use it to help the patient. Of all the analyst's interventions, therefore, transference interpretation (and the countertransference interpretation that so often precedes it, usually privately) plays the most significant role in establishing and maintaining the patient's feeling of safety (Hoffman, 1983).[5]

By repeatedly transforming the limits of her own understanding into thought, then, the analyst becomes able to offer the patient something more than interpretations of experience that are already known. As she disembeds herself, the analyst comes upon hitherto invisible possibilities for new experience. And thus, although spoken questions may be the most visible evidence of curiosity, they are the result of the phenomenon, not the phenomenon itself. I mean to emphasize the openness and unbidden perceptions from which inquisitiveness arises.

THE PLACE OF THE THERAPEUTIC COLLABORATION
IN THE PATIENT'S JUDGMENT OF "FIT"

Once a relatively thorough collaboration has developed (and it is always relative, of course, because even the best collaboration is inevitably shot through with holes that are unknown to both analyst and patient until the analysis itself reveals them), there is more experience available to the patient in this unique interpersonal setting than there is anywhere else in life. The patient is not only able to be more curious than usual; often she is eager to be, even about painful matters. When the patient feels that the interpersonal atmosphere is reliably safe, the rewards of knowing are often great enough to make the pain of knowing, and the uncertainty that precedes and often accompanies it, worth bearing. Merleau-Ponty (1962), for whom the analyst's interpretation is much more than the mere delivery of a packet of information, makes the point this way in a discussion of a patient with an hysterical aphonia.

> In treating this condition, psychological medicine does not act on the patient by making him know the origin of his illness. . . . [I]n psychological treatment of any kind, the coming to awareness would remain purely cognitive, the patient would not accept the meaning of his disturbances as revealed to him, without the personal relationship formed with the doctor, or without the confidence and friendship felt towards him, and the change of existence resulting from this friendship. Neither symptom nor cure is worked out at the level of objective or positing consciousness, but below that level [p. 163].

We can agree, then, on the centrality of the analytic relationship in the effectiveness of an interpretation. But what exactly is it that the patient senses about unconscious content that allows her to determine the "fit" of the analyst's interpretation?

Prior to the interpretation, it often makes sense to say that even the collaborative patient has had no conscious sense of the meaning conveyed in the analyst's interpretation of unconscious material. Even so, in response to a successful intervention, the patient working in a relatively safe-feeling analytic atmosphere senses (i.e., is *willing* to sense, is *interested* in sensing) a "place," a kind of empty meaning-mold of the same shape as the interpretation, a "place" that, despite its not having been felt before by the patient, may nevertheless feel, in the very moment of its appearance, as if it has been waiting for the interpretation to fill it. This "place" is not just a manifestation of the patient's acceptance of the new meaning; it is the simultaneous recognition of this meaning and the absence that is now suddenly understood to have preceded it. The painter Ben Shahn (1957) refers to "the shape of content"; the collaborative analytic patient, in response to the analyst's successful interpretation of unconscious meaning, senses a preexisting "shape of absence." In rare and exhilarating instances, the interpretation fits the absence as a hand fits a glove, or as Cinderella's foot fit the slipper. Most of the time, though, while the fit may be recognizable, it is not necessarily perfect—nor need it be. It needs only to be good enough to move the analytic inquiry forward. There is almost always room for further shaping of the new meaning, to say nothing of the inevitable changes over time we expect to find in the object of the analyst's interpretation. I have already quoted Herbert Fingarette's (1963) maxim that insight is like seeing a well-formed ship in a cloud instead of a poorly formed rabbit (see chapter 2). We can now add that the cloud itself changes with the passage of time, and so the ship inevitably disappears; and even before it does, if one keeps looking, perhaps one sees a tree in the cloud that is even better formed than the ship.

The analyst helps along the process by which the patient recognizes the new meaning by couching interpretations in a way that allows the patient, either explicitly or implicitly, to reconstruct the means by which the interpretation came into the analyst's head. The analyst, in other words, often conveys interpretations by helping the patient to grasp the analyst's subjectivity. She does this not to maintain democracy, even if she believes a certain kind of democracy is important in analysis (and I do), but because she knows that if the patient sees how the analyst arrived at her conclusion, it will be easier for the patient to recognize the interpretation in her own frame of reference. The analyst behaves this way whether the interpretation in question is a rearrangement of matters of which the patient is entirely aware, or is an attempt to give voice to material that has been dissociated in the more traditional fashion.

The patient is always listening to the analyst in a context, and this context is the ground on which the interpretation falls; this "ground" determines the kind and range of significance the interpretation can have. We might call the ground of an interpretation its "context of significance," or its "context of relevance." Or, adapting a term used by Heidegger and Gadamer to a slightly different, more prosaic purpose, we might call this context the momentary "horizon" of the patient's experience. The limits of this therapeutic horizon determine what can appear in the patient's experience, what meanings experience can have for her. The horizon is closely related to the interpersonal field. As a matter of fact, we might call the therapeutic horizon a manifestation of the field. And the interpersonal field in the psychoanalytic situation contains, in addition to the transference-countertransference, the atmosphere of safety, in whatever degree it has been realized. Actually, in consonance with those writers, ranging in orientation all the way from Brenner (1980) to Hoffman (1983, 1991, 1992a, b, 1994, 1996) and Levenson (1972, 1983, 1991), for whom the therapeutic collaboration and the transference must be understood as parts of a single, unitary relationship between analyst and patient, and so cannot possibly be considered in isolation from one another, it is more truthful to say that the atmosphere of safety *expresses* the transference-countertransference, or *is part* of it.

In discussing the patient's willingness to stretch her dynamic limits in response to the atmosphere of safety, we should not overlook the fact that, when the patient feels safe and the transference is positive, she may very well want to please the analyst. It would be dangerous if the outcome that derived from this motive were simple suggestion— that is, the patient's uncritical acceptance of the analyst's interpretations. But we know that, most of the time, even patients who feel warmly toward their analysts are uninterested in parrotting them. And if the analyst also watches and listens for uncritical acceptance, it is unlikely to go unanalyzed.

The patient in a positive transference, however, even if she has no particular wish to parrot the analyst, does have a powerful and unobjectionable reason to give serious consideration to anything the analyst says. This openness to the analyst is unobjectionable because it is essentially just a honing of the patient's curiosity, a willingness to look for the subjective evidence to substantiate or disprove the analyst's observations. Even patients in a negative transference, if they have managed to develop the rudiments of collaboration before (or even during) the time the angry or disappointed feelings set in, can recognize "fit." The angry patient may not be willing to give the analyst the satisfaction of sharing this acknowledgment of fit, at least not until some later time, and there are times during which even the capacity to recognize fit is compromised by the negatively tinged interaction. Except in the case of intransigent negative transference, or negative therapeutic reaction, the patient's interest in recognizing fit never disappears altogether, once the patient has accepted psychoanalysis as a collaborative endeavor.

As an example, consider the patient who begins arriving late to sessions and insists that her behavior is due only to traffic, business meetings, or some other factor exterior to the treatment. The analyst who tries to interpret the first or second instance of such lateness, unless the patient has been compulsively punctual up to that point, is liable to be met with outright rejection from the patient. Even if the analyst waits until the behavior goes on long enough to establish a convincing pattern, she often runs into a brick wall if she simply asserts a dynamic reason for the lateness in the face of the patient's denial of such a reason. On the other hand, if the patient understands and accepts the general outlines of the analytic task, and the analyst presents the interpretation by laying out the agreement between the two of them to understand whatever they can about the patient, the patient is liable to be able to see, when it is pointed out, that her lateness deprives her of some of the opportunity to carry out the task she is otherwise committed to pursue, and that it is at least plausible that something more than traffic or business meetings keeps her from arriving on time. The important thing is that even if the analyst's internal observation of the patient is "objective" and made in the third person, the interpretation most certainly is not. The patient accepts what the analyst has to say, not because it is an objective fact, but because the interpretation makes subjective sense to her.

After this initial intervention (if it is successful), and perhaps after examining lingering feelings that the analysis of lateness is really only a disguised slap on the wrist from the analyst (a common enough feeling, and commonly enough correct), the patient is in a much better position to judge the fit of any particular interpretation of the lateness the analyst might offer. Of course, the patient is also in a better position to develop her own hypotheses about the matter, because the analyst's convincing curiosity, her devotion to the analytic task, has relieved the patient and led to an increment in the feeling of safety. That allows the patient greater access to the kind of experience that might make a defensive measure like lateness understandable. Finally, once the patient has been able to see that it is reasonable to hypothesize that her lateness is defensive, analyst and patient are in a position to address why the patient was so insistent that the lateness could only have been a matter of external circumstance. All these steps, and more, are taken without the analyst doing anything that qualifies as the uncovering or labelling of absolute meaning.

THE ATMOSPHERE OF SAFETY IN THE PERCEPTION
OF FEELINGS OF TENDENCY

The analyst gears interpretations to the patient's subjectivity because she knows, without having to be told, that that is how people understand anything. And knowing this, the atmosphere of safety becomes crucial. In thinking about the process of interpretation, we find that a well-established therapeutic collaboration, rooted in the atmosphere of safety, has the effect of helping the patient attend (or cease inattending) to certain meanings, or to the possibility of making those meanings, that would otherwise remain outside the patient's conscious horizon. The therapeutic relationship increases the possibilities for articulating meanings. What I am suggesting is that the relationship, in fortunate instances, makes possible a direct breach of the patient's defenses. Defense, in other words, is an interpersonal process, not only an intrapsychic one. *No* part of the inner world is isolated from the social realm. As Fairbairn (1954) writes in regard to hysterical patients, "the resistance . . . is not so much a resistance to the psychotherapeutic process as a *resistance to the psychotherapist himself*" (p. 105). This point is in direct disagreement with Apel, Habermas, and Ricoeur, who understand the repressed internal world to be isolated, removed from social contact.

"FIT" AND UNFORMULATED EXPERIENCE

When the patient in a successful therapeutic collaboration begins to recognize the possibility of previously disavowed meaning, she is moving from the use of unformulated experience as familiar chaos (chapter 3) to its use as creative disorder (chapter 4). This means a move from the denial of curiosity (in certain circumstances, and about certain aspects of experience) toward its affirmation, and a move from the refusal to acknowledge (again, in particular circumstances and in regard to certain content) what William James (1890) referred to as "feelings of tendency" and "signs of direction" in thought toward an openness to these same parts of experience. As a matter of fact, what I have described in this chapter as the collaborative patient's capacity to judge the "fit" of the analyst's interpretation could just as well be presented as the patient's recognition, in response to the analyst's intervention, of the relevant feelings of tendency in her own experience. The patient in a well-established collaborative analytic relationship is beginning to think effectively, for the first time, about parts of life that had heretofore remained outside the range of reflection. It is this new curiosity and freedom, rather than any particular new interpretation, that is the truest reflection of the patient's therapeutic movement.

INTERPRETATION FROM THE ANALYST'S PERSPECTIVE

Modern interpersonal and relational psychoanalysis is built on the premise that anything the analyst does with or about the patient, including the formulation of private and public observations, is a participation in the relationship (see Hirsch, 1996, for a review), and all participation is inevitably influenced by the unconscious factors that structure the relationship—unconscious factors that it is the task of the analysis to grasp. Edgar Levenson (1972, 1983, 1991), who was among the first to make this point and has always made it forcefully, purposely provoked his psychoanalytic readership by titling his first book *The Fallacy of Understanding* (1972). From this perspective, which is shared by all the many writers who qualify as what Irwin Hoffman (1983) calls "radical critics of the blank screen model," there can be no such thing as a simple, "objective" observation or interpretation. We must be too skeptical and curious to accept anything the analyst observes about the patient as a simple, objective response from an unbiased observer. This point encompasses even the content of the analyst's empathic responsiveness (Spence, 1984, 1988b; Friedman, 1985; Moses, 1988; Stern, 1988, 1994).

We know from everyday experience in our consulting rooms that the analyst's informed subjectivity will often be useful to the patient; but there is no getting around the fact that subjectivity is what it is. To make an interpretation, private or public, requires the analyst to give shape to unformulated experience, and that is a task every human being has no choice but to do in a subjective way. Coming full circle, that is another way to say why every clinical intervention must be a participation in the relationship with the patient. After all, an interpretation is merely a particular instance of the analyst's generic human capacity to give verbal shape to unformulated experience. How could the analyst formulate an interpretation without being influenced by the interpersonal field? Such a thing cannot happen between any two people, as we saw in chapter 8.

The analyst evaluates the interpretation in the same way the patient will when she hears it; the analyst, that is, judges the degree to which she has been able to say something satisfying. For analysts, words either satisfy or disappoint. Good interpretations give the analyst the feeling that the chosen words have expressed what they were intended to say; they fill that "shape of absence," just as the interpretation will do, if it is useful, for the patient. We take it for granted, though, that the analyst's own feeling about the interpretation is not enough to make it successful. It is offered with the hope that it will arouse the patient's answering sense of recognition and conviction.

GADAMER'S PERSPECTIVISM
AND PSYCHOANALYTIC INTERPRETATION

In concluding this chapter, I turn to the perspectivistic hermeneutics of Hans-Georg Gadamer (1975, 1976; see also chapter 11), which entails a conception of the kind of reality that unifies and underlies both my phenomenology of psychoanalytic interpretation and my rejection of the objective, unitary, nonsocial unconscious. Gadamer is simultaneously a perspectivist, a phenomenologist, and a realist. He acknowledges that reality exists, but he also insists that it is inevitably understood from a social, historical, linguistic, and (we can add, from our psychoanalytic vantage point) individual perspective. Any interpretation, psychoanalytic or otherwise, is a perspective.

We can understand one view of perspective (but *not* Gadamer's) by means of a visual metaphor. If you hold in your hand an object, and you turn it this way and that, each time you turn it you will view it from a different perspective, and each perspective offers something new about the object that cannot be appreciated from any other perspective. Reality, if we were to understand it on the basis of such a model, would be made up of any number of such perspectives, couched in all the various modes in which we apprehend the world. Taken together, all these perspectives would be a complete picture. But because each era and each cultural tradition encourages access to only a portion of the perspectives that are possible, and because each individual has access to only a portion of the perspectives available in her time and social groups, an individual's view of reality, including the reality of what she herself is, must necessarily be highly selective. In this view, which is more or less traditionally essentialist, the task of psychoanalysis is to help the analysand lift the personal and cultural veils and reveal as much of internal and external reality as possible. This model is useful as far as it goes. Schachtel (1959, 1970) used it to great effect in articulating his conception of the allocentric mode of perception, in which what it means to know the object fully is to perceive it from every possible perspective.

The problem with the approach is twofold. First, it reduces the individual's role in the construction of experience to the selection of an angle of view on a preformulated object, and that, as far as I am concerned, unreasonably cramps our conception of the constitutive involvement of the individual in the genesis of her own experience. The construction of experience is not, like Saki's short story "The Lady and the Tiger," simply a matter of which doors to open. We are more involved in how to formulate the experience we encounter than that. Gadamer's perspectivism is as much about how we formulate the object as it is about how we view an object that already exists. Second, this "angle-of-view" perspectivism leads to a constricted view of reality. Such a reality is unitary and unacceptably concrete. It hides nothing, it implies nothing. It contains no particularly vague or unformulated truths. If you take the right "photograph" of it, it reveals anything, because all its truth is right there to see. To expose it, you need only observe it from the right angle.

As Gadamer envisioned it, reality is quite different than that. It is an inexhaustible resource. Like great works of art, it is so rich and allows so many perspectives—interpretations—that it is even possible for two contradictory perspectives to be true, or, in the slightly more conservative expression Gadamer sometimes uses, contradictory interpretations can each "have their truth." Think of Tevye's quandary in *Fiddler on the Roof.* He has just agreed with one neighbor's account of what would be a fair solution to a disagreement when the opposing neighbor offers a reasonable but diametrically opposed solution. With a good deal of beard-scratching, Tevye also agrees with the second neighbor. When a third neighbor objects that they can't both be right, Tevye says cheerfully, for emphasis stabbing the air with his forefinger, "You're right, too!"

Tevye's quandary is one of the core problems of the psychoanalytic situation. In conservative psychoanalytic thought, reality is as simple as the object one turns in one's hand, and the interpretations of both the patient (the transferential grasp of the analyst) and the analyst (the interpretation of the patient's transference) therefore can be judged simply by reference to reality. Analyst and patient simply have to be sure they are talking about the same angle; they can also verify that by comparing their experience with objective reality. In this scenario, Tevye is wrong: only one of his neighbors can be right.

For a growing number of contemporary psychoanalysts, though, the patient's idiosyncratic or problematic perceptions of the analyst and of people in outside life are seldom simply wrong (e.g., Racker, 1968; Levenson, 1972, 1983, 1991; Hoffman, 1983, 1991, 1992a, b). They are instead perspectives or interpretations with a certain validity of their own, and it is this validity (among other things) that it is the analytic task to articulate. Like Tevye's neighbors, the patient and the analyst are both right.

Tevye's position is Gadamer's position, too. For Gadamer, because the object of understanding is known only in light of the interpretations made of it, there is no independent comparison possible between interpretation and reality. We see what interpretations teach us to see; here we have a deep respect for the individual's constructive activity. We also have the manifestation of Gadamer's respect for the unimaginable richness of reality: it is so complex that it can accommodate multiple, even conflicting interpretations. In discussing Gadamer's thesis of the mimetic function of art, Georgia Warnke (1987) says it this way:

> One learns to see the object represented in terms of the truth that the representation reveals about it. Hence we learn to see the sea as a Turner seascape teaches us to see it, just as Rembrandt's work teaches us the depths of character a human face can reveal [p. 59].

The important thing here is that Turner is not teaching us to revise our perception of the sea in an arbitrary way. The painter, for Gadamer, is not merely introducing a visual convention that is some Derridean combination of the arbitrary and ultimately meaningless traditions available in her era. Gadamer's view of tradition is affirmative instead. On the basis of what is available in his time and place, Gadamer says, Turner reveals to us a bit of reality.

All understanding for Gadamer is dialogic. It occurs only in conversation; in fact, understanding *is* conversation. Now, conversation means something in particular to Gadamer: it means the mutual attempt of the two partners in the conversation, just as I have presented the collaboration of the two participants in the analytic situation, to see the perspective of the other.[6] And as I have already mentioned in passing, for Gadamer any perspective occurs within a set of horizons, or a context. That context is the set of conditions within which the perspective has its truth. If you wish to understand a perspective that is not your own, you must provoke within yourself an experience Gadamer calls a "fusion of horizons." That is, like Hegel, Gadamer sees in disagreement not just an obstacle, but an opportunity. The "fusion" is that moment when, after however much conversation is necessary, and from within your own horizon, you grasp the horizon of the other. In a famous passage, Gadamer (1975) writes:

> Our starting-point is the proposition that to understand means primarily for two people to understand one another. Understanding is primarily agreement or harmony with another person. Men generally understand each other directly, i.e., they are in dialogue until they reach agreement. Understanding, then, is always understanding about something [p. 158].

This agreement, however, should not necessarily be understood as the victory of one view over another, or even as the achievement of a synthesis, though it certainly may be either of these things as long as both parties in the conversation freely accept the solution. The essential aspect of agreement is the new capacity, given the context in which the interpretation is made, to grasp the truth in what the other has to say. If we add to this equation the element of the patient's feeling of safety, making it possible to understand how the patient might eventually find her way to a position within which she can grasp the truth in what the analyst says about aspects of her own (the patient's) unconscious experience, psychoanalysis is very much a dialogue in the spirit of Gadamer.

10

The Analyst's Unformulated Experience of the Patient

Interpersonal influence can be effective without being known. We take this point for granted. Constant and mutual influence is the rule. We do not have to know what we are doing to affect others, and we do not have to be able to think about influence to accept it. Quite the contrary. The most profound interpersonal influence goes as deep as it does *because* it is not known by either party. We are most likely to participate unwittingly in precisely those interpersonal patterns we would describe as problematic—that is, if we could see the patterns well enough to describe them. This is true in any relationship, no less inside the consulting room than outside it, and no less for the analyst than for the patient. We can only choose not to participate after we know what we have already been involved in. And by then the essential work has been done. This means that the spontaneous, unconsidered reactions of analyst and patient to one another may be the sole evidence, the footprints, so to speak, of the very influences which cannot be articulated by either participant, but which most need to be known. Sometimes, as with footprints, reconstructing the beast from the evidence would require so much speculation that the task is best left until more data accumulate. At these times, though analysts may suspect that their direct experience reflects an entanglement in unseen interactive realities, they cannot see how to use their reactions. The links between their experience and the patterns they wish they could describe remain obscure, and they must wait. Other times, analysts' reactions inform them immediately about the state of relatedness the patient intends to create. In any case, it is vital for analysts to know explicitly and continuously their direct experience of, and with, the patient.

Any difficulty we have in knowing countertransference is therefore of primary clinical significance. Operationally, for the working psychoanalyst, knowing one's experience of the patient means being able to formulate it in words, if only to oneself. Yet we all sometimes have trouble finding these words, in just knowing what our ongoing experience of the patient *is*, much less solving the additional problem of knowing what it means. For the time being, I will focus on those aspects of the question that are least influenced by the characterological difficulties the analyst brings to the interaction. Because they have been written about so often, and in fact are relatively rare in the everyday countertransference of seasoned analysts, I will not discuss the typical problems in which the analyst, for private reasons, refuses to know how she feels about a patient (Ehrenberg, 1985; Tauber, 1978).

THE NATURE OF THE ANALYST'S EXPERIENCE

The very nature of the analyst's experience of the patient contributes to her difficulty in knowing it. Reactions to others usually occur in a form with which words are not easily compatible. It is a different kind of experience than words—like music, say—and so grasping it in words is problematic, and the result of the attempt, though it has its own kind of claim to validity, is unquestionably different than the nonverbal form. We cannot speak music or painting. We cannot even describe them without a loss of content so thorough that the description is meaningless without direct acquaintance with the work itself. The analyst's experience of the patient is, like these forms, nonverbal and prelogical in nature (Tauber and Green, 1959). Its truth is not sequential or logical, but presentational, like artistic truth (Langer, 1942). What we glean from our reactions is not the propositional truth of language, but what Bertrand Russell called "knowledge by acquaintance" and what Tauber and Green reconceptualized as "prelogical experience."

THE FORMULATION OF THE ANALYST'S EXPERIENCE

That part of the analyst's experience which will eventually be most analytically useful feels as if it comes naturally. It is not experienced as intentional; it just happens. It is unbidden and, more often than not, unnoticed. Levenson (1988) puts it that what the analyst does not know about the patient *is* the countertransference. The most significant of our experiences of the patient are defined by this quality of being out of our grasp. Much of countertransference is embedded in that vast realm of experience that is seldom directly apprehended, but of which everyone is dimly aware, the inattended everyday–everything that is just the way of the world. It is in this part of the analyst's responsiveness to the patient that genuine surprises germinate.

Prior to being put into words, then, the analyst's experience of the patient is unformulated. And since the unformulated can be put into words in more than one way, countertransference experience that will later become useful is not inevitable. It remains to be constructed. Each time something new appears in the analyst's experience of the patient or the interaction, it is a sign that the process of transmutation from presentational and unformulated to articulation in language has been accomplished once again.

The psychoanalyst's primary problem is not how to select a correct interpretation. The primary problem is how to sense that there is something there to interpret. The problem of interpretation arises only when material is visible, speakable, available for understanding—an everyday state of affairs, of course, but not the most central or most difficult. Interpretation can be merely wrong, but experience itself can be absent, and absence is the greater difficulty. One has no reason to look for something the existence of which is not suspected.

Clinical examples of the unformulated nature of the analyst's experience of the patient are problematic. The lack of differentiation and indeterminacy of the unformulated are immediately changed by the verbal description one has no choice but to use. While it is impossible to imagine the material without formulating it, it is possible to describe the form of the analyst's experience and then try to imagine back to that which was not being articulated at the time.

A middle-aged academic had formerly had a satisfactory treatment experience elsewhere in the country with a highly regarded senior analyst. The analysis had ended prematurely because of the offer of a post that the patient felt he could not turn down. Academic posts were rare in his field; tenured positions, such as the one he was offered, were nearly nonexistent. The departure had been extremely painful for the patient, and the choice of a new analyst was difficult. He consulted several. After much indecision, and eight or ten meetings with me (interrupted by the consultations with other analysts, which he then returned to discuss), the patient felt comfortable enough with me to schedule hours. He remained somewhat unsure about his choice, he said, but felt that at some point he had to move ahead. His primary worry was that, since I was younger than his former analyst (I am middle-aged), I would lack a certain wisdom. On the superficial level, which was the only one I consciously consulted at the time, this suggestion did not seem unreasonable. I must have grasped the attitude that lay behind it, however, because, despite my superficial acceptance, I took in the observation with a kind of emotional cringe that became all too familiar to me in my work with this man.

The criticisms began as simple comparisons. The former analyst, for instance, had maintained more formality and emotional distance than the patient felt I did. Soon enough, though, questions about my professionalism arose. The other analyst's office had been austere, whereas mine had several watercolors and a colorful poster on the walls—improper decoration for an analyst. The other analyst spoke little, but was pithy; I talked too much. The other analyst was accommodating about scheduling and rescheduling hours; I was not. And so on. I charged too much. I was not worth my fee.

All these complaints were delivered in a calm, reasonable, almost regretful manner, as if the patient were terribly sorry to have to display bad manners in pointing out these gaffes of mine. He was also careful to point out his warm feelings about me and his positive observations, and in the first few weeks he asked himself several times whether his criticisms of me might make most sense as displacements from the past. This had less the quality of self-examination, though, than of protecting himself in advance against what he expected would be my interpretations. He concluded sadly that he had to stand by his observations.

In fact, it seemed to me that most of the attributes he complained about were real enough. My office is not bare, and given that the former analyst had been classical in orientation, it was plausible to believe that I talked more. Yet I was interested and puzzled about the patient's focus on these things, because he was not critical enough to leave, though he said often that his doubts about my skill made him question whether he should commit himself to the treatment. He did not merely stay, though. I sensed a budding attachment, and his involvement seemed clear. He was never late, usually early, and he worked hard, not at all as if he had the doubts he claimed.

One day, six or eight weeks after the initial consultation, the patient complained about a painting on my wall that he felt was derivative in style and inferior in execution. He said he realized that it would be "snotty" of him to conclude that I was shallow on the basis of my taste in art, but he nevertheless found himself, he said, having to contend with this perception of me. I would not be able to understand him in the necessary depth. His admission of having to worry about my lack of substance did not lead him to conclude that he was being "snotty," of course. It was, instead, another maneuver meant to defuse any defense I might have, analytic or otherwise, inasmuch as he would have interpreted anything I said, other than acceptance of his idea, as defensive. As I will indicate, it probably would have been.

I did not at this point understand any of this, so for the time being I said nothing. He went on to discuss something else, related, no doubt, but beyond my recall. I felt uncomfortable, a kind of pressure to respond that I usually hope to resist because of its very insistence. If I had responded, I think I would probably have said something about his worry that I was shallow.

As the patient talked I found myself wishing hazily that I could tell him that this painting was no longer of any real significance to me, which was in fact true. I then considered, in the same hazy state, removing the painting after the session. I no longer liked it anyway, I told myself, and after all, I had seen a piece just the day before that I had thought would be a nice replacement.

It was at roughly this juncture that I noticed what I was thinking. Why would I be thinking this way? What was I feeling that I wanted to mollify this man?

First, I realized that I had underestimated the extent of my worry about not living up to the standards of the former analyst, whose work I admired. But this explanation was insufficient until I realized that my patient, knowing that I recognized the name of his former analyst, had had reason to believe that I would feel this way. Similarly, the patient might have had reason to believe, from the fact that I had taken a good deal of care with the appearance of my office, and perhaps from something I had said or done, that I would respect his considerable knowledge of art. Perhaps he had reason to believe I would be vulnerable to his jibes about my painting. I saw that I had felt intimidated, and with this description to myself of my feeling state came relief from the pressure to respond. Knowing I was threatened made it unnecessary to protect myself.

My conclusion appears so obvious in the telling of the episode that it may seem a wonder that I did not see it before. It was not so obvious at the time, though, and that particular word, "intimidated," helped me. It was a form that articulated my experience, that held it in one place for me to reflect on. I could then ask why I had felt this way, and I could put into words (to myself) that my patient was not merely critical, but contemptuous. I had sometimes felt contemptible. It now came to me to put a word to the looks the patient had given me when decrying my possession of the painting: "withering." This, too, was helpful. I had withered under his glare, probably as many others had, maybe as he himself had under the glare of someone else—a parent? What kind of feeling state was this intimidation meant to effect in me? What did he then feel? Given the simultaneous presence of his attachment and his intimidation of me, did my being threatened play some important part in the kind of connectedness he sought with me? How? Why? Was this perhaps the best he could do to create an atmosphere of intimacy? Or maybe he wanted to distance me in order to prevent my behaving in a way that would provoke an intense attachment. Had I in fact threatened him (maybe interested him as well) by not maintaining the degree of distance and silence he had come to associate with psychoanalysis? These questions were eventually productive in the detailed description of the field and the patient's character.

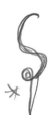

Until I began to question myself about my fantasies about the patient, an important aspect of my experience of the patient had been unformulated. I had been so buried in my direct experience of his intimidation and contempt that I could neither articulate it nor even know that something significant was invisible to me. My intimidation did not exist in an explicit verbal form, though, predescribed and ready to appear in awareness the moment I would accept it. The words to construct it had to be found.

Could the experience have come into being in a different form if I had used different words to describe it to myself? This question is impossible to answer conclusively, because experience can only be formulated once. The experience may be reformulated later, but this new articulation is the formulation of a different experience. After one has used satisfying words for it, the union of experience and word usually seems to have been inevitable, so inevitable, as a matter of fact, that the whole process of constructing reflective experience is very seldom noticed at all. Psychoanalysis is one of the few contexts that offer such an observational opportunity.

In addition, if I had formulated the experience in different words, I probably would also have described differently what led up to it, which means that to be convincing, an alternate formulation might have to be accompanied by an account of the prior events that would be different in ways I cannot know. I am now past the point of formulation, and so cannot re-create what came before it. But with these substantial provisos, imagine how the events following the formulation might have been different if I had said to myself that I felt ignorant and embarrassed, or disliked, both of which would have been true at that moment. Even assuming I had been able to observe these reactions before I acted on them, the inquiry that followed would have been different than the one that took place. The words we choose guide us more than we know. And the current situation, the interpersonal field described by Sullivan (1940) as "the physician, the patient, and the parataxic concomitants" (p. 190), guides our choice of words, and governs even whether we see that we are faced with the necessity for words at all.

THE GRIP OF THE FIELD

To this point I have presented the problem of countertransference awareness as a consequence of the nature of the analyst's experience. A second and more familiar approach derives from the study of the interpersonal field. Among the writers who have contributed to this literature are psychoanalysts from most major orientations. They share the view that, routinely, the patient unconsciously attempts to influence the analyst, and that the analyst's experience therefore contains valuable information not necessarily available in other forms. The analyst's experience of this influence, or reaction to it, also regularly occurs outside awareness. Thus, these writers' positions suggest that the grip of the interpersonal field on the participants is a second reason that the analyst may not put her experience of the patient into words. Hoffman (1983) describes these writers as "radical critics of the blank screen model," distinguishing them from "conservative critics" and from adherents of asocial, blank-screen conceptions of the analytic situation. In regard to the analyst's experience, Hoffman writes that,

> the analyst in the analytic situation is continuously having some sort of personal affective reaction that is a response to the patient's manner of relating to him. What is more, every patient knows that he is influencing the analyst's experience and that the freedom the analyst has to resist this influence is limited. Patients create atmospheres in analysis—atmos-

pheres which we sometimes actually speak of as though something were "in the air" between the participants. These atmospheres include the therapist's personal reaction to the patient, the patient guessing what the reaction is partly on the basis of what he thinks his own behavior is likely to have elicited, the analyst guessing what the patient is guessing, and so on [p. 411].

The reasons that the analyst may be unaware of her experience of, and reactions to, the patient vary from author to author. Sandler (1976), for instance, writes that "the irrational response of the analyst" is a "compromise-formation between his own tendencies and his *reflexive acceptance of the role which the patient is forcing on him*" (p. 276). The suggestion here is that lack of awareness has to do with the automatic, unthinking nature of the analyst's response. In Racker's (1968) view, on the other hand, the analyst regularly develops a countertransference neurosis, of which she must cure herself if the patient is to be cured. Here, the reasons for the analyst's lack of awareness are the familiar ones of the analyst's own neurosis, which are inevitably stimulated, though differently, by each patient.

Because of its flexibility and inclusiveness, however, I prefer for this purpose the description implicit in the work of Levenson (1972, 1983, 1991). Language and behavior are for Levenson transforms of one another, both containing the same information. Whatever analyst and patient are talking about is in some way being played out between them. The patient involves the analyst in the kinds of relationships the patient originally developed with family members. The patient employs these styles of relatedness continuously, and increasingly, the analyst does too. Even when the field is not the object of analytic attention, it is the structure of events. Everything that takes place is somehow meaningful in the terms of its structured exchanges. Analyst and patient create, and until it is discovered (over and over again), maintain the states of relatedness that brought the patient to analysis. Under these circumstances both analyst and patient are caught in the grip of the field. The analyst is influenced to be unaware of her reactions, and to that extent cannot understand her own participation, for the same dynamic reasons that the original family members did not understand *their* participation. (This is not to say that the analyst is not responsible, of course. Within the bounds of what the field offers (chapter 8), one shapes one's own response to the patient's influence.) The analyst's motivations for selective inattention, for keeping significant aspects of countertransference unformulated, are therefore as diverse as the patients she sees. We are reminded once again that the content of the analyst's awareness, like the patient's, is conditional, dependent on the real and illusory participants in the field. Learning why one has not seen one's involvement thus becomes an essential part of clarifying that very involvement.

There are, then, two reasons why the analyst may have difficulty being directly aware of her experience of the patient: the field grips the participants, motivations depending on the participants and the nature of the interaction; and the experience is unformulated, occurring in a form not conducive to language. The two reasons are interlocked, however. They are not alternate explanations. They explain the same phenomena at different levels of observation. The creation of states of relatedness, as Tauber and Green (1959) pointed out, is exactly the kind of experience that goes on in the presentational mode.

BREAKING THE GRIP

As long as patient and analyst are reacting to one another without questioning what they are doing, they are caught in the grip of the field. They may even believe they *are* questioning themselves and, unbeknownst to them until some later time, still be mired. As long as the grip is maintained, the participants' experience of the field remains unformulated. They simply do not see it. They generally do not even suspect there is something to see. Those of us whose theory leads us to expect to be mired, incidentally, are not innoculated by our expectations. The phenomenon is enough a matter of life that theory cannot protect us from it. Nor in fact would we want to be protected. To be gripped, or "transformed," as Levenson (1972) puts it, is not a problem to be avoided, but a reality to be accepted. If the analyst could not be gripped by the field, the patient would "have no respectable card of admission to the relationship" (Tauber and Green, 1959, p. 146). The analyst, in turn, would be denied firsthand experience of the patient's problems.

But of course the grip is only useful because sometimes it is broken. This happens only when patient or analyst becomes able to observe the interaction and question it, that is, formulate it. The one who questions is usually the analyst, of course, but this is by no means always the case, especially if the analyst is receptive to the patient's observations of the analyst. The patient's experience and the analyst's are reciprocal in this respect: If either participant can find a way to a true and felt reaction to the other, the work may proceed. In the patient's case, this reaction must be spoken to be useful; in the case of the analyst, the reaction is usually not spoken but serves as the instigation for renewed inquiry. If neither patient nor analyst can question the face value of what happens between them, there is a halt in the treatment until such questioning occurs, and the experience of the interaction remains unformulated for both parties until that time.

What determines whether and when the analyst will formulate her experience of herself and the patient? It requires work for the analyst to stop, reflect on the interaction, and see it well enough to put words to it. It requires that the analyst be able to imagine alternatives to the interaction as it is occurring. She may not know what she is feeling toward the patient until she can imagine feeling otherwise. For instance, she may not know that she is worried about a patient's suicide potential (i.e., she may not be able to say to herself that she is worried) until she can see that she feels anxious when the patient is even a minute or two late for an appointment. Until this happens, the analyst is buried in her own reaction. She does not see that she is worried until she can question herself about the source of her anxiety at the patient's tardiness, and she cannot question her reaction until she can imagine not having it. The analyst must be able to see that it would be possible to feel otherwise. She must be able to say to herself, "The patient's lateness does not demand this response from me." As long as only one way of seeing is available, this way of seeing must be experienced as "just the way things are," unnoticed and unremembered.[1]

Ernest Schachtel (1959), apparently influenced by Heidegger, described this kind of experience as *embeddedness,* a state of unthinking familiarity with which we must struggle throughout life. Originating in "the quasi-uterine embeddedness during which mother constitutes the infant's world" (p. 53), this way of being later becomes a retreat or protection from the existential anxiety that must be borne if one is to achieve "openness" to people and things. Emerging from embeddedness, finding and facing the unfamiliar, is the great task of life, accomplished over and over again in productive and satisfying lives, in ever more subtle and mature ways. One must emerge from embeddedness, or more properly, always be in the process of struggling with it, in order to "directly encounter" others and the world around one.

The analyst in the grip of the field is embedded in it. She formulates her experience and emerges from this particular episode of embeddedness when she maintains the *allocentric attitude.*

At any particular moment, the analyst can have one of two attitudes toward the patient, *autocentric* or *allocentric.* These are concepts developed by Schachtel in his work on perception, though he broadened them to describe more general attitudes with which one faces the world (1959). In the autocentric attitude, the other person is what Schachtel calls an object-of-use. One has some predetermined purpose for her. One looks for something in her rather than opening oneself to her. This is the attitude with which we necessarily approach the physician or the dry cleaner or anyone else from whom we want a particular thing or service—though in some of Schachtel's more extreme examples entire lives are constrained within the bounds of the familiar. Novelty is seldom experienced. Objects and people are merely registered as members of a category before attention flits on.

> We look around and say to ourselves, silently and implicitly: "This is the store at the corner of X street, this is the red house, this is the tree in front of it, these are people going to work, this is the bus stop; this is the chair and the floor lamp, the desk, the window, the bed, etc." While we see all these objects, in this perspective we do not see them fully, in their own right. What is the use we put them to when we just recognize them in this way and then let our glance pass on to some other object which, in turn, we quickly file away as "recognized"? We use the objects for orientation and reassurance that we are moving and being in our familiar, accustomed, everyday world [pp. 169–170].

The allocentric attitude, by contrast, is curiosity, an openness or receptivity that requires the tolerance of ambiguity and uncertainty, and sometimes pain.

> [T]his attitude is one of profound interest in the object, and complete openness and receptivity toward it, a full turning toward the object which makes possible the direct encounter with it and not merely a quick registration of its familiar features according to ready labels. The essential qualities of the interest in, the turning toward, the object are its *totality* and its *affirmativeness.* The totality of interest refers both to the

object in which the perceiver is interested and to the act of interest. The interest concerns the whole object, not merely a partial aspect of it; and the perceiver turns toward the object with his entire being, his whole personality, i.e., fully, not just with part of himself. The act of interest is total and it concerns the totality of its object [pp. 220–221].

To perceive another person allocentrically is to be as curious as possible, open to all the alternate formulations one finds unfinished in oneself, including one's reactions to the other. The uncertainty of the unformulated is preserved, even nurtured. Alternatives are allowed to percolate and glimmer, emerging as indeterminate shapes, some of which then attain enough form for words to give them coherence. The other person is seen from all sides. There occurs what Polanyi (1958, 1959), echoed in the psychoanalytic literature by George Klein (1976), called "indwelling"—dwelling within the experience of another through its reconstruction as one's own. The allocentric attitude is what makes possible the leap of the analyst's experience of the patient into words.

But the allocentric attitude, and the consequent attitude to the unformulated, is an ideal, possible to assume only part of the time, and not even desirable to assume continuously. One would never do anything else, for example, if every glance at a clock provoked absorption in the movement of the hands. One would never arrive at a destination unless it were possible to follow a familiar route without being drawn into contemplation of everything along the way. As a matter of fact, it is a background of familiarity that makes fresh encounter possible.

It is perhaps more feasible to maintain the allocentric attitude in the consulting room than in most other places, because as analysts we encourage ourselves during our hours with patients to become absorbed in their experience in a way that few, if any, other kinds of work allow their practitioners. Nevertheless, a constant allocentric attitude is an unreachable ideal for psychoanalysts too. We listen through the filters of our personalities and our theoretical commitments. We are selective, not merely receptive. We have to be so absorbed in what Levenson (1983) calls the "algorithm" of psychotherapy that we can work without having to become lost in thought about each thing we do. And being heir to the common human limitations, we have plenty of moments when we simply are not willing to set aside our own interests enough to be immersed in the patient's experience. And of course, the earliest understanding of countertransference remains valid: The analyst may develop prejudiced perceptions of the patient composed of details selected according to neurotic exigency.

And yet, in keeping with the paradox I have already mentioned, fresh encounter is possible only because of its contrast with the very familiarity from which it is an escape. Every figure must have a ground. New experience of the analyst is meaningful only against the background of transference. In a successful analysis, that which is so familiar to the patient that it is not seen (i.e., the transference) is seen for the first time, and in becoming the background for an experience other than itself, a background for an alternative to itself, it changes. It becomes one of the possibilities. Novelty arises.

The same process must occur in the countertransference. The analyst must somehow put words to her own reactions and thereby create alternate perceptions of the patient. Thus, we must have a way to understand how nurturing the allocentric attitude in oneself can be consistent with the recognition of irrational, autocentric countertransference.

A CLINICAL ILLUSTRATION

A young professional man in the early stage of treatment told me one day that he would not be coming to his next session. He was taking the day off from work and wanted to have no responsibilities at all. He said this matter-of-factly, finding nothing in it worthy of note. He assumed, he said, that he would be charged for the hour. My immediate response was frustration and annoyance. I inquired routinely about what the patient liked about having no responsibilities, and about his perception of the session as an obligation to be fulfilled or avoided, but privately I felt that there was no nonadversarial way to address the real question—why the patient insisted on feeling oppressed by me. As I perceived it, any time I had broached this question in the past, the patient had withdrawn from active participation, becoming overtly compliant but secretly sullen. The patient seemed to feel oppressed by, and resentful about, any inquiry into his feeling of oppression. However much I might have suspected myself of missing something, I simply saw no way to carry the inquiry further.

My reaction at this point was autocentric. I was in the common and contradictory position of feeling that the patient would not let me do my job. For the moment, the treatment was stymied.

The analyst's experience of the patient remains in the autocentric mode only as long as it is not directly represented in the analyst's awareness. If the analyst allows herself to formulate the experience, thus making it possible to hold it at a distance, reflect upon it and not merely react to it, she can maintain the allocentric attitude. Schachtel (1959) says that our capacity to experience in the autocentric mode, if we are receptive to it, is essential equipment in fully registering the other's presence. He writes, "It is the attempt to escape from such feelings, rather than the existence of them, which prevents man from turning fully, with his whole being, toward the object" (p. 227). In his belief that the autocentric can be a source of information about the other if it is treated allocentrically, Schachtel shows himself to be a psychoanalyst rather than a philosopher. The power of self-reflection to transform one's own experience is central to Schachtel's work. This aspect of his views makes the autocentric-allocentric dialectic more suitable for the present discussion than the existential distinctions that are similar to Schachtel's in other important respects, such as Buber's (1957, 1965) I–Thou or Sartre's (1956) being-in-itself and being-for-itself.

In my example, the problems in the interaction would probably have spiralled if I had not been successful in understanding this feeling I had that the patient was obstructing progress. Events were more favorable, however. It occurred to me to question myself about why I had not just accepted the patient's lead regarding the next session. I could have just waited to see what would happen. Inquiring about it may have made sense, but had I been attached to a particular outcome? It seemed so. I wanted the patient to come to that session. Actually, I realized, it was not only the idea of missing the session that had annoyed me, it was the matter-of-fact tone of the patient's voice. It now seemed to me that this tone had been *insistently* matter-of-fact. If I were to question this decision, being presented so reasonably by the patient, I would be cast as the oppressor. I had therefore avoided directly questioning it, but I apparently resented this control over me. However, I noted that by this point in the interaction I had in effect *become* the oppressor, because I had responded to the patient's challenge by at least feeling like imposing my will. By now, the patient was probably reacting to my suppressed annoyance as yet another instance of my intention to control him. A silent power struggle seemed to be taking place.

I now asked the patient if it was possible that he was feeling pushed around. I offered some of the details I have just reviewed as reasons why the idea had occurred to me. The patient was somewhat wary, probably of my intentions in bringing this up, but said that in fact he was feeling pushed around and that it had happened several times before. It seemed to him that at these times I became less responsive to him, less interested, but he had never considered the possibility that my reaction might have something to do with his own. I could then ask the patient if he could identify anything I had done, maybe in the previous session, that had made him feel that I was lording it over him. If I had done something like this, it might account for his feeling that it was necessary to wrest back from me control over the situation. The patient was able to remember such an incident, something subtle enough (hardly "lording," as a matter of fact, but that was the word I had used with him) for him to feel that his angry reaction, which had been only momentary, was unreasonable. He had swallowed his reaction, which of course had only increased his resentment about having to submit.

The inquiry did not stop here. Further questions were raised, including the characterization of my experience in the previous session: In what way might I have attempted to control the patient? And to what extent might the patient's seemingly collaborative approach to this investigation actually represent a more subtle version of the oppressor-oppressed scenario, the patient playing the compliant or obedient child, afraid of the parent-analyst? Perhaps, eager not to disappoint me, he was trying to please me and hating himself for it. All of these possibilities were plausible, given what I knew about the patient, and eventually I could feel that I knew whether they were true. By then, though, new questions had arisen. The recapture of the allocentric attitude and the formulation of the analyst's experience offer no permanent solutions, but they do allow both participants greater freedom to articulate the next problems.

A SEQUENCE OF EVENTS IN THE ANALYST'S EXPERIENCE

In the course of treatment, then, the analyst's experience repeatedly goes through the following sequence of transformations: (1) embeddedness in the grip of the field, which is formulated in the experience of neither patient nor analyst; (2) emergence from embeddedness and the regaining of the allocentric attitude; (3) formulation of the analyst's experience of the patient; (4) a break in the grip of the field. The following vignette illustrates one such sequence.

A single woman executive in her late 20s had entered treatment a year earlier in order to be able to establish and maintain a relationship with a man. We were bogged down in one important respect. The patient had no more than the average difficulty in finding appropriate and available men, but usually, to her surprise and dismay, the man left the budding relationship after a few weeks. These departures were sudden and mysterious, and left her feeling discouraged and sometimes hopeless. I suspected that the patient, who gave a first impression of self-reliance and resourcefulness, and who in fact did have these characteristics, very soon also conveyed to these men a bottled-up kind of desperation for their affection, and resentment at the absence of sufficient evidence of this feeling on their parts. It was my guess that these feelings were too intense for the early stage of a relationship, and that the men left precipitously because of their fear of this intensity, their resentment at some kind of demanding quality, and their guilt at being unwilling to offer what she wanted to someone they probably saw as warm and affectionate. At one time or another I conveyed all these speculations to the patient. Although she found them interesting and even probable, she could not experience them directly, and so was left unconvinced, though wishing to be.

It so happened that one of the major security operations used by this woman was to approach many topics with what she came to call her "fix-it" attitude. It was difficult and, consequently, unusual for her to explore freely a problem of her own, because she felt she was to blame for it, but she felt quite at home in immediately tackling a solution to it. By the time of the session I describe, we had already discussed this many times.

On the day in question the patient was telling me about a telephone conversation the night before with the man she was currently seeing. They had been talking about where to go on Saturday night, and the patient had expressed a preference. Immediately, and in response it seemed, the man's tone of voice became more distant. At that point the patient said, in a tone that sounded resentful in her report of it, "Do you think you could be nicer to me?"

I interrupted the patient here and asked her what she thought might have happened in that interchange. She had not thought about it, she said, because in her report to me she had merely been on the way to the point she wanted to make, and had not meant to give any special emphasis to this part of the interaction. Now that she thought about it, however, she could see that it had been at this point that the phone conversation became uncomfortable, which it had remained until the end. I asked her whether she thought the resentful tone of the remark, as she had told it to me, represented the feeling she had conveyed at the time. She said ruefully that she thought it probably did, though she had not been aware of it at the time and did not understand it now. Then she said, in a sad and resigned kind of way, "Look, I know I should think about what it means, but I just can't imagine what else I could have said to him." She drifted into silence.

My initial response to this, only peripherally noted by me, was a sinking feeling and frustration at what seemed to be another instance of her fix-it attitude. One more opportunity to explore something about this central problem seemed to be on the way down the drain. I said nothing, though. As moments passed I was aware of something else, of her apology to me for fixing it rather than thinking about it, and I began to see that I must many times have been subtly critical of this defense of hers. She must have anticipated this critical attitude just now, so that she felt discouraged and hopeless. I only saw at this moment what I had been feeling in these other instances because, at the same time, I felt an alternative to it. Her subtle apology, awakening in me an awareness of her difficulty in dealing with me about her defense, had made it possible for me to feel compassion, and this compassion was the alternative that made my previous frustration visible to me. Of course, prior to this I would not have known there was a gap in my compassion for this woman, nor would I have been able to see clearly that I felt critical. As is often the case, the grip of the field became visible only as it was broken.

The interaction I have characterized here between this woman and me—the patient repeatedly turning to me needily (to help her fix something) and me retreating critically, leaving her feeling discouraged—is precisely the interaction we had been trying to investigate elsewhere in her life. With my recognition of my reaction to the patient and my part in the interaction it was possible to rediscover an allocentric attitude toward her and to investigate the problem in the transference-countertransference field. It was natural to me at this point to change the nature of my participation, and, in fact, from then on it probably would have felt uncomfortable to maintain my participation as it had been. This new participation, in turn, encouraged the reciprocal formulation of new experience by the patient. Inadvertently, the patient had behaved in such a fashion that I was able to formulate an aspect of the field that, until then, had been invisible to both of us.

11

Gadamer's Hermeneutics

A Philosophy for the Embedded Analyst

So few analysts are willing any longer to defend the blank-screen metaphor of the analyst's role, at least in its stark form, *sans* qualifications, that to attack it has become a gratuitous act, useful only as a kind of chest beating. And yet every time one is ready to consign the issue to oblivion, one reads some new article, or hears about someone's defense of neutrality, and the tired old argument comes to life. So perhaps the distinction between those who adhere to the orthodox clinical view and those who don't retains meaning after all.

Be that as it may, it has become much less interesting to bash the blank-screen metaphor than to delineate differences within the group of analysts who already accept some kind of modification of the most conservative view. Work in this area has only just begun. One of the few comparisons of this sort is by Greenberg and Mitchell (1983), who describe three solutions to the problem of how to represent interpersonal relations in psychoanalytic theory. One can, like Freud himself, and along with Hartmann, Mahler, Jacobson, and Kernberg, try to change drive theory so that relational matters are accommodated, but in a way that is ultimately instinctual. Or, like Sullivan and Fairbairn, one can dispense with drive theory altogether and begin anew with interpersonal relations as the cornerstone. The third alternative is a mixed model in which relational and drive phenomena are explained separately, the kind of solution adopted, according to Greenberg and Mitchell, by Kohut and Sandler.

Another set of categories has been proposed by Hoffman (1983), whose work has particular appeal to the working psychoanalyst because of its exclusive focus on clinical theory. Hoffman discerns two ways clinical writers have taken issue with the blank-screen metaphor: the conservative critique and the radical critique. In the conservative critique, as in Greenberg and Mitchell's strategy of accommodation, the problematic aspects of the old idea may seem to be addressed, but actually the essence of the problem remains. The conservative critic emphasizes some aspect of the analyst's "real" influence on the patient (as opposed to influence "distorted" by the patient). The judgment that the patient has seen the "real" meaning of the analyst's behavior is based on how the patient reacts, the criterion being the patient's correspondingly "appropriate" or "undistorted" response. For example, to the analyst's genuine helpfulness and capability, the undistorting patient responds by joining the "real relationship" or the working alliance. Similarly, the "appropriate" response of the undistorting patient to the analyst's neurotic countertransference is the patient's accurate observation of the *analyst's* inappropriateness. The patient's capacity to assess accurately these influences from the analyst is therefore a social phenomenon; it is an effect of the interaction, "uncontaminated" by the nonrational inner world. But this capacity on the patient's part exists separately from the rest of the patient's experience of the analyst, which is conceived by the conservative critic to be distinctly nonsocial, nonrational, and transferential. In this sense, conservative critics continue to employ the blank-screen model and the associated *asocial paradigm*: "According to these conceptions, there is a stream of experience going on in the patient which is divorced to a significant extent from the immediate impact of the therapist's personal presence" (Hoffman, 1983, pp. 390–391). That is, some part of the patient's experience is continuously fantasy-based, an ongoing eruption of the inner life, perhaps catalyzed by current external events, but only indirectly related to them. Transference is routinely viewed as distortion.

The radical critic, on the other hand, who may be identified with interpersonal psychoanalysis, the object relations school, self psychology, or even classical Freudian psychoanalysis, espouses a truly *social* conception of the analytic situation. The therapist is inevitably involved in the interaction, usually in ways he does not suspect. Hence there is no single truth, and transference and countertransference are unformulated experience, to be articulated by the selection of an interpretive perspective. The analyst is in no position to claim that transference is distortion. Rather, writes Hoffman, "the perspective that the patient brings to bear in interpreting the therapist's inner attitudes is regarded as one among many perspectives that are relevant, each of which highlights different facets of the analyst's involvement" (p. 394). The patient may actually be able to observe aspects of the analyst's involvement which the analyst has not yet seen. "More than challenging the blank screen fallacy," writes Hoffman, "the radical critic challenges what might be termed the *naive patient fallacy*, the notion that the patient, insofar as he is rational, takes the analyst's behavior at face value even while his own is continually scrutinized for the most subtle indications of unspoken or unconscious meanings" (p. 395).

It is only by learning about himself that the radical critic believes the analyst can learn about the patient. Only in the act of disembedding himself from previously unseen aspects of the interaction is he able to experience—and perhaps say—something new. "At the very moment that he interprets, the analyst often extricates himself as much as he extricates the patient from transference-countertransference enactment" (p. 415). The radical critic assumes he is embedded in the interaction, that in certain important respects he is always blind to it. He continually queries himself about his participation, trying to create the possibility of a question, a foot in the door.

ISSUES OF KNOWING AND UNDERSTANDING

In the United States, we are in the midst of heightened psychoanalytic interest in the nature of knowing and understanding, led by the increasingly frequent citation of hermeneutic views.[1] It is no longer unusual for analysts to find clinical relevance in questions that only recently would have been deemed entirely metaphysical: What does it mean to know something about the patient? About one's experience of the patient? What is the nature of the material we are trying to understand? What is an interpretation? What qualifies as truth, and how can we recognize it? Who determines when we have reached it?

These new interests are natural and even necessary for radical critics, because as soon as one defines the basic unit as the interpersonal field and not the individual, one must replace the comforting assumption that the truth is already there, buried, awaiting discovery. The archaeological metaphor has outlived its usefulness. Like the blank screen, it is an image of stasis unsuited to represent the inevitable participation of both parties. For the radical critic, the "truth" about the patient is a mutual construction, an outcome of the interaction, always interpretive and only partially predetermined. And thus the definition of what it is for something to be unconscious is in a state of flux. For many analysts, lack of awareness now means the absence of explicit reflection, not the inaccessibility of a hidden reality. Besides unformulated experience, recent psychoanalytic concepts reflecting these trends are Stolorow's "prereflective unconscious" (Atwood and Stolorow, 1984; Stolorow, Brandchaft, and Atwood, 1987; Stolorow, 1988) and Bollas's (1987) "unthought known."

THE ASYMMETRY OF THE ANALYTIC RELATIONSHIP

The acceptance that the process of constructing truth is mutual does not mean that the analytic relationship should be conceptualized as symmetrical. Egalitarian, yes; symmetrical, no.

To make the decision to enter treatment means to accept that a certain set of differential roles is to be assigned to oneself and the analyst. Basically, these roles are interpretive perspectives. The patient's role is to say everything about his experience that he can, including his experience of the analyst. The analyst's role, though, is hardly limited to an appreciation of what the patient says—a stance that would amount to an asymmetry of a different sort. As a matter of fact, many or most patients would be disappointed if that is what the analyst did. It is the analyst's responsibility not only to develop an empathic appreciation of the patient's perspective, but to have a perspective of his own. If the analyst did not work that way, little would happen, because there would seldom be any reason for the patient to think in new ways about himself. It might seem that the empathic stance of the self psychologist or the containing function of the object relations analyst contradict this formulation, but they do not. Those analysts, too, would agree that their analytic functioning requires them to have an independent perspective about what they are doing with their patients. The reason they treat their patients as they do is hardly that they accept what patients say at face value, but precisely that they do not. Like all analysts, they have their own ideas about what is called for, ideas that their patients might very well disagree with in the most strenuous way if they knew about them, and if they understood what these prescriptions meant about the way their analysts privately characterized them.

For most analysts, though, we might say that analytic work is defined by a vacillation between the roles of empathizer and interpreter. In Racker's (1968) roughly equivalent terms, the analyst alternates between observing and acting on a modulated grasp of his own concordant and complementary identifications with the patient. This is what it *is* to be an analyst, and most patients who enter treatment thereby endorse their analysts to occupy that role. The patient is purchasing the analyst's specifically analytic services, and they include a set of interpretive perspectives that the patient appropriately considers whenever the analyst deems them useful to add to the conversation. This is a freely accepted asymmetry.

But there are also many cases in which the patient enters treatment without making such an endorsement, explicitly or implicitly. These people, who are more difficult for the analyst to deal with and are often characterized as borderline, narcissistic, and so on, would have reactions to knowing the analyst's formulations ranging from disorganizing disappointment and depression through utter rage. The analyst, under these circumstances, has no choice, of course, but to keep many or most of his own interpretive perspectives to himself, at least for the time being. But does that mean he does not develop them? Absolutely not. As a matter of fact, we are perfectly well aware that if he did not develop them, the treatment would blow up immediately (and it may, anyway, of course), because the only way the analyst imagines how he can effectively treat the patient is by reference to these private formulations. As I just mentioned, this is the situation of the self psychologist and of the analyst who works by containing the patient's projections; but it is also the situation of *any* analyst working with a patient who cannot tolerate a fully collaborative analytic relationship.

Where is the egalitarianism in this? Does this situation not sound a little like the relationship between an authority and a subject? The reason it is not is really very simple: besides the fact that the patient always has the power to terminate the relationship, of course, he also always has the right—even the responsibility, if he disagrees—to dispute what he knows of the analyst's understandings. In the work of the radical critic, what the patient has to say about himself or the analyst, or the two of them together, may be quite valuable; this depends on how convincing it is to the analyst, just as what the analyst says depends for its ultimate therapeutic value on the conviction it arouses in the patient (see chapter 9). The necessity for each participant to convince the other is the egalitarianism of the analytic relationship, and it exists despite the fact that the relationship is asymmetrical. In any particular case, the patient may have a more useful or coherent perspective on himself (or on the analyst) than the analyst does. Asymmetry does not imply the analyst's infallibility, after all, only the ongoing attempt of two people to occupy certain more or less cooperative and complementary stances relative to one another's participation. (For a view closely related to this one, see Aron, 1996.)

With all that said, I must return to the point that the analyst is always embedded in the analytic situation in such a way that the ideal distribution of roles, the ideal therapeutic collaboration, is utterly impossible, even for the analyst, almost all the time. But the ideal is there, and we try to meet it as best we can. Thus, in the following discussion of Gadamer's hermeneutics, wherein Gadamer implicitly portrays the conversation in which understanding takes place as not only egalitarian but symmetrical, the analytic reader must remember that Gadamer was a philosopher and not a psychoanalyst. He did not grapple with conversations in which, from the outset, it is recognized that one person has special reasons not to understand (at least we hope that the analyst's reasons not to know are usually less compelling than the patient's). The patient's special reasons are one of the factors that make the psychoanalytic conversation unique in all of life, and that build asymmetry into the analytic relationship's very foundation.

GADAMER: A PHILOSOPHER RELEVANT
TO CLINICAL PRACTICE

For Hans-Georg Gadamer, as for most modern hermeneutic philosophers, understanding (in the general sense, now, not the psychoanalytic one) is inevitably a matter of selecting and formulating one interpretation from the multiple plausible alternatives in any given situation. Reflective meaning cannot be said to have existed prior to its revelation in language, at least not in an apprehensible form. All of this, of course, is entirely consistent with the conception I have presented as the articulation of unformulated experience in language.

Gadamer claims that understanding requires us to disembed ourselves from our preconceptions—from what he calls "prejudice" or "prejudgment." New understanding emerges when we are able to make visible the expectations that have such a large role in the formulation of experience, and this can occur only in dialogue with the other. "In the last analysis," writes Gadamer (1962), echoing the radical critic, "*all* understanding is self understanding" (p. 55).

But the unique emphasis that makes Gadamer intriguing and useful to the embedded analyst is his view that prejudice is not only the bane of new experience, but the source of it. Gadamer looks to prejudice just as the radical critic looks to countertransference. It is not merely error. It is not noise in the system. Rather, it is both what makes possible new understanding and what stands in its way. Without prejudices we would be free to formulate anything at all and unable to make a single thought. Thus Gadamer (1975) can say, "Every experience worthy of the name runs counter to our expectation. . . . Insight is more than the knowledge of this or that situation. It always involves an escape from something that had deceived us and held us captive" (pp. 319–320). But he can state with equal conviction, "Prejudices are biases of our openness to the world. They are simply conditions whereby we experience something—whereby what we encounter says something to us" (1966, p. 8). Gadamer's philosophy is an exegesis of this paradox.

Reading Gadamer stimulates down-to-earth questions about clinical practice and clinical thinking. Because the aim of this chapter is to draw connections between Gadamer's thought, unformulated experience, and clinical psychoanalysis, much of what Gadamer has to say has been left out. His ideas are not discussed for their own sake. At the same time, though, a brief exposition of Gadamer's overall perspective and its historical context is unavoidable. The exposition follows in two sections, "From Schleiermacher to Gadamer" and "The Hermeneutic Circle," and to a lesser extent in a third, "Sharing a Tradition." The remainder of the chapter is focused on the implications for psychoanalysis practiced in the social paradigm. Chapter 12 takes up these views in a specifically clinical context.

FROM SCHLEIERMACHER TO GADAMER: REJECTING EMPATHIC KNOWING IN FAVOR OF MUTUAL INFLUENCE

Hermeneutics is the study of the process of understanding. Prior to the work of Schleiermacher, the father of modern hermeneutics (he wrote in the beginning and middle of the 19th century), it had been assumed that ease of understanding was the norm. The meaning of the text was treated as if it should be self-evident to the competent reader. Understanding could be taken for granted; *mis*understanding was the exceptional event that required explanation. Hermeneutics at that early time was really just the study of the practical problems involved in interpreting different kinds of texts. Schleiermacher, however, impressed with how difficult it is to grasp what an author really intended, reversed the original formula and originated the modern view, which still holds sway: *Mis*understanding is the natural state of affairs; it is *successful* understanding that requires explanation. In this way, hermeneutics metamorphosed from the clarification of isolated difficulties in grasping meaning—the correcting of errors in comprehension—to the much more general study of what it is to understand (Palmer, 1969).

It is more reasonable to assume misunderstanding than understanding, said Schleiermacher, because intervening between the text and the reader are time, history, custom, changes of language, and so on. The reader is faced with a document encrusted and obscured by the debris of change. Thus, in the Romantic tradition from which Freud also eventually emerged, Schleiermacher came to believe that the truth lay *behind* one's reading of the text, and had to be reconstructed. One needed to put together in one's own experience the historical context in which the text was written. If that could be accomplished, one could read the text from within the vantage point of the writer, and it would then be possible to grasp its original meaning. Palmer (1969) describes the process: "For Schleiermacher, understanding . . . is the reexperiencing of the mental processes of the text's author. It is the reverse of composition, for it starts with the fixed and finished expression and goes back to the mental life from which it arose" (p. 86). To the extent that the empathic reconstruction was accurate, the recreated meaning was accurate. There was a single truth in the text, and it preexisted the reader's encounter with it. The influence of the reader's present-day involvement in the world, to the degree that it interfered with a direct encounter of the writer's original intention, was a source of error. This is the most familiar model of bias, the traditional understanding of error forged in the Enlightenment: preconceptions veil and distort the truth; truth appears when error is removed. Thus, for Schleiermacher, hermeneutics was a set of procedures used to eliminate distortions. Though there was an undeniable role for intuition, the principles of understanding could be taught (Palmer, 1969).

Gadamer claims just the opposite, and in so doing he grounds his work in the phenomenological description of understanding, specifically eschewing any attempt to influence its practice. Because of the very nature of understanding, says Gadamer, it *cannot* be taught. It *happens*; it is unbidden. Understanding is not reconstruction to Gadamer, but mediation between reader and text, or between two participants in a conversation. Understanding takes place in dialogue: it requires the involvement of two parties, it goes on in the present moment, and it depends on present attitudes, not on recreating the past—all of which are consistent with the social paradigm.

We cannot understand, according to Gadamer, without reference to the tradition in which the understanding is meaningful; but that tradition is nowhere spelled out fully. Tradition exists in the innumerable unarticulated prejudices with which we approach the world. Tradition is actually the sum of all prejudice. Each person is an embodiment of tradition, a living expression of the history of cultures. And thus, to refer to prejudice is to refer to the basis of human existence. Gadamer writes, "It is not so much our judgments as it is our prejudgments that constitute our being."[2] We are at one and the same time, then, our own tool for understanding and the very substance of what must be understood. Since we embody what we wish to know, we cannot very well perform a directed search for truth. One does not know what to look for; one cannot see one's own eye. We are necessarily embedded in tradition because it represents the only possibilities we have.

It is language, and language only, that defines reflective meaning, and the limits of possible reflective meanings are precisely the same as the limits of language. If a meaning cannot yet be spoken, it does not yet exist in a form that could be reflectively understood; if it is not within the capacity of language to represent, it can never be reflective meaning at all. The sum total of all those meanings that are capable of linguistic representation is a second way Gadamer defines culture, or tradition. That is, the possibilities of language, the sum of prejudice, and tradition are all ways of referring to the same thing.

What we understand is not separate from us. The truth cannot be located and uncovered. Rather, says Gadamer, we must recognize that we already *are* the truth, that the problem is formulating the relevant aspects of our being. All we can do is to make a dialogue with another person in which we engage our prejudices in such a way that they become clear to us, and understanding emerges. The participants in what Gadamer calls a "genuine conversation" try to do just this by sensing the constraints that keep their dialogue from opening further. Thus the one who wishes to understand cannot set out knowing he will accomplish the task, as one could in making the decision to take a walk or watch television. Rather, one is attuned, as prepared as possible to see and sacrifice prejudices in the interest of receiving the other's message.

In all these ways, Gadamer rejects Schleiermacher's belief that the meaning of the text is hidden and preexisting, available only through empathic communion with the writer. Reflective meaning does not exist prior to the interaction in which it occurs. It is an event, not a thing. Because of our embeddedness in tradition and our consequent reliance on prejudice, we cannot, says Gadamer, depend on being able to produce an empathic communion just because such a connection is desired.

This disagreement sounds remarkably similar to the issue regarding empathic knowing which separates interpersonalists and some object-relations writers from self psychologists (e.g., Bromberg, 1989; Stern, 1988, 1994). The analyst who believes he has no choice but to work from a position of embeddedness cannot trust his own intention to enter the patient's inner world, to learn through empathic immersion. Neither the patient's experience nor his own is transparent to his scrutiny.

There is another connection worthy of note. For a psychoanalyst, Schleiermacher's position that truth lies underneath or behind the text immediately brings to mind the concepts of manifest and latent content. Schleiermacher's characterization of the reader trying to see beyond the appearance to the writer's true intention is like the classical analyst trying to penetrate defensive obscurities and distortions to reveal the patient's true motivations beneath. These are varieties of the "hidden reality" view (Neisser, 1967). On the other hand, Gadamer's characterization of meaning as an articulation and selection of possibilities dovetails nicely with the radical critic's rejection of transference and countertransference as distortion and the affirmation of these phenomena as legitimate, albeit individual and analyzable, selections of possibilities.

Thus the field of hermeneutics, like psychoanalysis, seems to be moving from an older conception of meaning as a static phenomenon, a thing that preexists its interpretation, to a newer understanding that meaning is an activity, an event, and can only take place in interaction. Some of the differences between Schleiermacher and Gadamer resurface in the contemporary dispute between Gadamer and Habermas, though in more subtle form. I will return to this famous debate later in the chapter.

THE HERMENEUTIC CIRCLE

The concept of the hermeneutic circle is the framework of hermeneutics. When modern hermeneutic writers differ, their disagreements center on its proper interpretation.

The idea arises from a paradox: We can understand only those communications that we can locate in their proper contexts. Unless an utterance can be placed in the appropriate configuration of tradition, its meaning remains obscure. Imagine trying to understand certain passages in Freud without knowing that he was taking issue with Jung; or trying to understand a dream without knowing the events of the day preceding it, or the patient's associations to it; or trying to understand a patient's barely supportable characterization of a co-worker as greedy without knowing that the patient himself is terribly afraid of being greedy.

But here is the rub: We cannot select the appropriate context without first having grasped what we claim we are trying to understand. How can one know, before understanding the dream, how to select the relevant events from the myriad possibilities of the previous day? How can one settle on the significant aspects of the patient's character without already having decided what the transference to the co-worker means? Palmer (1969) puts it this way: "How can a text be understood when the condition for its understanding is already to have understood what it is about?" (p. 25).

The hermeneutic answer is that we comprehend by means of continuously projecting complete understandings into communications from the other, communications we actually understand only partially. We extrapolate complete understandings on the basis of these partial understandings we already have. And where do the partial understandings come from? They are in turn stimulated by the complete understandings we project. Thus is the circle closed. But of course, something else must occur, or else comprehension would be nothing but self-reference. All comprehension is a process of projecting partial understandings into fully rounded ones, and then modifying these projections on the basis of what we actually come into contact with in conversation with the other person. In other words, when we understand, we have been able to treat our projections like hypotheses; and when we do not understand, it is because we have not managed to adopt this degree of uncertainty. This is the hermeneutical circle, and it is clear what the problem for the hermeneutic thinker is: One has to take a position about how we avoid seeing nothing more than we expect to see. Under what circumstances can projections be hypotheses and not givens?

At least this is the primary problem for Gadamer, because of the role of tradition in his conception of understanding. Whenever we explicitly understand something, what has happened is that we have made into expressive language some unexamined aspect of tradition. Productive prejudices are those that can be illuminated in such a way that new understandings come into view. They are capable of being disconfirmed.

SHARING A TRADITION: CULTURAL DIFFERENCES AND THE SPECIAL CASE OF PSYCHOANALYSIS

What is understood gains its meaning as much from what remains *un*articulated as it does from the words themselves. Each piece of understanding is surrounded and given meaning by "the infinity of the unsaid." Even around each word, giving context and relation, is a "circle of the unexpressed."[3] Over and over again, Gadamer emphasizes that understanding is as much a process of "concealment" as "revealment." In bringing one possibility into the light, experience is organized in such a way that other possibilities are "darkened." But those possibilities thus kept from the light are still significant in the making of meaning. To understand is not only to grasp what is said, but also to be so much a part of the tradition of the speaker that one also grasps the relation of what is said to all that is not said.

For example, consider a Chinese teacher of American literature, living in a rural area of China, who could talk with what seemed a respectable degree of familiarity about certain modern American novelists, but who could so little conceive of the tradition within which these writers work that, when the topic of conversation somehow turned to New York (he had heard of it, but knew no more than that), he could not understand how Manhattan skyscrapers could be taller than the single two-story structure in his own village. It was not so much that he refused to believe this fact, but rather that there was no way for him to make sense of it. It just could not be anchored in his own tradition. To paraphrase Gadamer, there were no conditions in this man's world whereby this encounter could speak to him. Needless to say, the friend who related this story, when she finally grasped that her interlocutor's attitude was due to bafflement and not to obstinacy, immediately reassessed the preceding conversation about novels, which she suddenly saw had been more a matter of verbal mimicry than real substance. She had unknowingly supplied the relevant context for whatever he had said.

Thus the process of understanding can go on only between people who share a tradition—or who are at least aware that they do not share one. Some years ago I offered to help a Japanese man with his English. Finding that we got along well, we decided to combine work and play by having lunch together once a week and going over cartoons in the *New Yorker*. I taught him vocabulary by naming the pictured objects, and I introduced grammatical points and matters of convention by explaining the thoughts the cartoons conveyed. But no matter how careful my explanations, most of the time my friend didn't get the jokes. I would fish around, trying to figure out what assumptions I brought to the situation that he did not. Trying to imagine how he saw, or didn't see, the most obvious parts of my world (how do you explain why it is funny for a man to bite a dog to someone for whom the very idea of a pet is uproarious?) led to hilariously concrete explanations of things I had never even thought to say. Eventually, at some moment that inevitably surprised me, I would learn that we had reached some meeting of the minds, because he would burst into laughter, more often than not right in the middle of my sober explanation of slippers or some such thing. He was frequently no more able than I to make sense out of why his understanding had come together in that particular moment.

Since analyst and patient generally share more or less the same set of cultural prejudices, the situation between them is often less baffling than it was between my Japanese friend and myself—often, but not always. My friend and I had the advantage of knowing how unfamiliar we were with each other's prejudices. We looked for misunderstanding in every sentence that passed between us. In psychoanalysis, on the other hand, even though the participants may share a culture, the relationship can seldom be as explicitly based on the mutual recognition of each other's prejudices. The most dedicated investigators of transference and countertransference are nevertheless inevitably involved in many conventional and unquestioned (and therefore masked) aspects of relatedness. They do not know what to look for. And even when something alerts them to the possibility of specific questions, the task of making visible the interweaving of the very tailored prejudices two people develop between them is more difficult than recognizing cultural differences. The clash of cultures, while it may be hard to understand, is at least unmistakable.

GENUINE CONVERSATION AND THE CREATION OF THE ANALYTIC FIELD

Gadamer differs from his predecessors in rejecting the possibility of prescribing a method of understanding. There is no way to describe how being comes into language—which is to say, there is no way to describe how one ought to approach the world to gain the truth. The concept of an exclusive method—a set of rules, such as the scientific method, prescribing how knowledge is to be determined—is legitimate only so long as what is learned is separate from the one who learns it. If the truth is separate, the question of the best way to approach it is a logical one. But if truth is the outcome of the grasp of being in language, there cannot be a superior way to accomplish it, because one cannot escape being part of the event one wants to capture. One method cannot be recommended over others. As a matter of fact, according to Gadamer (1962) the conscious application of a method can never result in revelation. He writes, "The real event of understanding goes beyond what we can bring to the understanding of the other person's words through methodical effort and critical self-control. Indeed, it goes far beyond what we ourselves can become aware of. Through every dialogue something different comes to be" (p. 58). Method to Gadamer is reification, the concretization of unexamined assumptions. Belief in method subverts the discovery of truth. Method should be questioned routinely, its assumptions understood and evaluated, never merely followed. And thus Gadamer's approach does not have specific technical implications for psychoanalytic practice. One could even make the case, on the basis of these ideas, that the concept of technique in psychoanalysis is specious.

Technique is not specious, however; we will always need it. Our recognition that it is a social construction, not an essence, hardly means we should wash our hands of it. What *is* specious (and here

Gadamer would undoubtedly agree) is the claim that one kind of technique is the true one, or that the analyst's participation is in error if it is not organized by technique. Hoffman (1994) suggests that whatever technique we use structures our participation, not by leading us in the paths of righteousness, but by setting up a dialectic between technique and spontaneous personal participation. Without technique, psychoanalysis would be no different than any other conversation; and without the analyst's spontaneous participation, psychoanalysis would be emotionally arid. Each of these kinds of participation on the part of the analyst can exist, however, only against the background of the other; technique and personal participation are both necessary if either is to be meaningful. The patient only cares about our spontaneity because of our usual demonstration of a commitment to a disciplined way of working; and our way of working is meaningful only because the patient knows this technique often puts a rein on our spontaneity.

As one interacts with a text or another person, the hermeneutic circle goes around and around. First, expectations develop, based on what one has brought to the encounter and on the history of the encounter itself. Each time (moment to moment) an understanding is called for, one projects into the future a preconception of what the other person or the text will disclose. This projection is based on the assumption that the other person or the text is internally consistent, and that the past is therefore a relevant basis on which to construct a possible future. One completes the partial meanings one has gleaned. To the extent that the expectations we form on this basis are explicitly known, one can see whether or not the situation with which one is faced confirms or disconfirms them. On the other hand, to the extent that one is not aware of one's expectations, one does not learn. "Understanding," says Gadamer, "is primarily agreement," by which he intends to say that to understand is to see what the other means. Yet this is an insufficient expression. Here is Warnke (1987), who has contributed a book-length study of Gadamer.

> Genuine understanding, on his [Gadamer's] view, derives not from an imposition of one's own prejudices or needs on the object to be understood . . . ; neither does it result in the abject acceptance of the views of that object, as the idea of anticipating completeness seems to imply. We have seen that the condition of true understanding is the same as that of genuine conversation: a recognition of one's own lack of knowledge and willingness to learn [p. 102].

Genuine conversation sounds like psychoanalysis. But doesn't the patient consult the analyst precisely because he cannot converse, cannot disconfirm his expectations, because he is caught in the endless stalemate that is transference? Well, yes, but this brings up something very interesting, an elusive point that happens to be especially clear from Gadamer's perspective. In treatment, the construction of transference and countertransference, even during the time when these interactions are still being blindly enacted by patient and analyst, is at least as significant as their eventual understanding in words. The relationship must be made; it must come into being. The participants in an analysis must develop a shared "tradition" to which to refer. Transference and countertransference need to feel so familiar to the participants, even if invisible and vaguely unwelcome, that when the right words emerge, they are recognized. It is only the familiarity of the relatedness, the way it fits and feels, that eventually makes it possible, in Gadamer's words, for something in the rush of events to "stand," to "come to a halt."

Psychoanalysis, no less than any other discipline, is limited by the culture at large in the possibilities its participants can envision, and in that sense tradition means the same thing between analyst and patient as it does between reader and text. The tradition that matters most in psychoanalysis, however, is that miniscule (relatively speaking) subset of invisible prejudices that analyst and patient create between them, the interpersonal field, what we might call the "being" of the analytic situation. It takes time (unless something dramatic and unfortunate occurs, usually only in the treatment of very disturbed patients) for analyst and patient to influence each other deeply and subtly enough to "have a relationship," to be in each other's presence in such a characteristic way that something can be said about it. The field must be created before it can be understood; it must be put together before it can be taken apart. Out of all the unformulated possibilities, two people come to a way of being together in which certain behaviors and experiences are allowed and others are prohibited, and in which the degree of recognition of, or enforced blindness to, various aspects of experience is prescribed. They make a history, complete with prejudices, and then they try to disconfirm them. And thus, Gadamer's scheme highlights the way in which, in psychoanalysis, prejudices are both one's blinders and the ground against which one is eventually able to discover a figure. This point has been recognized by those analysts who have seen that the analyst must regularly be able to play (and of course that means genuinely play, i.e., without awareness) a reciprocal role to the patient's transference—at least for a time—if the treatment is to be alive and helpful (e.g., Feiner, 1982; Jacobs, 1991; Levenson, 1972; Sandler, 1976; Racker, 1968; Searles, 1979; Tauber and Green, 1959).

Because it takes time to establish the pattern of what will be seen and what must not be seen—the distribution of light and darkness in the relationship—the analyst may be clearer about certain aspects of the patient's character in the first few sessions than he will be again until much later in the treatment. (This observation, the accuracy of which is unmistakable as soon as it is stated, was a personal communication from Earl Witenberg, reported by Bromberg, 1982.) At the beginning, analyst and patient have yet to establish their characteristic relatedness, and there is little reason for the analyst not to use all his observational powers. As time passes, however, he is caught in the grip of the interpersonal field constructed by the patient and himself, and it is only when the relevant issues can be analyzed that the analyst is again free to see. Of course, from the point of view of the radical critic, there is every reason to suspect that the same thing goes in the reverse direction as well. The patient, too, is probably freer to see the analyst at the beginning than when the pattern of prejudice is set in place.

If indeed we create a shared tradition and then discover it, coming to see the other person clearly in psychoanalysis is a more complex matter than understanding a text—more complex, too, than what Gadamer means by understanding the other in a conversation. The added complexity arises from the fact that in psychoanalysis, to see what the other means requires that one unveil the other's preconceptions of oneself, the preconceptions that interlock with one's own and contribute to maintaining one's blindness. As far as I know, Gadamer does not address this intriguing problem, which in fact might be expected to arise between any two people, not just participants in the analytic situation.

OPEN QUESTIONS, COMMITMENT, AND COUNTERTRANSFERENCE INVOLVEMENT

Prejudice is not necessarily inaccurate, only invisible. The questioning of prejudice may lead to disconfirmation, or it may lead to the conclusion that one's implicit assumption is in fact worthy of being consciously adopted. But prior to the decision regarding what to do with prejudice, there is that moment when one is suddenly capable of seeing it—and an alternative to it. It becomes possible to reflect on the prejudice one had been buried in until that moment, and one also sees the other's perspective. A comparison is available. The creation of such a comparison is what Gadamer calls finding an "open question." In an open question, a clear choice between alternatives appears, and answering the question therefore means learning something. Here is a brief illustration.

Recently, I wondered to myself whether the suddenness of a patient's decision to leave her job might have to do with a recent conflict with a supervisor (which she had discussed with me the week before), or whether, as in the patient's presentation of the issue, the new job itself was the sole motivating factor. I wondered whether the patient might have had more second thoughts if the conflict had not occurred. The new job paid better, but the old job carried more prestige. Notably, in discussing her decision with me, the patient did not mention the conflict with the supervisor at all. I brought up the question with the patient and, at least partly because my uncertainty about the answer was real, the patient accepted the question and was able to be curious about it. (She found it especially interesting that she had not even considered the problem with the supervisor.) In this case I formulated an open question in my own mind, and in conveying it to the patient, helped formulate the same open question in hers.

The questioner must mean the question if it is to be open; that is, the question may actually be an interpretation. For a question to be open, the one who asks must believe that both alternatives are possible, and this can only happen when the analytic work is going on right at the edge of what the participants know. The uncertainty must be genuine. So, for example, it would not have been an open question for me merely to have asked the patient whether there was anything more to the decision than met the eye. This question does not derive from genuine uncertainty, because it does not refer to a specific contrast between alternatives, only to the possibility of one. Genuine uncertainty for Gadamer requires particularity; one must know precisely what one is uncertain about.

Most open questions are not made explicit by questioners, not even to themselves. My example of the question asked by the analyst about the job change is cumbersome by comparison to the kinds of fleeting, subtle open questions that are more the rule. The kind of experience Gadamer refers to as an open question, as a matter of fact, is seldom actually spoken or even reflected upon. Gadamer means to describe a ubiquitous kind of experience, which is a precursor of every thought that qualifies as new. And here the process has been traced as far back toward its origins as it can be. This is the mystery at the heart of knowing. It cannot be said where open questions come from. And if we do notice them, they *appear*—we do not have the sensation of creating them.

Sometimes open questions are visible in hindsight. For instance, there was a particular moment I recall in the second or third hour I spent with a new patient when it occurred to me for the first time that this person spent very little time with friends and seemed not to care. How did this thought arise? The patient was referring to some upsetting news she had received the prior evening. She had been alone before, during, and after the event. I imagined her feeling lonely, but then I realized she was not conveying this feeling. Alternatives became available: perhaps she had the feeling, but was keeping it to herself; perhaps she was capable of the feeling, but was avoiding it (would it have made her too vulnerable in front of me, someone she did not yet really know?); or perhaps she characteristically did not experience loneliness. My expectation that she would have been lonely became visible to me at the same moment that I saw that she had not been. It took inquiry, of course, to establish which of the possibilities was most accurate, but the essential observation had emerged. The open question that preceded it can be reconstructed easily enough in this case. It would go something like, "Was the absence of companions painful to her, or did she feel no need for them?"

In what conditions do open questions arise? What can be done to encourage the perception of alternatives? (This, of course, is the radical critic's primary problem.) Gadamer says that any understanding requires commitment. "If there is any practical consequence of the present investigation," he says in the introduction to *Truth and Method* (1975)

> it certainly has nothing to do with an unscientific 'commitment' [that is, a commitment to some other system than science, such as the humanities]; instead it is concerned with the 'scientific' integrity of acknowledging the commitment involved in all understanding. My real concern was and is . . . not what we do or what we ought to do, but what happens to us over and above our wanting and doing [p. xvi].

Understanding requires commitment to a preconception, which means the willingness to give oneself over to a way of seeing. Before a prejudice can be known, before one can even know one has it—in fact, before it could even be said that a particular prejudice exists—

one must be committed to a way of understanding. And this commitment must be deep enough to be implicit (in Polanyi's, 1958, similar conception, *tacit*), so that in coming into awareness in language, it broadens one's horizon. What this means in psychoanalytic terms is that the analyst must be *involved* with the patient, willing to feel toward the patient as anyone else would, though of course not *only* as anyone else would (cf. Hoffman, 1994). It has long been taken for granted that the patient's emotional involvement in the analysis is crucial. But the shared tradition needed by the patient and analyst cannot be created without this same commitment from *both* participants. The analyst must be unafraid to commit himself to a whole-hearted experience of the countertransference. This point is hardly novel, but Gadamer's perspective offers us a new route of access to it.

THE FUSION OF HORIZONS: ANY UNDERSTANDING REFLECTS A CHANGE IN THE FIELD

Gadamer calls that moment in which a preconception and its alternative can be differentiated a "fusion of horizons." "Horizon," writes Weinsheimer (1985), paraphrasing Gadamer, "is another way of describing context. It includes everything of which one is not immediately aware and of which one must in fact remain unaware if there is to be a focus of attention; but one's horizon is also the context in terms of which the object of attention is understood" (p. 157). When horizons fuse, it is because the visibility of one's own preconceptions makes it possible to grasp the context in which the other's meaning exists. In seeing one's own expectations one falls into the other's. One simply finds oneself there, and a new experience is suddenly available; one has stepped into the configuration of prejudices the other occupies, the same distribution of light and darkness, the same relation of articulated possibility to unformulated being. This event is often described in psychoanalysis as empathy, though it is clear from Gadamer's stress on the analysis of preconceptions that he could not take such a view. At the same time, however, one can recognize in the fusion of horizons Gadamer's continuity with Schleiermacher. Although he may have rejected empathic knowing and reconstruction in favor of mediation, Gadamer must tackle the same problem. Somehow he must explain how one senses the context in which the other's statement is meaningful. The horizons fused are those of the person with the prejudice and the person who has provoked the possibility of alternative—for the present purpose, the analyst and the patient. And of course it happens in both directions. That is, analyst and patient at different times are each in the position of grasping preconceptions, as well as providing the conditions that makes the other's grasp possible. When the analysis is moving well, each is receptive to questions from the other, just as a reader, to understand, must not only put questions to the text, but must also allow himself to be questioned *by* the text. Gadamer's understanding of the hermeneutic task might double as a definition of the best moments of most analyses, at least those conducted by analysts for whom the equality of Gadamer's conversants does not represent a violation of the therapeutic situation. Prior to the following passage, Gadamer (1966) has just complained about the "leveling tendencies" of our industrial age, which influence language to become nothing more than a "technical sign-system."

> Yet in spite of (these leveling tendencies) the simultaneous building up of our own world in language still persists whenever we want to say something to each other. The result is the actual relationship of men to each other. Each one is at first a kind of linguistic circle, and these circles come into contact with each other, merging more and more. Language occurs once again, in vocabulary and grammar as always, and never without the inner infinity of the dialogue that is in progress between every speaker and his partner. That is the fundamental dimension of hermeneutics. Genuine speaking, which has something to say and hence does not give prearranged signals, but rather seeks words through which one reaches the other person, is the universal human task [p. 17].

Thus Gadamer implies that the process of understanding requires a successful interpersonal integration. Nothing can be grasped that the relationship between the parties does not allow. Here is another (1975) description of that integration. Once again, read it as if it applies to psychoanalysis.

> Coming to an understanding in conversation presupposes that the partners are ready for it and that they try to allow for the validity of what is alien and contrary to themselves. If this happens on a reciprocal basis and each of the partners, while holding to his ground simultaneously weighs the counter-

arguments, they can ultimately achieve a common language
and a common judgment in an imperceptible and non-arbi-
trary transfer of viewpoints. (We call this an exchange of
opinions.) [p. 303]

Of course, this kind of relatedness, while it may occur with some frequency in the interaction between a reader and a text, is the ideal in
psychoanalysis, one analysts are always glad to achieve but do not routinely expect. But in addition to drawing attention to this fact, these
passages carry a significant implication for psychoanalysis: *Any new
understanding is a crystallization of some aspect of the interpersonal field.*
That is, because understanding requires a genuine exchange, and
genuine exchange is precisely what is missing when patient and analyst are caught in the grip of the field, it follows that whenever some
new thought is available to either patient or analyst, a shift in the relationship must have occurred to allow it. This is true whether or not
the new thought is manifestly about the relationship. *Any* new
thought on the part of either analyst or patient is an occasion for the
analysis of transference and countertransference, because its very
existence means that the participants have stumbled into some kind
of freedom between them that was not there before. The successful
pursuit of psychoanalytic inquiry, no matter what the content under
discussion, is the same thing as expanding the possibilities of the
therapeutic relationship.

Along with the radical critic, one must conclude, on the basis of
Gadamer's view, that no analytic examination of the patient's history,
of a current relationship, or of anything else can occur outside the
influence of the field. Here the analyst finds himself on familiar
ground. There can be no such solitary entity as "the patient's past,"
for instance. It is not possible to tease out a person's history in the
abstract, "uncontaminated" by the context in which it becomes relevant. And neither can the interpersonal field be defined in a way that
separates it from anything that goes on in it. Every relationship
shapes the content that occurs in the conversations of its participants.
For "his past," one must substitute "his-past-in-our-present." But does
this mean that there is no reality outside ourselves to which we can
refer. Does anything go?

Definitely not, no more than in the work of Sullivan or any other
theorist whose work is inherently social, because Gadamer's criterion
of truth is consensual validation. Valid meaning is a construction
accepted by the community of interpreters, and it emerges in language—once again reminiscent of Sullivan. A meaning is not valid,

that is, unless it can be understood by someone else. For Gadamer, writes Linge (1976), as for the radical critic, "interpersonal communication . . . [is] the locus for the real determination of meaning" (p. xxxiii).

It is probably even more important to emphasize that, for Gadamer, this consensual validation is rooted in its capacity to represent reality. The world cannot simply be understood in any undisciplined way we feel like, because reality does exist. It is really there for Gadamer, though our routes of access to it are inevitably shaped and selected by history and culture. But as I have tried to say already, in Gadamer's thought, unlike much of postmodernism, our situatedness in history and culture is the key to the possibilities for understanding. Our embeddedness in our time and place is, if we use it creatively, our means of revelation, not merely a barrier to our knowing. It is our participation in the life of our cultures—whether in contentment or dissent—that underwrites our pursuit of the truth. Sass (1988) writes, in reference to Gadamer's perspective, "For, though it may be impossible to discover a single meaning, this does not mean that anything goes, that listeners can legitimately ascribe any meaning to any discourse. The hermeneutic approach is a sort of 'middle way' between objectivism and relativism" (p. 254).

THE PRIORITY OF PREJUDICE:
GADAMER AND HABERMAS

The hermeneuticists most cited in psychoanalytic literature are Ricoeur and Habermas, not Gadamer. And for good reason. Ricoeur (1970, 1977) published a book-length study of Freud's work and an influential essay, which appeared in a psychoanalytic journal, on the question of proof in Freud's writings. Habermas (1971, chapters 10–12) makes clinical psychoanalysis his model for what hermeneutics should be. For Gadamer, psychoanalysis is merely one variety of hermeneutic inquiry. Why, then, should the radical critic turn to Gadamer?

Answering this question requires a review of the debate between Gadamer and Habermas.[4] In Habermas's ideological analysis, Gadamer's acceptance of the value of tradition encourages a kind of conservatism. Habermas is concerned that when tradition is structured according to ideology oppressive to humankind, Gadamer's approach would never expose it, and would in fact capitulate to it, treating it as inescapable. Oppressive ideology, in other words, because for Gadamer it would be part of tradition or prejudice, would never be noted to *be* oppressive, but would be accepted—perhaps even honored—as part of the ground against which the figure of new understanding appears.

This problem with Gadamer's thought, says Habermas, is the result of Gadamer's belief that hermeneutics—that is, the act of inter- pretation—is primary, that it precludes preexisting objectivity. It is the result of Gadamer's position that we are always caught in tradition, that we are the product of our prejudices and our attempts to illumi- nate them. But Habermas argues that, if we agree on the primary and prehermeneutical value of emancipation, we *do* have a basis for objec- tivity. For if we can identify ways in which tradition acts to oppress us, we can change the conditions of our living. Therefore, objectivity comes before hermeneutics; an insistence on liberation, the objective "good," should shape our attempts to interpret and understand. Social science, to Habermas, is defined by its commitment to discover the invisible sources of oppression in the traditions we inherit. Social science is therefore based in objectivity, and psychoanalysis is the prime example. In this way, hermeneutics loses its primary status, and becomes instead the study of how the social sciences—which now become the primary discipline—make visible the restrictions on free- dom and equality that are embedded in our history.

Gadamer's reply to this argument is that we cannot legitimately exempt anything from examination, including our prejudices about freedom and equality. Why should we believe that such an exemption is not itself a prejudice in need of examination? Is Habermas not claiming that by believing in the absolute value of emancipation, and in our absolute ability to perceive it and to know how to accomplish it, we can transcend history and simply decide not to be involved in the event of understanding? Can we believe that it is possible to step outside history in this way? Can we *ever* conduct understanding with- out participating in it? The best way to ensure that we know as much as possible—about everything, oppressive ideology included—is not to make exceptions, but to attempt to bring into the light *all* our prej- udices. In this way, freedom and equality will ultimately be best served. For Gadamer, hermeneutic reflection devises the questions that are then directed to social science, not the other way around. We should not simply resist authority, as Gadamer believes Habermas encourages, but try to examine the prejudices that lead us to accept it. If we find that these prejudices are wrong, we should resist; but it is perfectly conceivable that they are acceptable and accurate in any particular case, and in that instance we have no reason to resist. It is hermeneutical reflection we must insist upon, not unreasoning resistance.

Yet we must grant that the explicit attention Habermas gives to the problems of power and oppression is welcome, and we must recognize that Gadamer's work falls short here. Gadamer's work, at least when it is applied to psychoanalysis, should be supplemented by the views of writers who, in the words of Jane Flax (1996, p. 577), attend to "the historical contingency, radical incompleteness, and intrinsic insufficiency" of the narratives through which we understand race, gender, and other constitutive aspects of our identities.

But when the problem of power is taken up in relation to Gadamer's work, as Philip Cushman (1995) has already started to do within psychoanalysis, it should not be taken up as the objective fact it is considered to be by Habermas. Conceptions of power do not have to preexist hermeneutic analysis to participate in shaping it.

Then how shall we bring our increasing awareness of these problems to bear on our clinical work? As far as I am concerned, the task is best accomplished in the same way I have described the patient and analyst dealing with unconscious resistance; that is, resistance is not dealt with as an objective fact, but as an aspect of subjectivity that has to be made phenomenologically appreciable (chapter 9). In an analogous way, patient and analyst need to converse about the likelihood of power relations until the presence of such influences becomes convincing to both analyst and patient, and until specific, contextually relevant shapes of power become clear and compelling. We need a phenomenology of power in psychoanalysis no less than a phenomenology of resistance. Once we are educated to the ubiquity of power relations, there is no reason that they cannot be approached hermeneutically, in dialogue.

There are unmistakable parallels between this dispute and the schism between the social and asocial paradigms of psychoanalysis, and it is probably now clear why the radical critic would side with Gadamer, agreeing that we cannot escape participation in the event of understanding—that we "cannot not interact" (Levenson, 1972). But it should also be pointed out that in the debate between Gadamer and Habermas the field of psychoanalysis is limited to the works of Freud, which means that a good deal of the argument ends up being irrelevant to the radical critic. If attention is restricted to Freud's asocial paradigm, there is no particular reason to challenge Habermas's argument. The conservative classical analyst, after all, does believe that interpretive schemes can be objectively applied to the patient's productions. The events to be understood occur inside the patient, separate from the analyst, so that the analyst does indeed stand outside the event of understanding. Far from being expectable, involvement with the patient (i.e., countertransference) outside the analyst's technically defined role is (at least more often than not) avoidable and problematic.

SCHAFER AND THE INTERPERSONAL FIELD

The prejudices between analyst and patient—the interpersonal field—is not where hermeneutic attention in psychoanalysis has been focused to date. The most extensive, sophisticated, and widely known writings on hermeneutics in clinical psychoanalysis, those by Roy Schafer (1983, 1988, 1992), focus on how hermeneutics aids analysts in their attempts to emancipate the patient from oppression by the internal, intrapsychically theorized unconscious. For Schafer (1983), a theory is an interpretation, not science: "it shapes the phenomena to be analyzed, and it selectively accentuates and organizes them" (p. 31). It is Schafer's theme that clinical conduct and understanding is inescapably theory-laden, and he encourages the comparative study of psychoanalytic theories as a means of deepening our appreciation of theory's role. He also accepts that comparative study can reach only so far, because "each analytic approach tends to be self-confirming, and its results cannot easily be compared to those obtained differently" (p. 31). But Schafer leaves unquestioned the assumption that competent analysts generally shape their work with patients according to a rational application of the theory they prefer. He leaves unexamined, in other words, the analyst's embeddedness in the field. Instead, for Schafer, the competent analyst can be trusted to make careful, (relatively) emotionally removed observations. The analyst's observations may be theory-laden, and we may need to choose our theories very carefully for that reason; but within the "self-confirming" realm of its own operation, each theory remains in this view a rationally applied mode of observation.

But our experience with our patients is laden with more than theory. I would argue that theory is not even the most significant of the factors that influence the analyst's understanding. After all, an analyst is already armed with theoretical commitments when he meets a patient for the first time. Though the particular way the theory is applied is a function of the analyst's unfolding experience with the patient, the theoretical commitments themselves are not developed in interaction. But consider personal prejudices: starting with the very first meeting, these begin to form and shape the experience analyst and patient have in one another's presence. At the outset, the effect of tailored personal prejudices is small; the field in these initial sessions is largely a reflection of the analyst's and patient's pasts, composed of one another's relatively global attributions about what "kind" of person the other is. Each participant has plenty of life experience to use in these early diagnostic assessments, and the analyst also has a theory. But these attributions, like the analyst's theoretical commitments, are not developed in interaction; they are imposed on the basis of preexisting points of view. As time passes, the influence on the field of the participants' initial diagnoses of one another declines, to be replaced by an intricately woven pattern of implicit personal prejudices. I have tried to say that it is prejudice that constitutes the field—the transference-countertransference—and that it is therefore prejudice that eventually must be analyzed. Of course, in this view, the analyst by this time is deeply involved, incapable of anything like the rational, emotionally detached application of a theory.

At some point along the way, some combination of the analyst's perspicacity, intuition, and prejudices begins to inform his theoretical grasp of the patient and the relationship; this changed use of theory then feeds back on the web of the analyst's prejudices, which influences the analyst to participate differently in the relationship. Eventually, theory and prejudice begin to bear a dialectical relation to one another in the analyst's mind. Each becomes so much the child of the other that it is difficult to know which was the original parent. Was it theory that shaped in its own image our eventual interpretation of the prejudice, or was it the unconscious influence of the prejudice that led us to think about the patient, ourselves, or the relationship in the terms of a particular bit of theory?

We usually cannot give neat answers to this question. But we can use this brief account to emphasize the dialectical nature of the process. The analyst's use of theory occurs within a social web that becomes so ubiquitous and immensely complex that it eventually weaves theory, too, into itself; in turn, theory continually plays a crucial role in shaping our perception of prejudice.

Schafer could not be called a radical critic, nor would he wish to be; accordingly, it should not be surprising that he approaches this problem in a way more consistent with Habermas than with

Gadamer. As a matter of fact, Schafer (1983, p. 234) cites Habermas as his primary hermeneutic influence.[5] Like Habermas, Schafer seems to accept that there are certain important ways in which the observer can remain separate from the observation. The analyst may be embedded in his theoretical commitment, but he is not necessarily embedded in the field. As a contrast to the view of the radical critic, consider one of Schafer's (1977) descriptions of transference, which conveys his confidence in the capacity of the well-functioning analyst to remain clear of unconscious entanglement in the field, and therefore to know the meaning (at least within the domain of the analyst's preferred theory) of the patient's experience and conduct. "The major transference phenomena represent the achievement of such simplified, focused ways of defining and acting within the analytic relationship that *there can be no mistaking their meanings or avoiding their emotional manifestations or implications*" (p. 124; my italics).

From the perspective of a radical critic armed with social constructionism, Schafer, while he alerts us to one half of the dialectic of theory and participation, never even considers the other, which lies in the web of personal prejudices. I must disagree with Schafer in this sense. But let me ignore for a moment the fact that Schafer does not structure the issue as a dialectic. In order to compare Schafer's position and my own, let us reformulate Schafer's as an emphasis on the theoretical pole of the dialectic and my own as an emphasis on the participatory one. If we put the issue this way, we must admit that neither position is simply right or wrong—though each position's advocates would certainly claim that their position better suits what we know. It is a matter of vantage point. A Gadamerian view encourages us to focus not only on the objects of understanding, but on the inevitable shaping influence of the dialogue itself, whereas Habermas encourages us to focus less on the dialogue and to step back to gain a more critical view of the things to be understood.

THE TRIPLE HERMENEUTIC

Gadamer's views are a particularly good way to deal with a related, knotty problem in the logic of social-scientific knowledge that has been noted by a number of philosophers (see Taylor, 1971). There are two parts to this problem. The first part, which applies to both social science (Taylor, 1971) and natural science (Kuhn, 1970, 1977), has to do with seeing theory as a cultural product. The argument goes that the understanding of science is "situated": it is a "language game" (Wittgenstein) or a "semantic field" (Taylor), which means that "the direction of research within a given field, the standards by which research hypotheses are confirmed and rejected, and the criteria for the relevance of data all refer to a normative framework of assumptions, conventions, and purposes" (Warnke, 1987, p. 109). The knowledge of science is therefore not objective, and it is certainly not free of values. On the contrary, in this view, as in Foucault's (1980), such knowledge actually represents the institutionalization of values. Schafer recognizes this point in his effort to establish a comparative psychoanalysis.

The second part of the argument, however, applies only to the social (or human) sciences. For these areas, it is not only fields of study that constitute language games. The subject matter itself—human living—is a language game. That is, the way we live every day—the common meanings our behavior and linguistic expressions have for us, the content of our everyday concepts, and all the rest of those taken-for-granted underpinnings that make life coherent and meaningful—requires its *own* hermeneutic exegesis. Just in order to *have* a subject matter, social sciences must assume this preexisting, socially constructed organization. We refer to this aspect of living by means of concepts such as as Mead's (1934) "generalized other," or Berger and Luckmann's (1967) "everyday life," which are socially constructed and yet experienced as inevitable and objectively real. Thus, any attempt to study human life inevitably requires what Anthony Giddens (1976) calls a "double hermeneutic," and any understanding in human science cannot be accomplished simply by applying a language to a content, but requires the convergence and mediation of *two different* languages.

The analyst comes to the analytic situation, then, with two hermeneutic tasks. Since each analytic pair's experience with one another is built from the same vocabulary of culturally defined elements available to us all, the analyst must grasp implicitly the common, everyday meanings of the interpersonal field; then the analyst must understand the way these meanings can be recombined in the realm of theory. This is the double hermeneutic. But soon another task arises, the one to which I have just drawn attention. Any interpersonal field is unique in its particular details, and it accrues more and more detail over time. As its particularity increases, to the first two tasks we must add the job of understanding the very particular selection of common meanings that have become habitual and invisible in the analytic situation. These are the very tiny and specific, socially constructed sets of organizing principles to which I have been referring as the interpersonal field. The field demands its own exegesis, an exegesis that requires, but is not accomplished by, a grasp of the social fabric the participants have in common. Any study of the events that take place in one particular relationship, then, requires something more of the researcher than the double hermeneutic refers to. Here we have a third level of the mediation of meaning, what Protter (1996), who makes the same point, calls a "triple hermeneutic." What this means for psychoanalysis is that, if we accept that any event in the treatment is embedded in the very particular set of prejudices that the analyst and patient have established in the field, then the act of understanding requires the convergence and mediation of not just two, but *three different* languages.

Because Gadamer believes understanding is consensus through dialogue, his work is particularly well suited to the conditions of the double hermeneutic. Consensus, after all, is defined as the understanding of what the other person means within the other's frame of reference—and that frame of reference, of course, is the everyday world. Think how much more necessary this kind of understanding becomes when the other's frame of reference is not just everyday life, but that tiny portion of it specific to a particular interpersonal field. Thus, Gadamer's work, essential when the hermeneutic is doubled, becomes even more crucial when it is tripled.

BUT WHAT SHOULD THE ANALYST ACTUALLY DO?

Gadamer does not offer a practical answer to what is, after all, the question of most import to psychoanalysts: How can prejudice be disconfirmed? How do we come to be able to ask open questions? To tackle these questions directly Gadamer would have had to contradict himself, because any answer he would give would amount to a recommended method. His final word on the matter is that we must develop and maintain what has been variously translated as "effective-historical consciousness," "consciousness of effective history," and "the consciousness in which history is ever at work." This unwieldy phrase simply means that one must remain receptive to the new and unfamiliar by being open to the effects of history (i.e., tradition) on one's understanding. History must be allowed to live in us, to direct our explicit awareness, to arrive at a knowledge of itself through our consciousness of prejudice. We must be a conduit for the conversion of being into language. I have tried to emphasize that in psychoanalysis the most crucial history to which we must be alive is the prejudices we develop in interaction with the patient.

That Gadamer offers nothing more concrete than this will be unsatisfying to anyone attached to the notion that psychoanalysis should be practiced according to a specifiable technique. It may seem that Gadamer's view encourages nihilism, or perhaps laziness, since there is no way to search out the truth. It may even seem to imply that psychoanalytic education is unnecessary. Why don't we just "converse?" But Gadamer's view does nothing to weaken the case for analytic discipline and education, because to adopt this perspective means placing great stress on the necessity for the analyst to question himself about whatever he takes for granted, to find a way into "seeing what is questionable" (Gadamer, 1966, p. 13). And seeing what is questionable requires a consistency of self-reflection that would be next to impossible without careful supervision and a training analysis that touches the analyst in the way he hopes his patients will be touched. To understand someone else requires innocence and openness, which are not only gifts, but accomplishments of education and experience.

To work from the view of understanding that Gadamer and the radical critic have in common, the analyst faces a high degree of uncertainty. All he can do is try to identify good questions (Levenson, 1988; Stern, 1992b), never being sure he is successfully pursuing even that limited aim. Whatever its difficulties, though, the perspective an analyst finds in the work of Gadamer will be familiar to the many analysts who already believe that in clinical practice one has no choice but to become part of something beyond one's ken, to be inhabited by the unbidden, to surrender to the mystery by which we formulate what we know. Gadamer's critique of method would suit Masud Khan (1969), for instance, in whose oft-quoted words, "We are all the servants of the patient's process" (p. xxxi). Levenson (1982), who cites the same remark of Khan's, also comes to mind: "some process is going on that they [patient and therapist] have not initiated or energized. There is the remarkable experience of being carried along by something larger than both therapist and patient: A true sense of an interpersonal field results. The therapist learns to ride the process rather than to carry the patient" (p. 13).

12

Courting Surprise

Unbidden Perceptions in Clinical Practice

The combination of unformulated experience, the social paradigm of psychoanalysis, and Gadamer's hermeneutics no doubt has nearly as many clinical ramifications as there are psychoanalysts to imagine them. I have imagined some of my own, a few of which have already come up in passing here and there throughout this book. This chapter, however, is devoted exclusively to them.

It is fitting here, in the last chapter, to return to the problem of the given and the made, the issue that defined the first one. All the clinical effects of unformulated experience and Gadamer's hermeneutics have something to do with this dialectic. On the one hand, we believe that, on the basis of our histories and our current interpersonal circumstances, we construct our own experience; on the other, we recognize (and frequently feel, in the most experience-near sort of way) that we do not create our experience at all, but receive it, that our experience simply arrives. We experience ourselves as constructors, makers or builders of our own experience, but also as constructed. When we experience ourselves as constructed, we have no sense of participating in the shape our experience takes. In fact, the more fully an experience is our own—the more it comes from what we like to call "deep down within us"—the more it usually feels, oddly enough, as if it comes from elsewhere.

But no matter how well we learn the lesson that we generate our experience, and no matter how clinically useful it is to us to see, as analysts and as analysands, how deeply involved we are in shaping what we experience, we never shake the impression of being mere recorders. However deeply we may feel what we experience, and however passionate our commitments may be, spontaneous thoughts, images, or feelings are unexpected. They seem to come to us; despite the fact that our formulations are our own, we feel like conduits; our articulations of unformulated experience are unbidden.

Patient and analyst work with unbidden perceptions routinely. Most significant perceptions of others—of ourselves, too—arise without conscious intention. They come from elsewhere, unbidden as symptoms or dreams. They are events that fall outside expectation, though seldom startling and not infrequent. Often they are the outcome of many small and half-noticed perceptions, the accretion of which, if it is noted at all, is seen only in retrospect. Because the experience occurs spontaneously—that is, because it is not constructed in a consciously calculated sort of way—it is inevitably authentic. It may be a distorted or ambiguous expression of whatever truth it contains, but it cannot be simply wrong. An unbidden thought can be no more wrong than a dream. The problem is to discover how it is right. How does the thought embody a real observation? (Fromm, 1951; Levenson, 1981; Tauber, 1954; Tauber and Green, 1959). Once such a thought—perhaps merely an inclination to think, a proto-thought—has arrived, conscious, willful effort is usually essential in evaluating it, honing it, and developing its ramifications. But the original, to be a real contribution, must arise from an intention so much of a piece with living that it is outside the bounds of reflection or control. As novelist John Fowles puts it, "a genuinely created world must be independent of its creator" (cited by Dworkin, 1985, p. 157). Authentic perceptions are not uncovered or figured out. The experience of the perception is that one simply *knows* something or sees something—something about how the other experiences the world, about how the other feels, about one's own experience of the other, and so on. This reactive experience is the most common method of interpersonal perception, unpurposeful and prelogical in nature (Tauber and Green, 1959). Though psychoanalysts may sometimes learn about patients in more consciously designed ways (e.g., conscious extrapolation from theory or developmental expectations), the great proportion of analytic observations, and all the most significant ones, are of the common human variety.

Take something as simple as suddenly knowing that the patient is sad. Seldom does this occur solely as the result of seeing the patient's tears and making an inference. When it does happen that way, the observation is liable to feel forced and unnatural, intellectualized. It feels like a lack of contact; patient and analyst are out of touch. The more usual course is that one simply finds oneself in possession of the information, along with some kind of responsive feeling. How the information has come into one's possession is seldom considered. And if the observation were then mentioned to the patient, and the patient were to deny it, one would not simply conclude that an error had been made. Rather, and again without having to wrangle over the decision, it would be natural to try to discover alternative ways in which the perception might be meaningful. Perhaps the perception represents a sense of something nascent or dissociated in the patient's experience. Or perhaps sadness is a common human expectation under the circumstances, in which case it is significant that the patient did not feel it. Or perhaps the analyst concludes the observation is just "wrong." Even in this last case, though, the analyst is unlikely to conclude that the mistake is meaningless. Instead, the experience is treated as if it were a dream, an indirect representation.

When a perception arrives unbidden, one seldom questions its veracity. One assumes there is truth in it; it is just not immediately clear what that truth is. Misperception of the patient is not based on putting too much faith in one's unbidden perceptions. That faith is justified. The failure lies in assuming that the truth in the unbidden perception is there at face value.

If the most important of the analyst's gleanings in the consulting room are unbidden, are strenuous efforts to understand misplaced? Should analysts resign themselves to a role as conduits for the wiser perceptions of their unconscious selves? Obviously not. Just because the experience of being a conduit sometimes accompanies the feeling of being deeply involved does not mean involvement can be artifically re-created by playing the part, clearing one's mind and waiting for inspiration to strike. This would not be what Freud (1912) meant by evenly suspended attention; it would be what Primo Levi (1989, p. 173) calls "lazy abandonment to the flow of the unconscious," or what Patricia Hampl (1989) refers to as "the lax habits of the free imagination."

It is easy to agree on this point. But it is not immediately apparent what the meaning of curiosity is in a world in which we have no means of getting exactly what we want from ourselves. Isn't the essence of curiosity the search within oneself for whatever one needs to know? How can that be so if there is no choice but to wait for our most salient thoughts to float into view? How can we look for that which must surprise us?

The fallacy here is the suggestion that unbidden learning is passive learning, that there is no way to influence what arrives in one's mind without conscious intention. Put this way, controversy again evaporates: though one cannot orchestrate one's own dreams, no one else is responsible for them. To accept the centrality of unbidden observations takes nothing away from the significance of precision, rigor, and curiosity in psychoanalytic inquiry. As a matter of fact, as I will argue in a later section of this chapter, holding the conviction that learning occurs in this way requires giving these attributes of our work even more emphasis than they already receive.

But before I can consider that point, the logic of unbidden learning must be established. How can it be that there is only an indirect relationship between the analyst's efforts and what is eventually understood? And for that matter, what is the evidence that most important understanding occurs in this way?

The answer to the latter question is simpler than it might seem. For in a careful analytic inquiry, what is learned must come unbidden. If it did not, if the analyst knew beforehand what could be expected as a result of questions and interpretations and the patient's responses to them, the work would be stale and intellectualized. Everyone is familiar with sessions like that. They are unsatisfying at best, often dispiriting, usually a reflection of some poorly comprehended aspect of the interpersonal field. When inquiry is more successful, it is because the question is clear and the answer is not. There is no way to know what will come next. This attitude is reflected in the way clinicians talk to one another, or put together a case report. When describing how a new thought about the patient or the field arose, for instance, an analyst is unlikely to say, "I figured out that . . ." or, "I reasoned that. . . ." Instead the passive voice tends to be used, indicating that one has *received* these thoughts, that one lacks a clear feeling of agency. One says, "It occurred to me that . . ." or, "It struck me that. . . ." Even when the manner of expression is more consistent with awareness of personal agency, such as, "I saw that . . ." or, "It seemed to me that . . . ," upon closer inspection it very often turns out that the sequence of cognitive events that led up to the observation cannot be recreated. It is sometimes possible to do so after the fact, and at times, in order to clarify the origin of a conclusion or speculation, the analyst makes a point of telling the patient as much of the thought process as can be recaptured. But this is the exception, not the rule. Most of the time the whole process takes place unnoticed. It is so natural for clinicians to practice this way—it is so natural for *all* humans to go about their living in this way—that little or no attention is paid to how seldom what one sets out to discover is what one ends up learning.

And yet there is no particular distinction in merely not knowing what will happen next. By itself, this is simply lack of discipline, Levi's lazy abandon. On the other side of the coin, it would be absurd to discount the necessity for consciously designed effort from patient and analyst, as if psychoanalysis, like an adolescent's notion of true love, were only genuine when it comes like a bolt out of the blue. Thus, there still needs to be a conceptual link drawn between the analyst's efforts in the inquiry—that is, expertise—and the eventually productive outcome. How does the inquiry result in observations that could not have been suspected?

Ernest Schachtel's answer to this question would probably be that the truth, unexpected or not, appears as soon as inquiry reveals one's incapacity and unwillingness to perceive the unfamiliar. For Schachtel (1959), truth is the spontaneous apprehension of the world as it really is, stripped of prior interpretations. One opens oneself to this truth through acts of existential courage, blazing a path beyond the socially sanctioned forms of "an already labelled world." Schachtel refers to the attitude within which such openness is possible as "allocentricity." In the allocentric attitude, one has no particular use or purpose for the other, and is therefore free to see him as he is.

Although Schachtel was one of the first to see that experience is not a given, but a construction, he believed, in accordance with the existential tradition to which he belonged, that the constructed aspects of experience were false, obscuring a truth that would otherwise be obvious. Allocentricity is a kind of innocence, more characteristic of what Schachtel understood as the pristine (though by no means sweet) perceptions of childhood than of the "closed world" of adulthood. Both Schachtel and Fromm would probably have looked fondly on unbidden experience as eruptions of truth through the veil of Marxist "false consciousness."

Today these views are less compelling, primarily because of the fundamental developments in our understanding of the nature of language that were discussed in chapter 1. Even in childhood, experience is an interpretation. There never was a raw form. All reflective experience can be constructed only according to the possibilities and limitations of language. There is no experience possible outside this range. Humans live within the world language encompasses, and it is meaningless, a misuse of language actually, to make reference to meaning beyond this boundary. As a result, the Marxist and existential call to throw off our shackles and accept the burden of freedom cannot be heeded with the same fervor and simplicity. It is not that the struggle for liberation means any less; rather, freedom now seems relative, and it is a more complicated task to reach what can be had of it. The radical choice and risk that were the core of the existential project are harder to believe in. No one can be rid of the assumed roles and received categories of thought that both Fromm (e.g., 1941, 1947) and Schachtel tried to see past. These same categories of thought, because they are embedded in language itself, become the very objects of study. Truth in this view is not understood as a correspondence between one's belief and an entity or principle with an independent existence in the external world. New truths cannot be approached directly, but only by exposing limitations in the understandings we already have.

Thus, contrary to what has been until recently the accepted view, the analyst's observational powers in the consulting room cannot be so simply directed at an unknown presumed to have been already present "in" the patient, independent of any structure contributed by the analyst. Because it cannot be assumed that there is a single truth, it cannot even be claimed that the patient could see it if his eyes were not blinkered by convention. What the patient does not yet know should no longer be portrayed only as substantive unconscious content, but instead also must be understood as unformulated, partially indeterminate, and actually absent. Its possibilities are the possibilities of language, and its formulation is an event that will be participated in by both patient and analyst. The unconscious should be conceived as something more than a container. It is more consistent with current practice to say, in line with Heidegger and those who followed him, that for something to be unconscious is for it to be so much *present* that we live in it instead of seeing it. To describe something as unconscious is to say that it is outside the range of explicit reflection.

In modern hermeneutic views of understanding, interest is directed at what is already known, with the intention of stating explicitly the implicit assumptions underlying its construction. Once these assumptions have been specified, gaps in the material become evident, and phenomena that have fallen through the cracks of the implicit interpretive scheme may become visible. The analyst pursues an awareness of absence by focusing the most detailed attention on what is present. The emphasis shifts from imposing yet another interpretation to specifying the schemes according to which the material has already been interpreted. Levenson (1988) presents such a view, concluding that, "the real task in therapy is not so much making sense of the data as it is, but resisting the temptation to make sense of the data!" (p. 5). Elsewhere, describing what he believes is the algorithm of psychotherapy, Levenson (1982) has this to say: "the therapist listens to the patient's story, gets a background, looks for what are essentially the lacunae—the holes in the Swiss cheese, the gaps in the continuity and coherence of the patient's life story" (p. 9). No less, as Levenson indicates later in the same paper, the analyst looks for lacunae in the continuity and coherence of the story of the treatment itself. The vital question here is how analysts come to an awareness of these gaps.

BETWEEN EXPERIENCE AND EXPECTATION

How do unbidden perceptions come about? It will be useful to approach this question from the other direction, with an examination of the circumstances in which experience is *not* known—in which the possibility of lacunae has not even become relevant yet. In this situation, experience disappears as fast as it takes place. There is no memory. Nothing can be reflected on because, at least in memory, nothing happened. There is only a present. These are the circumstances within which we live most of the time, as Schachtel saw. But it is a rare event to tune out completely, to remember nothing afterward, as in a fugue state. Rather, one is aware of experience of one kind, one is capable reflecting on it, while experience of a different kind just keeps going past, unnoted. For instance, most analysts would probably agree that they are involved in unseen patterns of interaction with the patient even during the moments when they are making progress on sorting out something else. Let us say, for example, that the analyst is laying out the details of the patient's relationship with Aunt Agatha in precisely the interactive style of this important person. (This is an instance of Levenson's 1983 dictum that what patient and analyst talk about and how they talk about it are "isomorphic transformations" of the same content.) And then, as the analyst eventually clarifies with the patient how the two of them are playing the Aunt Agatha scenario, perhaps something else remains unformulated—for instance, how the analyst may now be replicating the way the patient's mother, reacting to feeling deprived by Aunt Agatha, bitterly criticized the aunt, leaving the patient feeling disloyal whether she protested or assented. At this point, the analyst notices that the patient is suddenly in what seems to be low spirits, and he is mystified. What the analyst cannot see, of course, and probably the patient, too, cannot yet see, is that the patient is reacting to finding herself in the no-win situation he is presenting her with. Eventually this interaction, too, is untangled. Maybe it becomes clear, for instance, that the analyst was more proud than he realized about having been able to see himself playing the Aunt Agatha role, and the patient, reacting to this pressure to accept the new clarification, felt resentful but helpless, not being any more willing to hurt the analyst's feelings than her mother's. But as quickly as this is discovered, something else needs to be understood.

It is even simpler to say the same thing about content not explicitly concerned with the transference. That is, becoming able to reflect on one aspect of living does not necessarily raise the likelihood of being able to reflect upon another.

What happens, then, when experience does not register? What was going on when the analyst was acting out Aunt Agatha's part of the interaction? Why is it that the analyst often doesn't see what he is doing, even though he is sitting there with the express purpose of understanding?

At these times experience and expectation are indistinguishable. When nothing is learned, when things just happen, when experience passes by without being noted, it is because there is no space between what is (unconsciously) anticipated and what is (consciously) experienced. There is no gap between them. As long as that is so, experience disappears as fast as it takes place. It is invisible, not because it makes no impression on one's mind, but because the impression it makes coincides exactly with expectations one does not even know one has. One cannot spell it out because one has no reason to. It is taken for granted. There is no memory of it because whatever did happen had happened before in such a way that events will now be noticed only if they deviate. Generally, as Schachtel, and Bartlett (1932) before him, taught, the mere existence of expectations tends to preserve the status quo. Paradoxically, though the perception of deviations from expectation is the source of new experience, such perceptions are unlikely precisely to the extent that expectations have gelled. Once in place, anticipations influence the future to conform to their shape. We see what we expect to see—and we actually construct, too, what we expect to see. In interpersonal terms, this means that transference is not only an experience and a set of perceptions, but an influence that is quite often effective in provoking the anticipated response from the analyst. Even when the provocation is not so devastating in its effect that every observer would agree on its impact, the events of the analytic interaction, being as ambiguous as any other social intercourse, can usually be plausibly understood in this way (Gill, 1982; Hoffman, 1983; Levenson, 1972, 1983). Patient and analyst create expectations in interaction with each other, and responses to these expectations, and it is then the most significant task of the analysis to discover them.

Learning, in the form of an unbidden perception, is what happens when a space appears between experience and expectation. This is true, separately, for analyst and patient. New experience does not arise *de novo*—it emerges from what has come before, it becomes visible as a contrast to what is already known, against the background of the familiar. Gadamer (1966), for whom this is central, says it succinctly: "Only the support of familiar and common understanding makes possible the venture into the alien, the lifting up of something out of the alien, and thus the broadening and enrichment of our own experience of the world" (p. 15). It is from this vast fund of familiar and common understanding that unconscious expectations are drawn, and it is the articulation of these unformulated expectations that makes it possible to broaden and enrich our experience of the world. Learning is impossible precisely to the extent that expectations cannot be brought into language.

The identification and explicit description of expectations is the major task of the analysis. Analyst and patient find their way to speaking the familiar, and then they find, in what has been spoken, other gaps that can be worded, so that the description of experience moves always toward a greater degree of precision and subtlety. New experience emerges naturally and inevitably in the form of alternatives to the familiar.

CLINICAL ILLUSTRATION

The process of making expectations visible is not routinely difficult. The usual instances are the everyday bits of learning that go on between any two people, such as the earlier illustration of the sad patient. In that example, the expectation did not have to remain unformulated. To detail that very simple interaction will sound awkward and artificial, but with that proviso, perhaps the sequence went something like this: The analyst entered the moment with an expectation born of what had just happened. He simply expected, without conscious consideration, that the patient would feel as he had a moment before. There was no reason to expect otherwise. Suddenly the analyst saw tears, and the patient's tone of voice lowered and softened. His expression changed. Without explicit recognition of the event, the analyst now eased into a position in which his expectation was no longer valid. Immediately and naturally, the current expectation was as much taken for granted as the old one had been a moment before.

In this instance there was no interference in the analyst's awareness of his expectation; that is, neither the analyst nor the patient had any reason to object to the analyst knowing it. The expectation could be disconfirmed and discarded quite automatically. The patient had not been feeling anything obvious; suddenly he was. Seldom would one be directly aware of a preconception of this kind. It isn't necessary. Explicit reflection would quite often be a cumbersome intrusion into otherwise smoothly flowing experience. The important thing is whether one *could* be aware. Is the expectation knowable? Could it be seen if one had a reason to see it? This is the primary differentiation between those expectations which are problematic and those which are not.

Everyday examples of successful understanding do not draw clinical attention, though. Accounting for these events is primarily an epistemological problem, more properly the business of philosophers than psychoanalysts. Analysts are most interested in the pathology of understanding, especially those instances in which the analyst and the patient cannot see their expectations of one another, as in the following example.

A professional woman in her late 20s sought treatment because of depression over the death of an elderly relative, but it was soon clear that she had been depressed much of her life. We began psychoanalytic work. During the first several months of the treatment, as I got to know her and she got to know me, she relaxed—or so I thought—and a delightful, playful, mildly flirtatious kind of interaction began, and then became more frequent. I noted it, but did not try to say anything about it. It was a delicate and intimate way of relating, and I feared that I could not call attention to it without being clumsy, and that talking about it, at least at this point, could only be experienced by the patient as humiliating and rejecting. Perhaps, I thought, it was the kind of relatedness she needed in order to establish a reliable therapeutic situation with me. (This, incidentally, was not necessarily wrong, despite the later events I shall describe.) I felt I was participating in something that would eventually become clear—or perhaps it would not. Most of the time I was not aware enough of it for it to matter. I do recall having a suspicion from time to time that perhaps there *was* some reason to address the subject, a reason I ought to be able to think of and could not. I think this had less to do with an understanding of the field, though, than it did with a worry that I really should hold myself in check, since I was responding in kind without having thought through why.

In describing the interaction to this point, I may be making it sound as if my behavior was the result of conscious decision more often than was the case. It is true that I reflected on the interaction enough to gain the impression that there was nothing actively destructive about it. That much most analysts are able to do most of the time, even when they are caught in the grip of the field. The interaction was also in my focal awareness at those few moments during which I have described feeling a bit suspicious of my compliance—but even then, I did not see what I later learned was most relevant. Other than these partial exceptions, though, and a general attitude of tolerance about it, this aspect of what transpired between us became part of the unformulated background of the sessions, the medium within which we spent the hours. The experience was inattended. I was not curious about it at that time, for I was embedded in it, living it, taking it for granted. The work went on more or less unremarkably about one thing and another, including the patient's fear that I was critical of her and dissatisfied with her, just as she felt her highly accomplished, self-involved, and emotionally distant father was. The patient was well aware that she wanted to appeal to me, and on the one or two occasions when I was able to gently draw attention to the bantering between us, she said that indeed she derived some reassurance from this kind of interaction. It was also clear to her, as I had suspected, that she would be hurt if I did not respond in kind.

For my own part, I looked forward to the patient's hours. I felt helpful and appreciated. The inquiry seemed to be moving along smoothly. I assumed that eventually, after learning enough to make it safe to do so, we would be able to address the bantering more directly and thoroughly. In fact, at that time I am sure I would have guessed, if I had been asked to consider the question explicitly, that the patient probably even shared this prediction about the future course of the treatment.

Then, in the midst of such gentleness and good humor, the patient began to face me with complaints. She wondered whether she should have seen someone more "serious," perhaps someone who insisted on interrupting her playfulness. She was having too good a time. *I* was having too good a time. There was not enough going on in the treatment. Things should have been more solemn. Even if she initiated the interactions, she said, I should have refused to respond to them.

My first reaction was to feel that it was obvious that she was right. How could I have gone along with this? I was chagrined and somewhat guilty, feeling that my behavior had not been appropriate. And yet I could not see clearly how to handle the situation. The inconsistency between the patient's current attitude and her previous conviction that she wished me to respond to her playfully, that in fact she felt she needed such reassurance, did not occur to me yet. Whether or not I knew the very best thing to do, though, I decided that at the least I had to rein myself in.

This decision about my conduct was based upon the guilty application of a rule: Do not respond reciprocally to the transference. I do not even believe one can realistically adhere to this dictum. That is, my decision was (for me) not a sensible one, but a fallback position born of the wish to be a good and useful analyst. It may have relieved me of anxiety about the patient's sudden lack of appreciation of me, but it was not based upon an understanding of my part in the interpersonal situation. In retrospect, it is therefore not particularly surprising that it failed. I was merely continuing my participation in another guise, though of course this was completely beyond me at the time. To my horror, and despite my best intentions, I kept making slyly humorous remarks. These were inhibited and subtle enough to allow them to pass my lips before I really noted what I was doing, but were unmistakably playful—especially in the newly sensitive ambiance of our sessions. The patient did not miss my gaffes, either, and let me know that her unhappiness with me was mounting. I began to learn that she felt not only that I was not serious enough, but that I was not taking *her* seriously enough. I also saw that sometimes I had begun to initiate these playful sequences myself, not waiting for the patient, and that, in fact, I had been participating in this way for some time now. For instance, I might say, on seeing her, with a grin and an exaggerated sweep of the arm, "Well, come on in!" Or she might say she had had a bad day, with a shake of her head and humorous overdone woe, and I would say—in tune with the tone of her remark, but with more expressiveness than was really necessary—"A real lulu, huh?" The patient felt this conveyed that I was altogether too ready to have a nice time discussing events that were essentially miserable for her. Another time she was describing a frightening incident with a psychotic cabdriver. She told me how menacing he was. "He was so *big*," she said, wide-eyed. As was often the case, there was in her tone a kind of innocent wonder that usually struck me as intentionally cute, though not objectionable. I think—

again in retrospect—that I enjoyed it. In this instance I responded by saying, in the same tone, "And you're so *little!*" Now, this was not completely out of tune. It did convey an understanding of her feelings. But it is not the way I generally talk to patients. In fact, it is not the way two adults usually converse about a matter of gravity. It certainly is not what one would call sober. And, to her, it was therefore one more piece of evidence that I did not take her seriously.

However, I did not agree with the patient that my behavior *had* to mean that I was taking her lightly. Why did these *bon mots* of mine have to be interpreted in only this one way? I felt quite sure that I *did* take her seriously, no less seriously than I took any other patient.

As it turned out, this was wrong and she was right. On a Friday night, after emitting one of these distressing remarks in a session with the patient, I consulted a colleague whose judgment I respect. I told her the story with the aim of understanding how I could help the patient to look into the problem. My colleague's unexpected response, though, was, "Has it occurred to you that she might have a point?" That was enough to turn my perception of the situation on its head. Quite suddenly I saw that in a very important sense I was *not* taking the patient seriously, just as she said. The truth of this was underscored by the fact that I had seen the point immediately when my respected colleague had said it, but had not been able to accept the same thing from the patient. Over that weekend something else occurred to me, and it helped explain what I was doing. I saw that I had come to enjoy the patient's response to my humor, even to look forward to it. This was largely why I had enjoyed the patient's sessions so much. When she had begun to complain, I had felt deprived, a little betrayed, as if the rug had been pulled out from under me. It had felt a bit like being lured into a trap. Everything had been going so swimmingly, so pleasantly! She had been so appreciative!

There was no question that I now saw something I had not seen before about the grip of the field on us both. Since I had to explain the change in my views to the patient, I elected in the next session to lay out everything I had learned about how we had both participated in the establishment and maintenance of the problematic interaction. The patient, sensing my conviction, was greatly relieved. I had no doubt that I would now be able to change the nature of my participation, and in fact I did. It would now have been uncomfortable *not* to have participated differently (see also the clinical illustration at the end of chapter 10).

It was possible, too, for the patient to participate differently. Perhaps it was even as necessary for her as it had become for me. In short order, she and I discovered that indeed she did encourage me to continue bantering with her, that she had developed with her father the capacity to be the unusually gratifying audience I had found her to be, but that she had done so only out of a sense that this was her sole possibility. She could not be taken seriously by the men she wanted, and I, like her father, was one of that kind. Her bid for my attention had therefore been accompanied by resentment, and her expressions of delight and appreciation had been humiliating. Yet she had been no freer to present herself seriously than I had been to take her that way.

I had been operating on the implicit assumption that my claim to take the patient seriously was based on all the relevant data. I had been assuming (also implicitly) that I maintained this attitude only because it was true and reasonable, and that I disagreed with the patient only because her take on the situation was wrong. It might be said, then, that these assumptions constituted the unseen expectation. The problem with that interpretation is that it can be made in retrospect about any bind that analyst and patient work their way out of. The analyst (and the patient) always assume, incorrectly and without reflecting on it explicitly, that they are taking advantage of all relevant data. The unseen expectation needs to be stated more specifically in terms of the unformulated images the participants had of one another, such as the following: Like the father, I was treating the patient (to a degree) as if she were there to appreciate me, to be delighted by me. I was assuming, it turns out, that there was no good reason why she should object to being my audience. She, on the other side of this, was assuming that I was so self-involved that the only way she could make contact with me was by playing up her delight in me and encouraging me to behave in precisely the way she complained about. When these assumptions became visible—that is, once she and I gained the capability to see that we *had* expectations of one another—a series of new experiences occurred.

HERMENEUTICS AND THE INEVITABILITY
OF EMBEDDEDNESS

Many psychoanalysts have come to accept the inevitability of enactment, and some of us, especially those who conceive psychoanalysis to be rooted in a ceaselessly evolving interpersonal field, believe they are continuous. A hermeneutic perspective, however, adds something new to our understanding of the ubiquity of enactments. From a hermeneutic point of view, because *all* explicit understanding in life arises from a prior embeddedness in preconceptions or prejudice, the process by which patient and analyst work their way out of enactments is not an anomaly that happens only in powerful transference-countertransference fields, but is actually a phenomenon that exemplifies the very epitome of what it is to understand anything at all. That is, the way we disembed ourselves in the successful analysis of transference and countertransference is a paradigm for the way we grasp the world.

THE PROBLEM OF CURIOSITY:
SEEING WHAT IS QUESTIONABLE

In this particular clinical example I could point to the event—the consultation with my colleague—that allowed me to identify my expectation and formulate an alternative. Ongoing peer supervision is vital for analysts who believe they have no choice but to be embedded, since colleagues seldom have the same reasons to be buried in the interaction and may therefore be able to occupy that uninvolved position which the analyst simply cannot locate.[1]

But not always is it even clear which details to tell one's consultant, nor are colleagues always able to see the problem as clearly as mine did. And of course, even if the analyst knows what to describe, it is unfeasible to consult someone else every time it might be helpful to do so. Most of the time analysts fly solo, relying upon the desire to know, a desire that everything I have said to this point leads me to believe is only dubiously reliable. And thus, the problem of curiosity reappears. For if we have no means of getting exactly what we want from ourselves, if we must doubt that the truth even exists prior to the wish to know it, how does it make sense to think of curiosity?

To be curious is to be determined to know what is already there—what one is already aware of being confronted with—in the most detailed and complete way possible. It is receptivity to questions about matters that on the face of it may already seem fully understood. Curiosity means being in the process of differentiating whatever perceptions one has already identified; the unbidden emerges from that which has been meticulously described. The more fine-grained the grasp of what is already visible, the smaller the unexplained blip that can be noticed passing across it. When the analyst questions what he thinks he already knows about the patient, and about his reactions to the patient, uncertainty is preserved. It becomes harder to feel convinced of any single answer. These conditions constitute the climate in which unbidden perceptions flourish. In trying to create them, the analyst is doing what is possible to court surprise.

Sullivan probably would have believed it was not only unnecessary, but undesirable, to depend on perceptions arising outside volition. At the same time, though, he was very interested in meticulous description. He was committed to the idea that the treatment should assume the shape of a detailed inquiry. His method amounts to a continuous, long-term effort to drive a wedge between experience and expectation.[2] This way of conducting treatment depends less than classical technique on interpretation and more on finding good questions. The analyst seldom thinks he has an answer to offer. Previous understandings are continually subjected to study and review. Sullivan's (1954) procedure is today as easy to state, and as difficult to practice, as it was when he described it. Good questions are still harder to come by than good answers.

> [T]he psychiatrist listens to all statements with a certain critical interest, asking, "Could that mean anything except what first occurs to me?" He questions (at least to himself) much of what he hears, not on the assumption that the patient is a liar, or doesn't know how to express himself, or anything like that, but always with the simple query in mind, "Now, could this mean something that would not immediately occur to me? Do I know what he means by that?" [p. 19].

Curiosity is the imagination and discipline that lead to seeing what is questionable. To be curious is to be sensitive to the possibility of a question. It is the constant suspicion that one's own capacity for thought is woefully inadequate in ways that will eventually become painfully clear. It is a respect for particularity, a respect that for some attains the dimensions of love, or even reverence. For Mies van der Rohe, "God is in the details." Vladimir Nabokov admonishes writers to "Caress the detail, the divine detail."[3] Patricia Hampl (1989) comments:

> If, as Nabokov says, the detail is divine, there's nothing much to do but give yourself over to it as one properly does in worship. If there's any question about the divinity of detail, by

the way, think of that one thing that you can explain to no one but which is precious beyond expression. That is a divine detail. It is also a literary opportunity [p. 38].

Need it be added that it is an analytic opportunity as well?

When a guiding intelligence accumulates details, the result is clarity; thus clarity is the result of curiosity. But clarity and curiosity bear a reciprocal relation to one another, so that curiosity is also the result of clarity. To the extent that one cannot cite particulars about something—an event, a person, an interaction—one does not know how to be curious about that thing. Not knowing how to be curious, though, is not worthy of condemnation, at least not when it occurs, as it so frequently does, in the experience of someone who is dedicated to understanding. Often the closest one can come to being curious is wanting to be, or being puzzled about why one cannot be. The state of being unable to see what is questionable is a way station on the path to an open question. To be unclear can be as much an opportunity as a liability. Primo Levi (1989) tells us,

> It is obvious that perfectly lucid writing presupposes a totally conscious writer, and this does not correspond to reality. We are made up of ego and id, spirit and flesh, and furthermore nucleic acids, traditions, hormones, remote and recent experiences, and traumas; therefore we are condemned to carry from crib to grave a doppelganger, a mute and faceless brother who nevertheless is co-responsible for our actions, and so for all our pages [p. 170].

And so, too, responsible for all our psychoanalytic work. Curiosity is the never satisfied insistence on knowing the doppelganger, the unknown psychoanalyst who is there in the room, too, and who will always be just beyond acquaintance, forever moving and forever still, occupying the same shadows on the far side of every new understanding. No writer knows deeply what he has written, Levi tells us; and no analyst, we can echo, thoroughly understands the course of an analysis.

It should also be emphasized what curiosity is not: It is not mere inquisitiveness, the asking of questions. Questions are the most visible evidence that curiosity is operative, but they are an outcome and not the phenomenon itself. The answers given by the patient to the spoken questions in a detailed inquiry, for example, are not themselves the most interesting understandings. The most interesting and significant observations arrive unbidden, *following* the answers to questions. They become possible because of what is brought to light in the patient's response, but exactly how they are related to these concrete and volitional responses very often remains unknown.

Contrast all this to the conventional view of curiosity derived from the epistemology of correspondence: If the truth is out there somewhere, or maybe "in there" somewhere, curiosity is the desire to look for it, or at least the willingness to trip over it. Understanding should not depend on expectations, but on a direct link between what is perceived and what is actually out there. Expectations are not considered the soil in which understanding must root, but the source of distortion and error. They are to be exposed, excised, and cleanly done with, returning us to that unprejudiced state of being in which we can be inscribed by the impressions of the world around and within us. And when a very good and plausible explanation for something has been spoken, it can be said that curiosity has been satisfied. The truth is like buried treasure, and it has been found. We can stop looking. We can trust ourselves, actually, in a way we are forever deprived of by modern hermeneutics. If preconceptions are ubiquitous, and if the greatest clinical necessity is constantly to question them, then there is no final answer to any question that arises in the course of the treatment. Since each understanding is contextual, what Issacharoff and Hunt (1978) call a "new truth," it will be displaced by fresh understanding as the work proceeds. There is an excitement to this, but also a kind of sadness, because every new truth becomes a prejudice. Every understanding is eventually a betrayal. Analysts are always on the verge of relinquishing their proudest moments, understandings that sometimes have been hoped for and awaited over long periods of time. It is no accident that Gadamer often refers to disconfirmations as disappointments.

THE INNOCENT ANALYST

It is painful enough not to be able to believe any longer in the simplicity of the existential call to freedom. But what of the clinical values, anchored in those same existential views, that have guided the practice of generations of analysts? What of openness to the other? What of the authentic intention to see the other clearly? If human beings can never be rid of so-called distorting influences, if the patient's truth can never simply impress itself on the listening analyst, then is it realistic to maintain the ideal of the analyst's openness to the patient? Must we conclude that Schachtel's allocentric attitude and Buber's I-Thou are romantic illusions, the naive expressions of an outmoded epistemology?

If openness is illusory, it is not only Schachtel and Buber whose work will have to be dismissed. Other artists, philosophers, and critics have proposed similar ideas, each attempting to describe what Shattuck (1984a) calls "a subtle mental operation which seeks to achieve freshness and particularity of attention" (p. 416). Shattuck's list of these writers includes Keats ("Negative Capability"), Bergson ("a more direct vision of reality"), Ruskin ("innocence of the eye"), Laforgue ("the natural eye"), Husserl ("bracketing"), Shklovsky ("defamiliarization"), Brecht ("distancing"), Rilke ("let each germ of feeling come to completeness quite in itself"), and Heidegger ("releasement"). To be required to discard all these ideas in the service of the vision of some brave new epistemological world would be a good reason to throw out the vision instead. We *know* we experience openness to our patients, as these writers knew they experienced openness to the world around them. There are times when the patient's experience is as clear as one's own, and the more this happens (as long as the treatment bears out that one's grasp was accurate) the more effective the treatment. How can this be reconciled?

If there is a way to understand openness as an achievement, a result of knowledge and effort and not just a return to an imagined state of unfettered perception, then the clinical experience and the epistemology cease to be contradictory. And there is such a way. It requires, though, that the analyst give up any vestigial belief in being a sensor, in being capable of receiving the truth merely by being receptive. It requires sacrificing the reassuring view that the truth is really there behind the veils. If openness is redefined according to hermeneutic views, it becomes a more complex and uncomfortable matter, an accomplishment for which innocence is not required, at least not innocence as it is most commonly understood.

Shattuck (1984a), though addressing himself to literature and not to psychoanalysis, takes on similar questions in the same essay in which he cited the writers listed previously.

By the time we can talk seriously about literature, it is too late to find a natural starting point in any direct, spontaneous response to the act of reading. . . . We live all our lives in the prison house of language, from whose codes and conventions no particle of our experience can escape . . . The armed vision is the only vision [p. 413].

Similarly, it is always too late to find a response to the patient which is not rooted in preconception. Is innocence, then, the illusion it seems? Is the innocent analyst a myth?[4] Shattuck continues:

> Yes, of course [it is a myth], as long as that term is construed to mean not damaging falsehood but useful fiction. We have a whole set of such devices that allow us to live beyond our immediate experience—the state of nature in philosophy, the corporation in economics and law, infinity in mathematics, salvation in religion. . . . We are dealing with the most subtle of all hermeneutics. Candor is a goal, not a given . . . the attitude does not result from a lapse back into inexperience, a newly costumed anti-intellectualism. On the contrary, the "new" in Rilke and the "remaking" in Laforgue point toward an advance beyond experience, an ulterior innocence derived from and building on our encounter with life, not know-nothingism, but a tolerant wisdom in the face of what we both know and don't know [p. 416].

Innocence does not have to be pristine to be meaningful. It is not a return to a child's-eye view of the world, as in the romantic conception. On the contrary, it is the result of learning. The capacity for innocence is an accomplishment. To psychoanalysts, whose work and commitment require constant exposure to the difficulty of self-knowledge, this way of understanding openness is not only fitting but just. Analytic ideals survive intact. As a matter of fact, bringing together faith in the value of openness with the respect for learning that runs so deep in psychoanalysis actually strengthens the ideal.

Openness is that same ongoing willingness to question everyday expectations that has come up over and over again in this book, a state of explicit familiarity with, and acceptance of, the strictures of one's own character and culture. Openness is, in a word, wisdom. This is obviously not to claim that analysts qualify as wise, just because analytic work requires the formulation of expectations. But clinical practice does demand a high level of openness. The analyst develops a "work ego" in the course of treatment and training, a capacity for self-containment and self-reflection, which may originally have been the training analyst's, but is now the analyst's own, and will become the patient's (though most patients will never have reason to employ it as consistently as the analyst needs to during sessions). Analysts are at their bests in the office. There is a minimum of interruption in the capacity to disconfirm the preconceptions emerging in interaction with the patient. The freedom to disconfirm varies, of course, with the mood one brings to the hour, the content under discussion, and most of all, with the vagaries of the interaction. But the foundation of psychoanalytic competence is that analysts are *relatively* free, within the special analytic setting, to allow themselves the unbidden experience that marks the formulation of expectations.

Notes

CHAPTER 1

1. I have not mentioned structuralism in this list, despite the fact that it was the structuralists who were more responsible than any other group of theorists for the view that experience is fundamentally linguistic. The reason I have not mentioned these writers (e.g., Lévi-Strauss, Barthes) is that their underlying objectivism is inconsistent with the interpretivist, hermeneutic perspective I am adopting here. Structuralism was not based in social constructionism, as postmodernism is, but in the position that objectively existing universal elements underlie experience and are responsible for its shape everywhere, although that shape varies according to the kinds of adaptations required in particular environments.

For the relevant philosophy of science, see, for example, Kuhn (1970, 1977) and Feyerabend (1974), and in the social sciences, Taylor (1971). For reviews of hermeneutics and references to the primary texts, see Palmer (1969), Howard (1982), and Bernstein (1983). Sarup (1989) and Best and Kellner (1991) offer overviews of poststructuralist and postmodern thought that suit the same purposes. The relationship between hermeneutics and psychoanalysis is presented in chapter 11, and by Steele (1979), Strenger (1991), Sass (1988), and, with special clarity and conciseness, by Phillips (1991). Barratt (1993) offers an extensive survey of what postmodernism means for psychoanalysis. Pragmatism in contemporary philosophy is widely associated with Richard Rorty (1979, 1982, 1991a, b).

2. Notice that the change that has taken place here is not a change in the relation between the signifier (the sound of the word "art") and the signified (the image or idea of art). The reason we now consider earthworks to be art is not that assemblages of mud mean something different than they used to; the reason is that the signifier "art" has been redefined by changing the relation between "art" and "nonart." The union between signified and signifier, which composes what Saussure called the sign, and which he believed was relatively stable, has been dissolved in poststructuralism. Now, signifiers are defined only by their relation to other signifiers.

3. Sapir and Whorf did not consider the existence and significance of unworded languages, nor did they question the epistemological hege-

mony of science and objectivity. Thus, although the excerpt from Whorf that I use is charming, and useful as a demonstration of the constitutive properties of language, it is not actually written from a postmodern perspective.

CHAPTER 2

1. Freud (1915, pp. 177–179) did leave room in his theory for a nonrepresentational unconscious. The contents of this part of the unconscious, however, are "unconscious affects" or "unconscious emotions," never unconscious ideas. Ideas were for Freud the only targets repression could ever have, because instinct itself cannot be represented, only connected to ideas and affects—and, as we have just seen, affects cannot be repressed because they cannot be pinned down clearly enough to be expelled.

2. Freud makes this point in the following way. A certain kind of nonverbal representation, what Freud calls the *thing-presentation*, is unique to the unconscious. Thing-presentations comprise the vocabulary of the *primary process*, which is Freud's term for the special kind of cognition that goes on only in the unconscious. The *secondary process* is the rational, verbal cognition characteristic of consciousness and the preconscious. When the secondary process connects to (*cathects*) a thing-presentation, verbal language is attached to the thing-presentation, transforming it into a *word-presentation* and bringing it into the *preconscious*. But the word-presentation is by no means a faithful copy of the thing-presentation; the language of the unconscious and verbal language are incommensurable; translation cannot be accomplished without a significant loss of meaning.

Once the representation gains access to the preconscious in this way, it can be brought into consciousness by a simple act of attention. The preconscious is simply that part of experience that could be conscious, but that has not fallen within the range of one's conscious attention. For the purposes of the argument I am making, the most important point is that, in Freud's view, what one becomes aware of in this way is a *diluted* form of the original unconscious representation.

CHAPTER 4

1. See Polkinghorne (1988) for a review of the controversies surrounding constructivism in history.

2. There are many collections describing the unbidden discoveries of artists, scientists, and mathematicians. Those I have come across are

Bruner (1979), Burnshaw (1970), Ghiselin (1952), Hadamard (1945), Hampl (1989), Kris (1952), Poincaré (1952), Raft and Andresen (1986), Rosner and Abt (1974), Rothenberg (1979), and Shattuck (1984a). For more material on relevant dreams, see Garfield (1974) and Woods (1947).

3. I have taken this phrase from Jean Piaget (though the reference escapes me). Emulating Henri Bergson, whom he greatly admired, Piaget apparently was fond of making reference to the "creative disorder" of his office, implying a link between his tolerance for ambiguity and messiness and his capacity for creative endeavor.

4. Mozart's words are reported by Ghiselin (1952, p. 44); Tsvetaeva is quoted by Muchnic (1980, p. 7); Frankenthaler's words appear in a piece by Loos (1997, p. 19). The remainder of the quotations in this paragraph appear in Burnshaw (1970).

5. The quotation from Rilke appears in Burnshaw (1970). The others in this paragraph are from Ghiselin (1952).

CHAPTER 6

1. Being subject to the same principles as any other type of engagement includes being subject to conflict. I have not discussed conflict thus far, and I do not address it elsewhere in the book. That absence of consideration, however, does not mean I eschew it, but that I take its presence for granted. In the passage just quoted, Fingarette points out that spelling-out and not-spelling-out are events that reflect decisions between conflicting alternatives. A large proportion of these considerations are what psychoanalysts would consider unconscious conflict. Unconscious conflict in the terms I am using here is best understood as a clash of purposes over whether or not to spell-out a particular interpretation. Just as in traditional theory, the conflict need not be known to be effective in provoking indecision over whether to spell-out in any particular instance. If such a conflict does become known, of course, that knowledge would represent an interpretation, not merely the revelation of preexisting content.

CHAPTER 7

1. Culture and person should not really be discussed separately, and probably one should try to avoid reference to things like the "influence" of culture on the individual, a wording suggesting that the person is already "there" for culture to have an influence "on." Persons, after all, *are* cultures. The understanding to which I am most sympathetic defines culture simply

as human practice, which makes it hard to know when one is talking about culture and when about an individual—and that is as it should be. In that case, though, one has to decide what to do about the idea of self, to which I am also committed. This problem of self and agency in a postmodern world is key for all the intellectual disciplines, but for none more than psychoanalysis, which can only survive if it negotiates postmodernism while preserving some notion of what is personal and authentic. Throughout this book, I have tried to use the plural when discussing culture, since we never exist in "a" cultural context, but at the intersection of many.

2. Bartlett got the same kind of results I am about to describe when he substituted visual material for verbal material.

3. Important exponents of this view include Racker (1968), Levenson (1972, 1983, 1991), Hoffman (1983, 1991, 1992a, b, 1994, 1996), Mitchell (1988, 1993), Ehrenberg (1992), Hirsch (1993, 1996), Renik (1993), Greenberg (1995), Aron (1996).

4. For the purposes I address here, I could cite Berger and Luckmann's (1967) *The Social Construction of Reality* with nearly the same effect as citing Foucault. Berger and Luckmann take the position that everyday reality, which we take for granted and treat as objective, is actually a social construction. Processes that began as subjective (think of any discredited idea that once was taken for granted) come to be thought of as part of the natural world. These pieces of reality are described as "objectivations," a term that bears a close relation to Bartlett's "conventionalisation" and to Foucault's "normalization." I prefer Foucault's account, though. Whereas Berger and Luckmann preserve the removed and "objective" stance of the traditional social scientist, someone who is simply describing the way things are, political and moral questions are the driving force of Foucault's thought.

5. Schachtel, in fact, in his magnum opus, *Metamorphosis* (1959), presages much of this discussion of convention. The general tone of his work is similar to what I present here, and it is probably fair to say that a long and respectful acquaintance with Schachtel's work inspired this part of the chapter.

6. The dream also had to do with the transference, but that part of the session is not immediately relevant to the illustration.

CHAPTER 8

1. Despite his field theory, Sullivan took for granted the existence of an objective reality separate from the observer. Interaction in the interpersonal field, therefore, results in a version of reality that is either accurate or distorted. Sullivan, then, was no constructivist. On the other

hand, he was committed to the idea that one's vision of reality is determined by the field in which one observes it, and he argued that our perceptions are more often personal and autistic (i.e., parataxic) than objective and consensually validated (syntaxic). See chapter 3.

2. Sullivan's thought, while it is not itself psychoanalysis, is nevertheless at the heart of the thinking of many of the psychoanalysts who have developed the interpersonal perspective (e.g., Lionells et al., 1995). Levenson (1992) has recently laid out this sequence of events in instructive fashion, showing the very particular ways in which Sullivan's thought is not psychoanalytic, and then detailing the developments, beginning in countertransference theory, that acknowledged the full import of Sullivan's conception of the interpersonal field (a task he himself never undertook) and built a psychoanalysis around that conception.

3. The references to this point would fill a substantial syllabus. In addition to Geertz, for accessible introductions to the most interesting of this psychological literature, see Harré (1984), Gergen (1985, 1991, 1992), Sampson (1989), Flax (1990), Cushman (1991, 1994, 1995), Kitzinger (1992), Kvale (1992), Shotter (1993), and Shotter and Gergen (1989). For those who wish to pursue them, these sources list the relevant philosophical references.

4. Philip Cushman (1994, 1995) argues that psychoanalysis and psychotherapy are inevitably political and moral activities, with their own embeddedness in various cultural surrounds. Cushman sees Sullivan's thought as an alternative to Winnicott's and Kohut's, in both of whose writings Cushman believes the self appears as a real entity, a "thing." Such ahistorical and nonpolitical two-person psychologies, says Cushman (1991) although they add to our understanding of interaction, raise the dangers of "reifying, interiorizing, and historically decontextualizing the self, locating the self's origins in the 'natural' development of infancy, depoliticizing the self's illnesses, and commodifying its cures" (p. 838). In Sullivan's work, on the other hand, with its recognition of the interpersonal field and its dereification of the self, Cushman sees the opportunity to create a three-person psychology in which the third participant in the interpersonal field is the recognition that each person is an "intersection" of traditions. The third participant, that is, is culture. Such a conception is consistent with what I am trying to say, with the proviso that the effect of cultures is, of course, never separate from that of the two people involved. As Cushman says, it is not as if each of us is a self *influenced* by culture, as if culture were something that came along after the self already existed. Rather, each of us *is* an intersection of traditions.

5. See Greenberg (1991) for a carefully worked out theoretical description of exactly how the interaction of the interpersonal and the intrapsychic might occur.

6. See Sass (1988) for a convincing description of the humanism that lingers in psychoanalysis. Sass also shows why the best remedy for humanism is hermeneutics.

CHAPTER 9

1. I have discussed this issue elsewhere (Stern, 1985).

2. See also the responses to Spence (1993) by Bruner (1993) and Rorty (1993), and the analysis of Spence's (1982) first book by Sass and Woolfolk (1988), who point out the contradiction between Spence's objectivism and his stated purpose of introducing hermeneutics into clinical psychoanalysis.

3. On the other hand, if one counts the contributions of object-relations theory and self psychology as elaborations of the observation, one would have to say that the literature on the problem is vast. Object-relations theory and self psychology have alerted us that what we have called resistance can be an expression by the patient of a certain kind of therapeutic need, and have suggested that under some circumstances the analyst should respond to this need in the here and now. For instance, the analyst may "contain" the patient's projected internal objects; or, upon understanding what it is to be the patient's selfobject, the analyst may accept the patient's use of him in this way; and so on. But these conceptions, however clinically vital they may have become, are not really ways of dealing with resistance as much as they are redefinitions of some instances of resistance. And we are therefore back at square one when it comes to the interpretation of the unconscious.

4. This point and the evidence to support it is in the tradition of James Strachey's (1934) theory of therapeutic action. In his classic contribution, Strachey suggested that the patient changed by installing the analyst as "auxiliary super-ego," which then allowed the patient to experience more than he would have been capable of without the treatment. I am also in debt to Strachey's contemporary, Richard Sterba (1934), the author of the other significant theory of therapeutic action of the day. For him, the therapeutic collaboration was not merely an aspect of the therapeutic process, as it tended to become in the work of later writers who emphasized it (e.g., Greenson, 1965, and Zetzel, 1956), but was a goal in its own right, and the key to therapeutic change.

The problem with Strachey's perspective is that he believed the analyst, in order to serve as the best stand-in for the patient's superego, should be neither a good object nor a bad one. I do not believe that the patient's feeling of safety can be adequately supported by a neutral object relation with the analyst, even if such a thing were possible. What I am advocating in what follows is, in this respect, closer to the developmentally oriented analysts of the Edinburgh Congress (Gitelson, 1962; Nacht, 1962) and various early writers of the object-relations school (e.g., Winnicott, 1958, 1965; Guntrip, 1969), who are unabashed in their advocacy of the analyst's attempt to be a good object. These writers, however, do not necessarily take the perspective, as I do here, that that attempt is best served by the analyst's consistent and compassionate curiosity.

5. Hoffman (1983) is responsible for the compelling argument about the place of transference interpretation in the patient's feeling of safety. Hoffman also makes the companion argument about the place of countertranference interpretation in the making of transference interpretations, which he derived from Racker (1968).

6. Conversation does not necessarily require two human beings. It can occur between a reader and a text, a listener and a piece of music, a viewer and a work of art. See chapter 11.

CHAPTER 10

1. I emphasize the analyst's use of her experience for diagnostic purposes in this example, but it is equally important that the analyst see that the patient, by not saying anything directly, yet influencing the analyst to worry, is trying to create some specific kind of relatedness. The analyst needs to learn the specific way she was influenced, and she needs to consider how she might actually have discouraged the patient from being more direct. If such aspects of the interaction were discovered, then one might also want to question whether there were ways in which the patient had influenced the analyst to be less available than she might otherwise have been, thus making the patient feel less safe in being direct. And so on.

CHAPTER 11

1. Cushman (1995) makes Gadamer a mainstay of his examination of the self and psychotherapy in social context, and Sass (1988) discusses the relation of certain aspects of Heidegger and Gadamer to psychoanalysis. Orange (1995) gives Gadamer's thought an important role in

her discussion of epistemology and self psychology. Strenger (1991) charts a path for psychoanalysis that runs between science and hermeneutics, and finds a place for both. A collection of articles edited by Messer, Sass, and Woolfolk (1988) addresses hermeneutics and psychological theory, including psychoanalysis. The introductory essay by Woolfolk, Sass, and Messer (1988) is a good, brief introduction to some of the basics of hermeneutics for psychologists who have had no previous exposure to the field. For presentations of the work of Gadamer, see Warnke (1987), whose book-length discussion, structured as a dialogue, is nontechnical. See also Bernstein's (1983) readable account of a way of understanding that falls between objectivism and relativism, in which Gadamer's work plays a leading role, and Weinsheimer's (1985) point-by-point exegesis of *Truth and Method,* Gadamer's major work. Other hermeneuticists who have been of particular interest to psychoanalysts are Habermas (1968), Taylor (1985a, 1985b), and Ricoeur (1970, 1981).

2. Translated and quoted by Linge (1976, p. xvii) from Gadamer's *Truth and Method.*

3. The first phrase is from Gadamer's *Truth and Method;* the second is from Hans Lipp's *Untersuchungen zu einer hermeneutische Logik* (1938). Both are translated and quoted by Linge (1976, p. xxxii).

4. I am relying here primarily on one of Gadamer's two major replies to Habermas (Gadamer, 1967) and on accounts by Warnke (1987) and Woolfolk, Sass, and Messer (1988).

5. I should add, however, that Schafer (1983) does write (p. 234) that he has found Habermas's view so useful because it is more moderate than the view of Ricoeur (1977), by whom the unconscious is conceived to be more fully a natural phenomenon of cause and force than Habermas understands it to be.

CHAPTER 12

1. Adherents of the concept of parallel process in supervision would have it otherwise, claiming that the supervisor is often buried in an analogue of the therapeutic situation, which is unconsciously created between therapist and supervisor. This view, so popular a few years ago that almost every article on supervision referred to it, seems already to have faded in significance. It makes better sense to argue, as Bromberg (1982) and Grey and Fiscalini (1987) have, that when supervisor and therapist become embedded, it is in a mire of their own making—a separate relationship, independent of the therapy being supervised.

2. This is not say that Sullivan would have agreed with the emphasis here. In fact, he would have argued, and emphatically, that one helps one's patients precisely to the extent that one *does* perform a directed search for the truth. Sullivan had a deep conviction about the accuracy of positivism. Thus it may seem contradictory to cite him in support of the view being developed here. To this objection the best reply is that Sullivan's clinical attitude and his ideas retain liveliness and relevance even in a different epistemology. Sullivan's interest in the complexities of the clinical interaction, which he focused on because of his belief in the significance of the observable, happens to be the same emphasis one has to take from a hermeneutic view.

3. Van der Rohe is quoted by Bruner (1987), Nabokov by Hampl (1989).

4. Spence (1987) examines some of the same questions from a hermeneutic point of view. As a matter of fact, he entitles one of his chapters "The Myth of the Innocent Analyst," by which he means that anyone, analysts included, in order to understand, must work from a prior commitment to some grasp of the material to be interpreted. Ergo, a loss of innocence, at least in the blank-slate sense. But Spence does not then go on to redefine innocence in terms consistent with his hermeneutic point of view. He really does mean that the innocent analyst must now be considered a myth. As the following text indicates, I believe the description of the analyst as innocent remains meaningful.

References

Archard, D. (1984), *Consciousness and the Unconscious*. La Salle, IL: Open Court.

Argyris, C. & Schön, D. A. (1976), *Theory in Practice*. San Francisco: Jossey-Bass.

Arieti, S. (1962), The microgeny of thought and perception. In: *On Schizophrenia, Phobias, Depression, Psychotherapy and the Farther Shores of Psychiatry*. New York: Brunner/Mazel, 1978, pp. 277–299.

——— (1976), *Creativity*. New York: Basic.

Aron, L. (1996), *A Meeting of Minds*. Hillsdale, NJ: The Analytic Press.

Atlas, J. (1995), Pinpointing a moment on the map of history. *The New York Times*, Section 4, Sunday March 19, pp. 1 & 5.

Atwood, G. E. & Stolorow, R. D. (1984), *Structures of Subjectivity*. Hillsdale, NJ: The Analytic Press. Edited from the second (1965) edition.

Barnett, J. (1980), Interpersonal processes, cognition, and the analysis of character. *Contemp. Psychoanal.*, 16:397–416.

Barratt, B. B. (1993), *Psychoanalysis and the Postmodern Impulse*. Baltimore, MD: Johns Hopkins University Press.

Bartlett, F. C. (1932), *Remembering*. Cambridge: Cambridge University Press.

Bateson, G. (1972), *Steps to an Ecology of Mind*. New York: Chandler.

Benjamin, J. (1988), *The Bonds of Love*. New York: Pantheon.

Berger, P. & Luckmann, T. (1967), *The Social Construction of Reality*. New York: Doubleday.

Bernstein, R. J. (1983), *Beyond Objectivism and Relativism*. Philadelphia, PA: University of Pennsylvania Press.

Best, S. & Kellner, D. (1991), *Postmodern Theory*. New York: Guilford.

Bibring, E. (1954), Psychoanalysis and the dynamic psychotherapies. *J. Amer. Psychoanal. Assn.*, 2:745–770.

Bollas, C. (1987), *The Shadow of the Object*. New York: Columbia University Press.

——— (1989), *Forces of Destiny*. London: Free Association Books.

Boring, E. G. (1950), *A History of Experimental Psychology*, 2nd ed. New York: Appleton-Century-Crofts.

Bowie, M. (1991), *Lacan.* Cambridge, MA: Harvard University Press.

Brenner, C. (1980), Working alliance, therapeutic alliance, and transference. In: *Psychoanalytic Explorations of Technique,* ed. H. P. Blum. New York: International Universities Press, pp. 137–157.

Bromberg, P. M. (1982), The supervisory process and parallel process. *Contemp. Psychoanal.,* 18:92–111.

——— (1989), Interpersonal psychoanalysis and self psychology: A clinical comparison. In: *Self Psychology,* ed. D. Detrick & S. Detrick. Hillsdale, NJ: The Analytic Press.

——— (1993), Shadow and substance: A relational perspective on clinical process. *Psychoanal. Psychol.,* 10:147–168.

——— (1994), "Speak! That I may see you": Some reflections on dissociation, reality, and psychoanalytic listening. *Psychoanal. Dial.,* 4:517–547.

——— (1996a), Hysteria, dissociation, and cure: Emmy von N revisited. *Psychoanal. Dial.,* 6:55–71.

——— (1996b), Standing in the spaces: The multiplicity of self and the psychoanalytic relationship. *Contemp. Psychoanal.,* 32: 509–535.

Bruner, J. (1979), The conditions of creativity. In: *On Knowing,* expanded ed. Cambridge, MA: Harvard University Press, pp. 17–30.

——— (1986), *Actual Minds, Possible Worlds.* Cambridge, MA: Harvard University Press.

——— (1987), Foreword. In: *The Freudian Metaphor.* New York: Norton, pp. ix–xvi.

——— (1990), *Acts of Meaning.* Cambridge, MA: Harvard University Press.

——— (1993), Loyal opposition and the clarity of dissent: Commentary on Donald P. Spence's "The hermeneutic turn." *Psychoanal. Dial.,* 3:11–19.

Buber, M. (1957), *I and Thou,* 2nd ed., trans. W. Kaufmann. New York: Scribner's, 1970.

——— (1965), *The Knowledge of Man,* trans. M. Friedman & R. G. Smith. New York: Harper & Row.

Bucci, W. (1985), Dual coding: A cognitive model for psychoanalytic research. *J. Amer. Psychoanal. Assn.,* 33:571–607.

Burnshaw, S. (1970), *The Seamless Web.* New York: Braziller.

Butler, J. (1990), *Gender Trouble.* New York: Routledge.

Chodorow, N. J. (1989), *Feminism and Psychoanalytic Theory.* New Haven, CT: Yale University Press.

Coleridge, S. T. (1816), Kubla Khan: Or a vision in a dream. A fragment. In: *Selected Poetry and Prose of Coleridge,* ed. D. Stauffer. New York: Modern Library, 1941, pp. 43–45.

Culler, J. (1976), *Saussure.* London: Fontana.

Cushman, P. (1991), Ideology obscured: Political uses of Daniel Stern's infant. *Amer. Psychol.,* 46:206–219.

——— (1994), Confronting Sullivan's spider: Hermeneutics and the politics of therapy. *Contemp. Psychoanal.,* 30:800–844.

——— (1995), *Constructing the Self, Constructing America.* Reading, MA: Addison-Wesley.

Damasio, A. R. (1994), *Descartes' Error.* New York: Grosset/Putnam.

Davies, J. M. (1996a), Dissociation, repression, and reality testing in the transference: The controversy over memory and false memory in the psychoanalytic treatment of adult survivors of childhood sexual abuse. *Psychoanal. Dial.,* 6:189–218.

——— (1996b), Linking the "pre-analytic" with the postclassical: Integration, dissociation, and multiplicity of unconscious process. *Contemp. Psychoanal.,* 32:553–576.

——— & Frawley, M. G. (1994), *Treating the Adult Survivor of Childhood Sexual Abuse.* New York: Basic Books.

deGroot, A. D. (1965), *Thought and Mind in Chess.* The Hague: Mouton.

Dinnerstein, D. (1976), *The Mermaid and the Minotaur.* New York: Harper & Row.

Donoghue, D. (1981), *Ferocious Alphabets.* Boston: Little, Brown.

Duffy, B. (1987), *The World as I Found It.* Boston: Houghton Mifflin.

Dworkin, R. (1985), How law is like literature. In: *A Matter of Principle.* Cambridge, MA: Harvard University Press, pp. 157–158.

Eccles, J. C. (1970), *Facing Reality.* New York: Springer-Verlag.

Ehrenberg, D. B. (1985), Countertransference resistance. *Contemp. Psychoanal.,* 21:563–576.

——— (1992) *The Intimate Edge.* New York: Norton.

Eiseley, L. (1969), *The Unexpected Universe.* New York: Harcourt Brace Jovanovich.

Fairbairn, W. R. D. (1954), Observations on the nature of hysterical states. *Brit. J. Med. Psychol.,* 27:105–125.

Farber, L. (1966), *The Ways of the Will.* New York: Basic Books.

Fast, I. (1984), *Gender Identity.* Hillsdale, NJ: The Analytic Press.

Feffer, M. (1982), *The Structure of Freudian Thought.* New York: International Universities Press.

——— (1988), *Radical Constructionism.* New York: New York University Press.

Feiner, A. H. (1982), Comments on the difficult patient. *Contemp. Psychoanal.,* 18:397–411.

Feyerabend, D. V. (1974), *Against Method.* London: New Left Books.

Fingarette, H. (1963), *The Self in Transformation.* New York: Basic.
———— (1969), *Self-Deception.* London: Routledge & Kegan-Paul.
Flax, J. (1990), *Thinking Fragments.* Berkeley, CA: University of California Press.
———— (1996), The conceptual power of multiplicity. *Contemp. Psychoanal.,* 32:577–593.
Foucault, M. (1973), *Madness and Civilization.* Vintage Books.
———— (1980), *Power/Knowledge,* ed. C. Gordon. New York: Pantheon.
———— (1988a), Truth, power, self. In: *Technologies of the Self,* ed. L. H. Martin, H. Gutman & P. Hutton. Amherst, MA: University of Massachusetts Press.
———— (1988b), Technologies of the self. In: *Technologies of the Self,* ed. L. H. Martin, H. Gutman & P. Hutton. Amherst, MA: University of Massachusetts Press.
———— (1988c), The political technology of individuals. In: *Technologies of the Self,* ed. L. H. Martin, H. Gutman & P. Hutton. Amherst, MA: University of Massachusetts Press.
Fourcher, L. A. (1992), Interpreting the relative and absolute unconscious. *Psychoanal. Dial.,* 3:317–329.
———— (1996), The authority of logic and the logic of authority: The import of the Grünbaum debate for psychoanalytically informed psychotherapy. *Psychoanal. Dial.,* 6:515–532.
Freud, S. (1900), The interpretation of dreams. *Standard Edition,* 4 & 5. London: Hogarth Press, 1953.
———— (1905), Fragment of an analysis of a case of hysteria. *Standard Edition,* 7:3–122. London: Hogarth Press, 1953.
———— (1912), Recommendations to physicians practising psycho-analysis. *Standard Edition,* 12:109–120, London: Hogarth Press, 1958.
———— (1913), On beginning the treatment. *Standard Edition,* 12:123–144. London: Hogarth Press, 1958.
———— (1915), The unconscious. *Standard Edition,* 14:159–216. London: Hogarth Press, 1957.
———— (1923), The ego and the id. *Standard Edition,* 19:12–59. London: Hogarth Press, 1961.
———— (1925), A note upon the "mystic writing-pad." *Standard Edition,* 19:227–234. London: Hogarth Press, 1961.
———— (1937), Constructions in analysis. *Standard Edition,* 23:255–270. London: Hogarth Press, 1964.
Friedman, L. (1985), Potentiality shrouded: How the newer theories work. *Psychoanal. Quart.,* 54:379–414.
Fromm, E. (1941), *Escape from Freedom.* New York: Rinehart.
———— (1947), *Man for Himself.* New York: Rinehart.

—— (1951), *The Forgotten Language.* New York: Holt, Rinehart & Winston.

Gadamer, H.-G. (1962), On the problem of self-understanding. In: *Philosophical Hermeneutics*, trans. & ed. D. E. Linge. Berkeley, CA: University of California Press, 1976, pp. 44–58.

—— (1966), The universality of the hermeneutical problem. In: *Philosophical Hermeneutics*, trans. & ed. D. E. Linge. Berkeley, CA: University of California Press, 1976, pp. 3–17.

—— (1967), On the scope and function of hermeneutical reflection, trans. G. B. Hess & R. E. Palmer. In: *Philosophical Hermeneutics*, ed. D. E. Linge. Berkeley, CA: University of California Press, pp. 18–43.

—— (1975), *Truth and Method*, trans. & ed. G. Barden & J. Cumming. New York: Seabury Press. Orig. pub. German, 1960.

—— (1976), *Philosophical Hermeneutics*, ed. D. E. Linge. Berkeley, CA: University of California Press.

Garfield, P. (1974), *Creative Dreaming.* New York: Simon & Schuster.

Geertz, C. (1974), "From the native's point of view": On the nature of anthropological understanding. In: *Local Knowledge.* New York: Basic Books, 1983, pp. 55–70.

Gendlin, E. T. (1962), *Experiencing and the Creation of Meaning.* Glencoe, IL: The Free Press.

—— (1964), A theory of personality change. In: *Personality Change*, ed. P. Worchel & D. Byrne. New York: Wiley, pp. 100–148.

Gergen, K. J. (1985), The social constructionist movement in modern psychology. *Amer. Psychol.*, 40:266–275.

—— (1991), *The Saturated Self.* New York: Basic Books.

—— (1992), Toward a postmodern psychology. In: *Psychology and Postmodernism*, ed. S. Kvale. London: Sage, pp. 17–30.

Ghiselin, B. (1952), *The Creative Process.* Berkeley, CA: University of California Press.

Giddens, A. (1976), *New Rules of Sociological Method.* New York: Basic Books.

Gill, M. M. (1963), Topography and systems in psychoanalytic theory. *Psychological Issues*, Monogr. 10. New York: International Universities Press.

—— (1982), *The Analysis of Transference, Vol. 1.* New York: International Universities Press.

—— (1995), *Psychoanalysis in Transition.* Hillsdale, NJ: The Analytic Press.

Gitelson, M. (1962), The curative factors in psychoanalysis: The first phase of psychoanalysis. *Internat. J. Psychol-Anal.*, 43:194–205.

Greenberg, J. (1991), *Oedipus and Beyond.* Cambridge, MA: Harvard University Press.

—— (1995), Psychoanalytic technique and the interactive matrix. *Psychoanal. Quart.*, 64:1–22.

—— & Mitchell, S. A. (1983), *Object Relations in Psychoanalytic Theory.* Cambridge, MA: Harvard University Press.

Greenson, R. R. (1965), The working alliance and the transference neurosis. In: *Explorations in Psychoanalysis.* New York: International Universities Press, 1978, pp. 199–224.

Grey, A. & Fiscalini, J. (1987), Parallel process as transference-countertransference interaction. *Psychoanal. Psychol.*, 4:131–144.

Guntrip, H. (1969), *Schizoid Phenomena, Object Relations, and the Self.* New York: International Universities Press.

Habermas, J. (1971), *Knowledge and Human Interests*, trans. J. Shapiro. Boston: Beacon Press.

Hadamard, J. (1945), *The Psychology of Invention in the Mathematical Field.* New York: Dover, 1954.

Hampl, P. (1989), The lax habits of the free imagination. *The New York Times Book Review*, March 5, pp. 1, 37–38.

Harré, R. (1984), *Personal Being.* Cambridge, MA: Harvard University Press.

Harris, A. (1996a), False memory? False memory syndrome? The so-called false memory syndrome? *Psychoanal. Dial.*, 6:155–187.

—— (1996b), The conceptual power of multiplicity. *Contemp. Psychoanal.*, 32:537–552.

Hawkes, T. (1977), *Structuralism and Semiotics.* London: Methuen.

Herman, J. L. (1992), *Trauma and Recovery.* New York: Basic.

Hirsch, I. (1993), Countertransference enactments and some issues related to external factors in the analyst's life. *Psychoanal. Dial.*, 3:343–366.

—— (1994), Dissociation and the interpersonal self. *Contemp. Psychoanal.*, 30:777–799.

—— (1996), Observing-participation, mutual enactments, and the new classical models. *Contemp. Psychoanal.*, 32:359–383.

Hirshberg, L. M. (1989), Remembering: Reproduction or construction? *Psychoanal. Contemp. Thought*, 12:313–381.

Hoffman, I. Z. (1983), The patient as interpreter of the analyst's experience. *Contemp. Psychoanal.*, 19:389–422.

—— (1987), The value of uncertainty in psychoanalytic practice. *Contemp. Psychoanal.*, 23:205–215.

—— (1990), In the eye of the beholder: A reply to Levenson. *Contemp. Psychoanal.*, 26:291–299.

—— (1991), Discussion: Toward a social-constructivist view of the psychoanalytic situation. *Psychoanal. Dial.*, 1:74–105.

—— (1992a), Some practical implications of a social-constructivist view of the psychoanalytic situation. *Psychoanal. Dial.*, 2:287–304.

—— (1992b), Expressive participation and psychoanalytic discipline. *Contemp. Psychoanal.*, 28:1–15.

—— (1994), Dialectical thinking and therapeutic action in the psychoanalytic process. *Psychoanal. Quart.*, 63:187–218.

—— (1996), The intimate and ironic authority of the psychoanalyst's presence. *Psychoanal. Quart.*, 65:102–136.

Horowitz, M. (1986), *Stress Response Syndromes.* Northvale, NJ: Aronson.

Howard, R. J. (1982), *Three Faces of Hermeneutics.* Berkeley, CA: University of California Press.

Irigaray, L. (1985), *This Sex Which Is Not One.* Ithaca, NY: Cornell University Press.

Issacharoff, A. & Hunt, W. (1978), Beyond countertransference. *Contemp. Psychoanal.*, 14:291–310.

Jacob, F. (1982), *The Possible and the Actual.* Seattle: University of Washington Press.

Jacobs, T. (1991), *The Use of the Self.* New York: International Universities Press.

Jacobson, L. (1997), The soul of psychoanalysis in the modern world: Reflections on the work of Christopher Bollas. *Psychoanal. Dial.*, 7:81–115.

James, W. (1890), *Principles of Psychology.* New York: Henry Holt, 1899.

Kermode, F. (1985), Freud and interpretation. *Internat. Rev. Psycho-Anal.*, 12:3–12.

Kernberg, O. F. (1980), Some implications of object relations theory for psychoanalytic technique. In: *Psychoanalytic Explorations of Technique*, ed. H. P. Blum. New York: International Universities Press, pp. 207–240.

Khan, M. M. R. (1969), Introduction. In: *Hands of the Living God*, by M. Milner. New York: International Universities Press.

Kitzinger, C. (1992), The individuated self-concept: A critical analysis of social constructionist writing on individualism. In: *Social Psychology of Identity and the Self Concept*, ed. G. Breakwell. London: Surrey University Press/Academic Press.

Klein, G. (1976), *Psychoanalytic Theory.* New York: International Universities Press.

Kris, E. (1952), *Psychoanalytic Explorations in Art.* New York: International Universities Press.

Kristeva, J. (1980), *Desire in Language.* New York: Columbia University Press.

Kuhn, T. S. (1970), *The Structure of Scientific Revolutions.* Chicago: University of Chicago Press.

———— (1977), *The Essential Tension.* Chicago: University of Chicago Press.

Kvale, S., ed. (1992), *Psychology and Postmodernism.* London: Sage.

Langer, S. K. (1942), *Philosophy in a New Key.* Cambridge, MA: Harvard University Press.

Levenson, E. A. (1972), *The Fallacy of Understanding.* New York: Basic Books.

———— (1979), Language and healing. *J. Amer. Acad. Psychoanal.,* 7:271–282.

———— (1981), Facts or fantasies: The nature of psychoanalytic data. *Contemp. Psychoanal.,* 17:486–500.

———— (1982), Follow the fox. *Contemp. Psychoanal.,* 18:1–15.

———— (1983), *The Ambiguity of Change.* New York: Basic Books.

———— (1988), The pursuit of the particular. *Contemp. Psychoanal.,* 24:1–16.

———— (1990), Reply to Hoffman. *Contemp. Psychoanal.,* 25:299–304.

———— (1991), *The Purloined Self.* New York: Contemporary Psychoanalysis Books.

———— (1992), Harry Stack Sullivan: From interpersonal psychiatry to interpersonal psychoanalysis. *Contemp. Psychoanal.,* 28:450–466.

Levi, P. (1989), On obscure writing. In: *Other People's Trades,* trans. R. Rosenthal. New York: Summit Books, pp. 169–175.

Lewicki, P. (1986), *Nonconscious Social Information Processing.* New York: Academic Press.

Lewy, E. & Rapaport, D. (1944), The psychoanalytic concept of memory and its relation to recent memory theories. In: *The Collected Papers of David Rapaport,* ed. M. M. Gill. New York: Basic Books, 1967, pp. 136–159.

Linge, D. E. (1976), Editor's Introduction. In: *Philosophical Hermeneutics,* ed. D. E. Linge. Berkeley, CA: University of California Press, pp. xi–lviii.

Lionells, M., Fiscalini, J., Mann, C. H. & Stern, D. B. (1995), *The Handbook of Interpersonal Psychoanalysis.* Hillsdale, NJ: The Analytic Press.

Loewald, H. (1960), On the therapeutic action of psychoanalysis. In: *Papers on Psychoanalysis.* New Haven, CT: Yale University Press, pp. 221–256.

———— (1976), Perspectives on memory. In: *Papers on Psychoanalysis.* New Haven, CT: Yale University Press, pp. 148–173.

———— (1980), *Papers on Psychoanalysis.* New Haven, CT: Yale University Press.

Loos, T. (1997), Tinkering for effect. *The New York Times Book Review,* January 19, p. 19.

MacKenzie, N. (1965), *Dreams and Dreaming.* London: Aldus Books.

Maritain, J. M. (1953), *Creative Intuition in Art and Poetry.* Princeton: Princeton University Press.

McCleary, R. C. (1964), Preface. In: *Signs,* M. Merleau-Ponty, trans. R. C. McCleary. Evanston, IL: Northwestern University Press, pp. ix–xxxii.

Mead, G. H. (1934), *Mind, Self, and Society.* Chicago: University of Chicago Press.

Merleau-Ponty, M. (1962), *The Phenomenology of Perception,* trans. C. Smith. London: Routledge & Kegan-Paul.

———— (1964a), Introduction. In: *Signs,* trans. R. C. McCleary. Evanston, IL: Northwestern University Press, pp. 3–35.

———— (1964b), Indirect language and the voices of silence. In: *Signs,* trans. R. C. McCleary. Evanston, IL. Northwestern University Press, pp. 39–97.

———— (1970), *Themes from the lectures at the Collège de France, 1952–1960,* trans. J. O'Neill. Evanston, IL: Northwestern University Press.

Messer, S. B., Sass, L. A. & Woolfolk, R. L., eds. (1988), *Hermeneutics and Psychological Theory.* New Brunswick, NJ: Rutgers University Press.

Mitchell, J. (1974), *Psychoanalysis and Feminism.* New York: Pantheon.

Mitchell, S. A. (1984), Object relations theories and the developmental tilt. *Contemp. Psychoanal.,* 20:473–499.

———— (1988), *Relational Concepts in Psychoanalysis.* Cambridge, MA: Harvard University Press.

———— (1991), Contemporary perspectives on self: Toward an integration. *Psychoanal. Dial.,* 1:121–147.

———— (1993), *Hope and Dread in Psychoanalysis.* Cambridge, MA: Harvard University Press.

Morse, M. (1951), Mathematics and the arts. *The Yale Review,* Summer.

Moses, I. (1988), The misuse of empathy. *Contemp. Psychoanal.,* 24:577–594.

Muchnic, H. (1980), Chosen and used by art. *The New York Times Book Review,* October 12, pp. 7, 32–33.

Mullahy, P. (1948), *Oedipus.* New York: Grove Press.

Nacht, S. (1962), The curative factors in psycho-analysis. *Internat. J. Psycho-Anal.*, 43:206–211.

Neisser, U. (1967), *Cognitive Psychology.* Englewood Cliffs, NJ: Prentice-Hall.

Newbold, W. R. (1896), A dream detective solves Professor Hilprecht's famous dream. In: *The World of Dreams*, ed. R. L. Woods. New York: Random House, 1947, pp. 525–530.

Oates, J. C. (1982), Stories that define me. *The New York Times Book Review*, July 11, pp. 1, 15–16.

O'Brien, T. (1990), *The Things They Carried.* New York: Houghton Mifflin/Seymour Lawrence.

Orange, D. M. (1995), *Emotional Understanding.* New York: Guilford.

Paivio, A. (1986), *Mental Representations.* New York: Oxford University Press.

——— (1991), Dual coding theory: Retrospect and current status. *Canad. J. Psychol.*, 45:255–287.

Palmer, R. E. (1969), *Hermeneutics.* Evanston, IL: Northwestern University Press.

Paul, I. H. (1957), Studies in Remembering: The Reproduction of Connected and Extended Verbal Material. *Psychological Issues*, Monogr. 2. New York: International Universities Press.

——— (1967), The concept of schema in memory theory. In: *Motives and thought: Psychoanalytic essays in honor of David Rapaport*, ed. R. R. Holt. *Psychological Issues*, Monogr. 18/19. New York: International Universities Press, pp. 219–258.

Phillips, J. (1991), Hermeneutics in psychoanalysis: Review and reconsideration. *Psychoanal. Contemp. Thought*, 14:371–424.

Poincaré, H. (1908), Mathematical creation. In: *The Creative Process*, ed. B. Ghiselin. Berkeley, CA: University of California Press, 1952, pp. 33–42.

——— (1952), *Science and Method*, trans. F. Maitland. New York: Dover.

Polanyi, M. (1958), *Personal Knowledge*, revised ed. New York: Harper Torchbooks, 1964.

——— (1959), *The Study of Man.* Chicago: University of Chicago Press.

Polkinghorne, D. E. (1988), *Narrative Knowing and the Human Sciences.* Albany: State University of New York Press.

Price, M. (1997), The power of enactments and the enactments of power. Paper delivered to the Karen Horney Institute, March 20.

Protter, B. (1985), Toward an emergent psychoanalytic epistemology. *Contemp. Psychoanal.*, 21:208–227.

———— (1988), Ways of knowing in psychoanalysis. *Contemp. Psychoanal.*, 24:498–526.

———— (1996), Classical, modern, and postmodern psychoanalysis: Epistemic transformations. *Psychoanal. Dial.*, 6:533–562.

Racker, H. (1968), *Transference and Countertransference.* New York: International Universities Press.

Raft, D. & Andresen, J. (1986), Transformations in self-understanding after near-death experiences. *Contemp. Psychoanal.*, 22:319–346.

Raine, K. (1971), *William Blake.* New York: Praeger.

Renik, O. (1993), Analytic interaction: Conceptualizing technique in light of the analyst's irreducible subjectivity. *Psychoanal. Quart.*, 62:553–571.

Ricoeur, P. (1970), *Freud and Philosophy.* New Haven, CT: Yale University Press.

———— (1977), The question of proof in Freud's psychoanalytic writings. *J. Amer. Psychoanal. Assn.*, 25:835–871.

———— (1981), *Hermeneutics and the Human Sciences.* Cambridge: Cambridge University Press.

Rorty, R. (1979), *Philosophy and the Mirror of Nature.* Princeton, NJ: Princeton University Press.

———— (1982), *Consequences of Pragmatism.* Minneapolis: University of Minnesota Press.

———— (1991a), *Objectivity, Relativism, and Truth. Philosophical Papers, Vol. 1.* Cambridge: Cambridge University Press.

———— (1991b), *Essays on Heidegger and Others. Philosophical Papers, Vol. 2.* Cambridge: Cambridge University Press.

———— (1993), Centers of moral gravity: Commentary on Donald Spence's "The hermeneutic turn." *Psychoanal. Dial.*, 3:21–28.

Rosner, S. & Abt, L. E., eds. (1974), *Essays in Creativity.* Croton-on-Hudson, NY: North River Press.

Rothenberg, A. (1979), *The Emerging Goddess.* Chicago: University of Chicago Press.

Sampson, E. E. (1989), The deconstruction of self. In: *Texts of Identity,* ed. J. Shotter & K. J. Gergen. London: Sage, pp. 1–19.

Sandler, J. (1976), Countertransference and role-responsiveness. *Internat. Rev. Psycho-Anal.*, 3:43–47.

Sarbin, T. R., ed. (1986a), *Narrative Psychology.* New York: Praeger.

———— (1986b), The narrative as a root metaphor for psychology. In: *Narrative Psychology,* ed. T. R. Sarbin. New York: Praeger, pp. 3–21.

Sarraute, N. (1939), *Tropisms*, trans. M. Jolas. New York: Braziller.

Sartre, J-P. (1956), *Being and Nothingness*, trans. H. E. Barnes. New York: Philosophical Library.

Sarup, M. (1989), *An Introductory Guide to Poststructuralism and Postmodernism*. Athens: GA: University of Georgia Press.

Sass, L. A. (1988), Humanism, hermeneutics, and humanistic psychoanalysis: Differing conceptions of subjectivity. *Psychoanal. Contemp. Thought*, 12:433–504.

——— (1992), The epic of disbelief: The postmodernist turn in contemporary psychoanalysis. In: *Psychology and Postmodernism*, ed. S. Kvale. London: Sage, pp. 166–182.

——— & Woolfolk, R. (1988), Psychoanalysis and the hermeneutic turn: A critique of *Narrative Truth and Historical Truth*. *J. Amer. Psychoanal. Assn.*, 36:429–454.

Saussure, F. de (1966), *Course in General Linguistics*, trans. W. Baskin. New York: McGraw-Hill.

Schachtel, E. (1959), *Metamorphosis*. New York: Basic Books.

——— (1970), On attention, selective inattention, and experience. An inquiry into attention as an attitude. In: *Interpersonal Explorations in Psychoanalysis*, ed. E. G. Witenberg. New York: Basic Books, pp. 40–66.

Schafer, R. (1976), *A New Language for Psychoanalysis*. New Haven, CT: Yale University Press.

——— (1977), The interpretation of transference and the conditions for loving. In: *The Analytic Attitude*. New York: Basic Books, 1983, pp. 113–133.

——— (1978), *Language and Insight*. New Haven, CT: Yale University Press.

——— (1983), *The Analytic Attitude*. New York: Basic Books.

——— (1988), The sense of an answer: Ambiguities of interpretation in clinical and applied psychoanalysis. In: *The Future of Literary Criticism*, ed. R. Cohen. London: Methuen.

——— (1992), *Retelling a Life*. New York: Basic Books.

Schama, S. (1995), *Landscape and Memory*. New York: Random House.

Schimek, J. G. (1975), A critical re-examination of Freud's concept of unconscious mental representations. *Internat. J. Psycho-Anal.*, 2:171–187.

Searles, H. F. (1979), *Countertransference and Related Subjects*. New York: International Universities Press.

Shahn, B. (1957), *The Shape of Content*. Cambridge, MA: Harvard University Press.

Shattuck, R. (1984a), The innocent eye and the armed vision. In: *The Innocent Eye.* New York: Washington Square Press, 1986, pp. 413–424.

―――― (1984b), Life before language. *The New York Times Book Review,* April 1, pp. 1, 31.

Shotter, J. (1993), *Cultural Politics of Everyday Life.* Toronto: University of Toronto Press.

―――― & Gergen, K. J., eds. (1989), *Texts of Identity.* London: Sage.

Sibley, B. (1986), Afterword. In: *Alice's Adventures in Wonderland,* by Lewis Carroll. New York: Little Simon (Simon & Schuster), pp. 139–158.

Simons, M. (1985), Love and age: A talk with Garcia Marquez. *The New York Times Book Review,* April 7, pp. 1, 18–19.

Slavin, M. & Kriegman, D. (1992), *The Adaptive Design of the Human Psyche.* New York: Guilford.

Spence, D. P. (1982), *Narrative Truth and Historical Truth.* New York: Norton.

―――― (1984), Perils and pitfalls of free-floating attention. *Contemp. Psychoanal.,* 20:37–76.

―――― (1987), *The Freudian Metaphor.* New York: Norton.

―――― (1988a), Tough and tender-minded hermeneutics. In: *Hermeneutics and Psychological Theory,* ed. S. B. Messer, L. A. Sass & R. L. Woolfolk. Newark, NJ: Rutgers University Press, pp. 62–84.

―――― (1988b), Discussion of Moses's "The misuse of empathy." *Contemp. Psychoanal.,* 24:594–598.

―――― (1990), The rhetorical voice of psychoanalysis. *J. Amer. Psychoanal. Assn.,* 38:579–603.

―――― (1993), The hermeneutic turn: Soft science or loyal opposition? *Psychoanal. Dial.,* 3:1–10.

Steele, R. S. (1979), Psychoanalysis and hermeneutics. *Internat. Rev. Psycho-Anal.,* 6:389–411.

Sterba, R. F. (1934), The fate of the ego in analytic therapy. *Internat. J. Psycho-Anal.,* 15:117–126.

Stern, D. B. (1983), Unformulated experience. *Contemp. Psychoanal.,* 19:71–99.

―――― (1985), Some controversies regarding constructivism and psychoanalysis. *Contemp. Psychoanal.,* 21:201–208.

―――― (1987), Unformulated experience and transference. *Contemp. Psychoanal.,* 23:484–491.

―――― (1988), Not misusing empathy. *Contemp. Psychoanal.,* 24:598–611.

——— (1989), The analyst's unformulated experience of the patient. *Contemp. Psychoanal.*, 25:1–33.

——— (1990), Courting surprise: Unbidden perceptions in clinical practice. *Contemp. Psychoanal.*, 26:452–478.

——— (1991), A philosophy for the embedded analyst: Gadamer's hermeneutics and the social paradigm of psychoanalysis. *Contemp. Psychoanal.*, 27:51–80.

——— (1992a), Commentary on constructivism in clinical psycho-analysis. *Psychoanal. Dial.*, 2:331–363.

——— (1992b), What makes a good question? *Contemp. Psychoanal.*, 28:326–336.

——— (1994), Empathy is interpretation (and who ever said it wasn't?). *Psychoanal. Dial.*, 4:441–471.

——— (1996a), The social construction of therapeutic action. *Psychoanal. Inq.*, 16:265–293.

——— (1996b), Dissociation and constructivism: Discussion of Davies and Harris. *Psychoanal. Dial.*, 6:251–266.

Stevenson, R. L. (1925), A chapter on dreams. In: *Memories and Portraits, Random Memories, Memories of Himself.* New York: Scribner.

Stolorow, R. D. (1988), Intersubjectivity, psychoanalytic knowing, and reality. *Contemp. Psychoanal.*, 24:331–338.

——— Brandchaft, B. & Atwood, G. E. (1987), *Psychoanalytic Treatment.* Hillsdale, NJ: The Analytic Press.

Strachey, J. (1934), The nature of the therapeutic action of psycho-analysis. *Internat. J. Psycho-Anal.*, 15:127–159.

Strenger, C. (1991), Between hermeneutics and science: An essay on the epistemology of psychoanalysis. *Psychological Issues*, Monogr. 59. New York: International Universities Press.

Sullivan, H. S. (1936–1937), A note on the implications of psychiatry, the study of interpersonal relations, for investigations in the social sciences. In: *The Fusion of Psychiatry and Social Science.* New York: Norton, 1971, pp. 15–29.

——— (1938), The data of psychiatry. In: *The Fusion of Psychiatry and Social Science.* New York: Norton, 1971, pp. 32–55.

——— (1940), *Conceptions of Modern Psychiatry.* New York: Norton, 1953.

——— (1950), The illusion of personal individuality. In: *The Fusion of Psychiatry and Social Science.* New York: Norton, 1971, pp. 198–226.

——— (1953), *The Interpersonal Theory of Psychiatry*, ed. H. S. Perry & M. L. Gawel. New York: Norton.

———— (1954), *The Psychiatric Interview*, ed. H. S. Perry & M. L. Gawel. New York: Norton, (1970).

———— (1956), Selective inattention. In: *Clinical Studies in Psychiatry*, ed. H. S. Perry, M. L. Gawel & M. Gibbon. New York: Norton, pp. 38–76.

———— (1964), *The Fusion of Psychiatry and Social Science.* New York: Norton.

Tauber, E. S. (1954), Exploring the therapeutic use of counter-transference data. *Psychiatry*, 17:332–336.

———— (1978), Countertransference reexamined. *Contemp. Psychoanal.*, 14:38–47, 59–69.

———— & Green, M. R. (1959), *Prelogical Experience.* New York: Basic Books.

Taylor, C. (1971), Interpretation and the sciences of man. In: *Philosophy and the Human Sciences, Philosophical Papers, Vol. 2.* Cambridge: Cambridge University Press, pp. 15–57.

———— (1985a), *Human Agency and Language, Philosophical Papers, Vol. 1.* Cambridge: Cambridge University Press.

———— (1985b), *Philosophy and the Human Sciences, Philosophical Papers, Vol. 2.* Cambridge: Cambridge University Press.

Valéry, P. (1920), With reference to Adonis (fragment of a preface), trans. L. Varése. In: *Selected Writings of Paul Valéry.* New York: New Directions, 1950, pp. 139–142.

———— (1950), Fragments from "Introduction to the work of Leonardo da Vinci," trans. T. McGreevy. In: *Selected Writings of Paul Valéry.* New York: New Directions, 1950, pp. 89–107.

———— (1952), The course in poetics: First lesson, trans. J. Mathews. In: *The Creative Process*, ed. B. Ghiselin. Berkeley, CA: University of California Press, 1952, pp. 92–106.

Warnke, G. (1987), *Gadamer.* Stanford, CA: Stanford University Press.

Weinsheimer, J. C. (1985), *Gadamer's Hermeneutics.* New Haven, CT: Yale University Press.

Werner, H. (1956), Microgenesis and aphasia. *J. Abnorm. Soc. Psychol.*, 52:347–353.

Whorf, B. L. (1942), Language, mind, and reality. In: *Language, Thought and Reality*, ed. J. B. Carroll. Cambridge, MA: M.I.T. Press, 1956, pp. 246–270.

Winnicott, D. W. (1958), *Collected Papers.* New York: Basic Books.

———— (1965), *The Maturational Processes and the Facilitating Environment.* New York: International Universities Press.

———— (1969), The use of an object and relating through identifications. In: *Playing and Reality.* London: Tavistock, 1971, pp. 101–111.

———— (1971), *Playing and Reality.* London: Tavistock.

Witenberg, E. G. (1978), The inevitability of uncertainty. *J. Amer. Acad. Psychoanal.*, 6:275–279.

Woods, R. L. (1947), *The World of Dreams.* New York: Random House.

Woolfolk, R. L., Sass, L. A. & Messer, S. B. (1988), Introduction to hermeneutics. In: *Hermeneutics and Psychological Science*, ed. S. B. Messer, L. A. Sass & R. L. Woolfolk. New Brunswick, NJ: Rutgers University Press, pp. 2–26.

Zetzel, E. R. (1956), The concept of transference. In: *The Capacity for Emotional Growth.* New York: International Universities Press, 1970, pp. 168–181.

Index

Abt, L. E., 259*n*
abuse, sexual
  defensive responses to, 124–125
action. *See also* practice
  knowledge *vs.*, 19
action images, 21–22
  public
    personal reworking of, 20–23
affect
  dissociation and, 126
  isolation of, 39–41
  thought and, 39–40
agency, personal, 158. *See also* will
  interpersonal field and, 153–156
analysts. *See also* countertransference
  classical
    on unformulated experience, 53
  curiosity of
    and patient's feeling of safety,
      172–174
  experience of
    clinical illustration of, 187–190,
      199–201
    formulation of, 186–191
    unformulated, 187–190
  influence on patient, 204
  openness of, 252–254
analytic field. *See* analytic relation-
    ship; interpersonal field
analytic relationship, 31–32, 39, 206–
    208. *See also* enactments; inter-
    personal field; psychoanalytic
    treatment
  blank-screen metaphor
    criticism of, 203–205
  cocreation in, 82
  creation of, 216–219
    and creation of genuine conver-
      sation, 216–219
  curiosity facilitated by, 175
  dissociation and, 101–102
  egalitarian

co-existing with asymmetry of,
    206–208
constructivism and, 82
fusion of horizons in, 224–226
gender dynamics in, 80
influence on analyst, 191–193
  breaking of the grip of, 193–197
multiple truths and realities in,
    182–183
personal agency and, 153–156
personal responsibility and, 154
power *vs.* curiosity in, 80
reflection and, 30–32
unconscious influence in treat-
    ment, 110–111
unformulated experience and
    multiplicity and, 147–151
analytic situation. *See* analytic relation-
    ship
Andresen, J., 259*n*
Apel, K.-O., 163
Archard, D., 117
Argyris, C., 54
Arieti, S., 74
Aron, L., 5, 260*n*
art, 257*n*
  as defined by linguistic process,
    13, 18
associations and constructions, 53–55
Atlas, J., 145
Atwood, G. E., 206
autocentricity, secondary (Schachtel),
    58–59
autonomy. *See* agency, personal
avowal
  disavowal and spelling-out, 123–126
  sexual abuse and, 124–125
awareness. *See also* interpretation;
    understanding
  consciousness, 85–87
  nondefensive motivations for lack
    of, 145

CPSIA information can be obtained at www.ICGtesting.com
Printed in the USA
LVOW10s0237180316

479723LV00020B/312/P